MEANING-CENTERED EDUCATION

"*Meaning-Centered Education* is an outstanding collection of rich, compelling, and thoughtfully written chapters. Indeed, it is a most important work that educators worldwide will find of enormous value, reflection, and application."

John M. Carfora, Associate Provost, Loyola Marymount University, USA

"This book is an excellent addition to those resources available on learning and teaching. The uniqueness of its approach will make a positive difference to the teaching of students and to academics interested in understanding more about their practice and ability to enhance the student learning experience."

Craig Mahoney, Chief Executive, Higher Education Academy, UK

In a time of globally changing environments and economic challenges, many institutions of higher education are attempting to reform by promoting standardization approaches. *Meaning-Centered Education* explores the counter-tide for an alternative vision of education, where students and instructors engage in open meaning-making processes and self-organizing educational practices. In one contributed volume, *Meaning-Centered Education* provides a comprehensive introduction to current scholarship and pedagogical practice on meaning-centered education. International contributors explore how modern educational scholars and practitioners all around the world are implementing a comprehensive framework that supports meaning making in a classroom. This edited collection is a valuable resource for higher education faculty and scholars interested in renewing the deep purposes of higher education.

Olga Kovbasyuk is Co-Founder of the Institute for Meaning Centered Education, and Professor of Intercultural Communication at Khabarovsk State Academy of Economics and Law (KSAEL), Russia.

Patrick Blessinger is Founder and Executive Director of the Higher Education Teaching and Learning Association (HETL), as well as a lecturer and researcher in education.

MEANING-CENTERED EDUCATION

International Perspectives and
Explorations in Higher Education

*Edited by Olga Kovbasyuk and
Patrick Blessinger*

Routledge
Taylor & Francis Group

NEW YORK AND LONDON

First published 2013
by Routledge
711 Third Avenue, New York, NY 10017

Simultaneously published in the UK
by Routledge
2 Park Square, Milton Park, Abingdon, Oxon OX14 4RN

Routledge is an imprint of the Taylor & Francis Group, an informa business

Library of Congress Cataloging in Publication Data
    Meaning-centered education : international perspectives and explorations in higher education /
    edited by Olga Kovbasyuk and Patrick Blessinger.
    pages cm
    Includes bibliographical references and index.
    1. Education, Higher—Philosophy. 2. Inquiry-based learning.
    I. Kovbasyuk, Olga, editor of compilation. II. Blessinger, Patrick, editor of compilation.
    LB14.7.M42 2013
    370.1—dc23
    2012044229

ISBN: 978–0–415–53203–7 (hbk)
ISBN: 978–0–415–53204–4 (pbk)
ISBN: 978–0–203–11508–4 (ebk)

Typeset in Bembo
by Swales & Willis Ltd, Exeter, Devon

SUSTAINABLE **Certified Sourcing**
FORESTRY   www.sfiprogram.org
INITIATIVE   SFI-01234
SFI label applies to the text stock

Printed and bound in the United States of
America by IBT Global

This book is dedicated to educators all over the world and to the members of the International Higher Education Teaching and Learning Association whose passion for teaching, learning, research, and service are helping to transform the academy in many positive ways.

Vision, Mission, and Values Statement

The long-term vision of HETL is to improve educational outcomes in higher education by creating new knowledge and advancing the scholarship and practice of teaching and learning.

To bring that vision to reality, the present mission of HETL is to develop a global community of higher education professionals who come together to share their knowledge and expertise in teaching and learning.

To effectively fulfill that mission, HETL adheres to the values of academic integrity, collegiality, and diversity. As such, HETL supports academic and pedagogical pluralism, diversity of learning, as well as practices that promote sustainable learning and peace.

Membership, Conference, Publishing, and Research Information

For information, please contact:

Patrick Blessinger
Founder & Executive Director
The HETL Association
E-mail: director@hetl.org
Web: hetl.org

CONTENTS

ABOUT THE AUTHORS

The Editors

Olga Kovbasyuk is Professor of Intercultural Communication. Her Ph.D. at the Far East University of Humanities, Russia, was concerned with personality self-development theory and practice. She has been teaching, and doing research for 30 years in a wide range of academic institutions. Dr. Kovbasyuk has presented papers on meaning-centered approach to education at international conferences in Russia, Poland, Japan, Germany, Greece, and the USA. She has over 70 publications, including 34 peer-reviewed articles in conference proceedings and chapters in books and professional journals. Her work has been recognized through numerous awards and prizes, including a national medal "For Excellence in Work," Teachers Excellence Award from the State Department, USA, Fulbright and DAAD institutional fellowships.

Patrick Blessinger is the founder and Executive Director of the International Higher Education Teaching and Learning Association and a Research Fellow at the School of Education at St. John's University in Queens, New York, USA. He has taught over 150 college and university courses and he has served as a program chair at colleges and universities in the USA and EU. He consults with higher education institutions and has served as an external academic advisor and accreditation advisor. He is the co-founder and co-director of the Institute for Meaning-Centered Education. He is the founder and editor of the *International HETL Review* and co-editor of the *Journal of Applied Research in Higher Education*. He is co-editor of several volumes within the *Cutting-edge Technologies in Higher Education* book series by Emerald Publishing. He attended Auburn University, the Georgia Institute of Technology, and the University of Georgia. He has received several academic awards including a Fulbright Scholarship from the US Department of State and a Governor's Teaching Fellowship from the State of Georgia, USA.

The Contributing Authors

María Luisa Pérez Cañado is Associate Professor at the Department of English Philology of the University of Jáen, Spain, where she is also Vice Dean of the Faculty of Humanities and Education. Her research interests are in Applied Linguistics, English for Specific Purposes, and the intercultural component in language teaching. Her work has appeared in over 80 scholarly journals and edited volumes published by Elsevier, Peter Lang, Cambridge Scholars Publishing, Multilingual Matters, Wiley-Blackwell, Routledge, and Springer, among others. She is also author of four books on the interface of second language acquisition and second language teaching and editor of seven books and one ELT journal. María Luisa has taught and lectured in Belgium, Poland, Germany, Portugal, Ireland, England, Mexico, USA, and all over Spain. She has recently been granted the Ben Massey Award for the quality of her scholarly contributions regarding issues that make a difference in higher education.

Anne Ellen Geller is Associate Professor, English, and Director of Writing Across the Curriculum, Institute for Writing Studies at St. John's University in Queens, New York. She teaches undergraduate and graduate courses in English, and her research focuses on writing centers, writing across the curriculum, support for faculty and student writers, and co-authorship.

Russell A. Hunt is Professor of English at St. Thomas University. He has taught English since 1963, mostly at St. Thomas University, though he has taught and lectured in Germany, Australia, Britain, and the USA. Trained as a specialist in the literature of the eighteenth century, he has been concerned for most of his career with reading, writing, and literacy development, and with pedagogical strategies which support learning in those areas. He is winner of a number of teaching awards, and has published widely as a journalist, reading researcher, and scholar of literacy learning.

John Juzbasich is CEO of Merit Systems LLC, a professional training company located in Wayne, Pennsylvania, USA. He is an Adjunct Professor of Management and Organization at the Pennsylvania State University's Great Valley School of Graduate Professional Studies and an Adjunct Professor of Leadership at the Campolo College of Graduate and Professional Studies, Eastern University, USA. He teaches graduate and undergraduate courses in strategic leadership, leading change, and cross-cultural studies. He is completing his D.Ed. degree in Adult Education from the Pennsylvania State University; he earned a Master's in Leadership Development from the Pennsylvania State University and a Baccalaureate in Economics from the Wharton School, University of Pennsylvania. His research interests include the role of temperament in adult leadership education, remote (virtual) instructor-led training, and multi-national and cross-cultural instruction. He is a member of the Society for Industrial and Organizational Psychology, the American Association for Adult and Continuing Education, and the International Leadership Association.

Virginia S. Lee is principal and senior consultant of Virginia S. Lee & Associates, a consulting firm based in Durham, NC, specializing in teaching, learning, and assessment in higher education. She has special expertise in faculty/educational development, inquiry-guided learning, course and curriculum development, and the planning and implementation of institution-wide undergraduate education reform efforts including quality enhancement plans. Over the past five years she has worked with approximately 70 colleges and universities in the United States, Canada, Qatar, and Turkey. She is a Former President (2007–2010) of the Professional & Organizational Development Network in Higher Education, the largest professional organization for faculty and educational developers in higher education in the world. She was selected as a Fulbright Specialist in 2010 for a term of five years.

Dmitry Leontiev is Professor at the Psychology Department of Lomonosov Moscow State University, Russia. He has earned both Ph.D. and Dr.Sc. degrees. He is also Head of the Research Lab of Personality Development of the Physically Challenged at Moscow State University for Psychology and Education and Head of the Research Lab of Positive Psychology and Quality of Life Studies at Higher School of Economics, Moscow, and Director of the Institute for Existential Psychology and Life Enhancement (EXPLIEN). He is author of numerous publications on the psychology of personality, motivation and self-regulation, psychology of art and personality assessment, including "Psychology of personal meaning" (1999, in Russian). National representative of Russia at the European Network of Positive Psychology, associate editor of the *Journal of Positive Psychology*, invited speaker at many national and international conferences, Promotional Award of Victor Frankl Foundation of the city of Vienna (2004).

Alyssa J. O'Brien is a lecturer at Stanford University, where she teaches in the Program in Writing and Rhetoric, the Public Policy Program, and Stanford's Continuing Studies Program. Since arriving at Stanford in 2001, Alyssa has written or co-authored several textbooks as well as many articles and conference papers. She has been an invited speaker in Asia, Europe, and the Middle East on subjects such as global learning, communication for leadership, visual rhetoric, and "mapping a change in writing." Over the past six years, she has directed the Cross-Cultural Rhetoric project (CCR), a research and teaching endeavor originally funded by the Wallenberg Global Learning Network. CCR now connects students across five continents and involves universities from ten countries through video-conference technology and blogs. Alyssa won the Phi Beta Kappa Outstanding Teaching Award in 2006, and what she enjoys most is helping people discover their voices in writing of all kinds.

Denise Potosky is Professor of Management and Organization at the Pennsylvania State University's Great Valley School of Graduate Professional Studies, USA. She earned a Ph.D. in Industrial Relations and Human Resources from Rutgers University, a Master's in Communication from the University of Delaware, and a Baccalaureate in Speech Communication with a minor in business from the Pennsylvania State University. She was a recipient of a Fulbright Scholar Alsace Regional Research Award in 2011 and is invited to conduct seminars and research internationally. She teaches graduate-level courses in global intercultural management, human resources management, leadership communication, and organizational behavior. Her research, published in leading journals, focuses on personnel staffing, with expertise in measurement and web-based assessment. Her research interests also include the individual, relational, and contextual factors associated with cross-cultural adaptation and leadership. She is a member of the Academy of Management, the American Psychological Association, and the Society for Industrial and Organizational Psychology.

Harriet Shenkman is Professor of Education at Bronx Community College, City University of New York. She is Founding Director of the Center for Teaching Excellence and Director of the First-Year Learning Communities, Office of Academic Affairs and former Chairperson and Deputy Chairperson of the Department of Education and Reading. Her research interests and areas of expertise include college-level pedagogy and faculty development, learning and cognition, developmental reading, learning communities and closing the assessment loop. She consults on building and sustaining Centers for Teaching Excellence, Learning Communities, Incorporating Cognitive Strategies into Teaching, and Closing the Assessment Loop.

Jim Spaulding is Senior Consultant and President of Lenape Associates, Inc., and is an experienced corporate educator. He also teaches a variety of subjects, including instructional design, database design, project management, and computer technology, at the Pennsylvania State University's Great Valley School of Graduate Professional Studies in Malvern, Pennsylvania, USA. He earned a Doctorate in Adult Education from Pennsylvania State University, a Master's in Educational Leadership from Immaculata University, and Bachelor of Science in Mathematics from Villanova University. He has published over 30 educational software titles for personal computers utilizing CBT and Simulation technology and is experienced in the computer industry as a systems engineer, project manager, consultant, and executive. He designs and delivers workshops and programs with instructor-led, virtual/hybrid, web-based, and computer-based training, and he maintains memberships in several professional organizations including IEEE, ACM, Project Management Institute, and American Association for Adult and Continuing Education.

Peter Charles Taylor is Associate Professor of Transformative Education at the Science and Mathematics Education Centre, Curtin University, Australia. His research focuses on exploring the role of new paradigms of research for professional development of teachers, cultural adaptation of science and mathematics curricula, and developing socially responsible science and mathematics education for sustainable development. He has published on these topics in numerous book chapters and journal articles and in his recent edited book, *Contemporary Qualitative Research: Exemplars for Science and Mathematics Educators* (2007, Springer). He has undertaken research consultancies in South Africa, Mozambique, Qatar, and Nepal and has presented keynote addresses at international conferences in Taiwan, Russia, and Iran.

Rupert Wegerif is Professor of Education and Director of Research at the Graduate School of Education in the University of Exeter in the UK. He has researched and published widely on dialogic approaches to education usually with technology and sometimes in relation to teaching thinking. He is currently directing and working on several projects investigating (1) talk in classrooms, (2) tools to support computer supported collaborative learning, and (3) dialogue across cultural differences in science education. He is co-editor of *Thinking Skills and Creativity*, an international journal with Elsevier. His new book entitled *Dialogic: Education for the Internet Age* will be published shortly by Routledge.

FOREWORD

Famously (if apocryphally), a question in the entrance examination for the University of Oxford (or was it Cambridge?) read: 'What is meant by "meant"?' Hugely bright English eighteen-year-old school pupils were intended to be taxed by it. And not surprisingly, for the idea of meaning is notoriously troublesome (and has been taxing philosophers for at least two thousand years). A book that sets out to tackle 'Meaning-Centred Education' is, therefore, taking on a very large task. What, after all, might be meant by 'meaning-centred education'?

What can surely be said uncontroversially is that there is hardly a more important concept in education—especially in a genuinely higher education—than that of meaning. For a genuine higher education has in part to be a process of education in which students come to handle concepts and ideas, and participate in tasks and activities, that have meaning to them. Of course, even then, we are hardly any further forward since the meaning of 'meaning' there remains unclear. To what degree does meaning have to imply personal meaning? And what might 'personal meaning' mean? Is the idea of personal meaning to be restricted to cognitive meaning or could it be widened to include a connection with a student's wider life (and so be 'meaningful')? And what of the idea of collective meaning: could it make any sense in this context? And even further, are there ideas of meaning that reflect cross-cultural differences, perhaps springing from different ideas as to the good life or well-being?

There are, therefore, manifold and highly complex matters afoot here. They are made more complex, in a way, in that they have hardly—to my knowledge—been hitherto exposed to a systematic unravelling. We are much in the debt, accordingly, of Olga Kovbasyuk and Patrick Blessinger, both in their discernment of key issues and in their marshalling of the contributions to this volume.

There is surely a particular timeliness to the publication of *Meaning-Centred Education*. For this is a world in which—so we are told—individuals are searching for meaning. It is also a world in which, as we see played out daily, different communities seek to impose their own frames of meaning upon each other, and even resort to violence in the process. It seems as if we are in a world that is both characterised by an evacuation of meaning and by strident efforts to fill that vacuum at the same time. But what connections might there be between such reflections about our age—at once secular and religious and at once scientistic and post-metaphysical—and a volume concerned with student learning? Does the promotion of meaning among students really have such societal and global considerations as its context?

Surely yes. For students are human beings, who are participating in higher education while simultaneously negotiating their own dilemmas and even traumas in their wider life. Characteristically, students' wider life is often very full, constituting many opportunities for their lifewide learning. Not just through their social networking (electronically and directly) but also through their multiple endeavours beyond the campus, students are interweaving with the wider world. Students are increasingly taking or forging opportunities to engage in experiences—paid and unpaid, in the private sector and in the public sector, for personal reward and financial gain, locally and globally—that not merely complement their formal learning experiences but abut them and even invade them. Students' lifeworlds and their university worlds intermingle so much so that their studies are affected by those wider experiences. The literature is as yet sparse on the matter but we may conjecture that students' reception of their formal learning experiences is not immune from their awareness and even experiences of profound ethical, social, gender, racial, religious and political matters. Students rarely live entirely separate lives in this respect.

It follows that the meaning that their course experiences have for students is influenced by the way students feel about their wider lives. In this highly fluid world, it is difficult if not impossible for tight boundaries to be maintained across different regions of life. Indeed, contemporary thinking about higher education—for example, the idea of students becoming 'global citizens'—trades upon this infiltration of life-zones; and so has thinking about education from the Greeks to the more modern German conception of Bildung and the English idea of liberal education. In these traditions, we see a sense that a genuine education is edifying for the individual as a person in the wider world. How this carry-over into the lifeworld of the student might be brought about is a further matter; and this volume helps us there, in offering chapters on the pedagogical challenges of enhancing the potential for meaning that students might derive from their studies.

Such considerations surely throw into high relief both the possibilities and the challenges in developing meaning-centred education. Perhaps, though, we should not feel daunted at the conceptual and practical challenges ahead of us. After all, it is not unknown for students at moments such as graduation day—in proudly introducing their parents to their tutors—to state somewhat animatedly that 'being here [at this university for these past three years] has changed my life'. That a life can be changed in this way surely denotes that higher education can reach deeply into a person's being; into the way they are in the world and the way they understand themselves as persons in the world. But all of this requires, as a necessary condition, that their experience of being a student has profound meaning.

'Meaning', therefore, has multiple meanings! A signal value of *Meaning-Centered Education* is that it draws the meaning of meaning-centred education very widely, encompassing both the more *interior* interpretations of meaning (in the student's immediate pedagogical experiences) and the more *exterior* interpretations (in the student's lifeworld). An issue that deserves even further study is that of the relationship between these two forms of meaning: is it that, typically, a student's progress (and meaning that she has found) in her studies imparts meaning to her wider life, or is it that a student's sense of well-being in her wider life (the meaning she finds in it) helps to impart energies to her in her studies and so enhances the possibilities for meaning that she finds there? Doubtless, there is an interweaving of these interior and exterior forms of meaning, and perhaps they have yet fully to be unravelled.

In a liquid age, meaning is elusive and even mysterious; and it is even being marginalised, through audit mechanisms that look for explicitness in programme descriptions. And yet, in a turbulent age, there is, as stated, probably no more significant issue in higher education; without meaning, the very enterprise of higher education is prejudiced. We are much in debt, therefore, to Olga Kovbasyuk and Patrick Blessinger for opening the space afforded by this volume for inquiry into meaning-centred education, and for the wide-ranging explorations of its contributors.

Ronald Barnett (r.barnett@ioe.ac.uk)
London, September, 2012

PREFACE

Olga Kovbasyuk and Patrick Blessinger

The Book

In recent years education in general and higher education in particular has undergone considerable changes and challenges due to the rapidly changing world. There appear new trends, paradigms, and philosophies (Asmolov, 2007; Ausubel, 2000; Lobok, 2001; Shuell, 1990) that reveal that educators all over the world are concerned about what directions to go in order to be better prepared for the challenges of the twenty-first century. The interest of the global society to education is increasing since the future of our planet depends on present and future graduates and how well they function in the local and global arenas.

Purpose

This book represents an increasing interest in meaning-centered education (MCE) and meaning-centered learning (MCL). The reason, as we view it, lies in the epistemological crises within social, humanitarian, and cultural sciences, which face paradigm shifts (Wulf, 2012). This situation provides urgency to view education from multiple perspectives, since discourses about humanity and education usually depend on the time, culture, and perspectives of how sciences interpret the notions of the individual and personality development. This leads to certain simplifications, since an individual is à complex phenomenon that requires multiple aspects of interpretation and research, across diverse disciplines and paradigms. This requires continual re-evaluation of knowledge and classifications about human beings and education, which reveal that the major notions of education, such as meaning and personality, often remain implicit under the conditions of epistemological and historical changes.

As editors of the book, and as educators and researchers operating in the international arena for many years, we first intended to gather diverse thoughts and practices related to meaning making and meaning-centered learning in education, to supplement them with theoretical foundations, and to offer this work as a mini reference on MCE-MCL scholarship and practice. In the process of our collaboration with each other and with our international colleagues, we expanded the initial task and generated a refined interpretation and explanation of MCE-MCL. In such a way, the book may serve as an interdisciplinary and transdisciplinary dialogue with scholars and educators from different countries and from different disciplines to provide multiple perspectives about MCE-MCL.

We provide an introductory psychological, philosophical, sociological, pedagogical, and scientific analysis of the dynamics of personal meaning making in educational processes to construct a theoretical framing of the MCE philosophy. The book also includes practical recommendations on how to apply the meaning-centered approach in a variety of teaching–learning situations. For example, how to build meaning in learning through sharing power with students (Tolman, this volume) and how to use reading and writing to develop meaningful contexts for learners (Geller, this volume). The book chapters are organized into three thematic parts that provide an overview for those not familiar with MCE-MCL as well as a rich and diverse set of new knowledge for those already familiar with MCE-MCL.

Structure

The first part, Theory and Principles of Meaning-Centered Education, presents the theoretical and methodological foundation of MCE, from historical to the present times, focusing on the psychological, philosophical, and experiential aspects of MCE. The second part, Worldwide Successful Practices: Voices of Experience, draws on the expertise of prominent researchers and practitioners of various academic disciplines and schools from around the world to illustrate examples of MCE in practice. The third part, Enhancing Meaning-Centered Teaching and Learning, while continuing the focus on teaching and learning, brings together findings and explorations of the cultural, social, and other factors which may be useful for the further development and research of MCE. The book structure is intended to reflect the dynamism and diversity of contemporary research of MCE. Each chapter attempts to provide a balanced overview of current knowledge and combine theoretical perspectives with recent empirical evidence. The style of the chapters is analytical but also engaging and accessible to anyone working in higher education or to students in schools of education. The authors also reflect on where the research agenda will likely advance in the future.

Aims

Some educational professionals in the post-industrial era question the soundness of contemporary higher education and its ability to respond to globally changing environments, including increasing cultural interaction, and the growing inter-dependence relative to policy making, technology, and economics, all of which affect the attitudes, values, and behaviors of learners. "Modern society is con-cerned that colleges and universities have given up on the meaning of life," and that, "exploring the questions of life's purpose and meaning appear to be hostile to a research ideal" (Kronman, 2007, p. 17). As a result, "the young people don't have any expectations regarding their future life, and they don't see any meaning in what they are going to do in that future" (Chudnovsky, 2009, p. 43).

However, many educators are making sincere attempts to renew their foci and ways of teaching in order to meet the needs of the new generation of learners. Within this context, many scholars and educators around the world have been increasingly interested in how to place personal meaning making at the center of teaching and learning and help make the teaching–learning process more personally meaningful to each participant. Glover (1997) has been developing a meaning-centered curriculum from everyday life. Barnes, Todd, and Heinemann (1995) elaborated on meaning making through talk. Zepke and Leach (2002) researched contextualized meaning making within experiential and self-directed learning.

There have been many publications on the related topics of transformative learning, student-centered learning, active learning, inquiry guided learning, problem-based learning, and dialogic strategies in education. It is our intention to broaden the territory of MCE-MCL by bringing together various perspec-tives on the subject, and developing a framework of MCE-MCL for teacher and learner scaffolding and support as we move towards new educational challenges in the new twenty-first century. To that end, MCE-MCL may help to enrich the teaching–learning process by expanding our thinking about how we can enhance learning opportunities and roles for participants.

Chapter Overviews

Part I: Theory and Principles of Meaning-Centered Education

These chapters address the theoretical perspectives of MCE, its philosophical knowledge base, and its underlying and related concepts, principles, and theories.

Chapter 1. In this chapter, The Nature and Origins of Meaning-Centered Education, Kovbasyuk and Blessinger examine the evolution of learning theo-ries to conceptualize the nature and origin of the meaning-centered educational philosophy, which remains an ongoing challenge due to its interdisciplinary and transdisciplinary character. They provide a theoretical foundation of meaning and meaning making, presenting different views and definitions of meaning. In addition, as viewed through the lens of the chapter authors' perspectives, they explore how MCE involves elements of constructivist, learner-centered, and transformative approaches and discuss the basis for a theory of meaning-centered learning (MCL), which they will articulate in more detail in Chapter 13.

Chapter 2. In this chapter, Emerging Contexts and Meanings of Human Education, Leontiev discusses how MCE supports varied life contexts and value relevance. Leontiev discusses the principle of MCE in the context of person–centered education, positive education, probabilistic education, and variational education.

Chapter 3. In this chapter, Dialogic Education in the Age of the Internet, Wegerif begins with a critical review of the major approaches to education called dialogic, including those inspired by Friere and Bakhtin. This leads Wegrif to the argument that the phrase "dialogic education" is best used to refer to education for dialogue as well as education through dialogue.

Chapter 4. In this chapter, Meaning-Centered Experiential Learning: Learning as an Outcome of Reconstructed Experiences, Potosky, Spaulding, and Juzbasich focus on the intersection of experiential learning, education theories, and meaning-centered communication perspectives and they argue that all experiential learning theories propose that learners derive meaning from their experiences, and that instructors can facilitate the meaning–making process in several ways.

Part II: Worldwide Successful Practices: Voices of Experience

These chapters explain recent empirical evidence and describe how MCE is currently being implemented in various curricula and in different cultural settings across the globe.

Chapter 5. In this chapter, Fostering Intercultural Dialogue via Communication Technologies, O'Brien and Kovbasyuk present the results of a case study that used MCE principles to enhance intercultural communication competencies and global awareness among students from several different universities on different continents.

Chapter 6. In this chapter, Making the Shift Towards a Meaning-Based Paradigm in European Higher Education: A Spanish Case Study, Cañado analyzes the creation of the European Higher Education Area (EHEA), known as the Bologna Process, and how EHEA is serving as a powerful lever for a meaning-based shift in teaching and learning.

Chapter 7. In this chapter, Meaning-Centered Integrative Instruction in Learning Communities, Shenkman explains how learning communities allow MCE to take place on many different levels in higher education and how they can foster cognitive skills, a sense of belonging, a connection with others, and a thematic and integrated approach to content instruction.

Chapter 8. In this chapter, True Collaboration: Building Meaning in Learning Through Sharing Power With Students, Tolman and Lee explain why facilitating a collaborative classroom environment and providing students with choices that impact their education is vital in order to fully enable genuine construction of personal meaning.

Part III: Enhancing Meaning-Centered Teaching and Learning

These chapters provide summaries of findings and additional recommendations of how MCE could be further enhanced in various curricula. These chapters provide insight for faculty, course and program designers, and learning architects on how to implement MCE strategy in a variety of teaching–learning spaces.

Chapter 9. In this chapter, Meaning's Secret Identity, Hunt explains the the-oretical and practical basis of thinking about language, and demonstrates some of the ways in which putting meaning at the center of classroom practice and developing an active relationship between the text creator and the text reader opens up new ways of approaching learning.

Chapter 10. In this chapter, How to Enhance Meaning-Centered Writing and Reading, Geller considers the question: What might university students' perceptions of their meaningful reading and writing experiences tell us about students' learning? Using insights gained from student perspectives this chapter suggests practical recommendations for crafting meaningful reading and writing activities.

Chapter 11. In this chapter, Supporting Students' Search for a Meaningful Life Through Inquiry-Guided Learning, Lee explains that inquiry is an inherently meaning-seeking activity driven by our innate desire to explain and make sense of our lives and the world around us. She explains it is a natural way of learning through the investigation of questions and issues relevant to learners.

Chapter 12. In this chapter, Research as Transformative Learning for Meaning-Centered Professional Development, Taylor explains how researchers can engage in transformative learning by using their own meaningful life experiences as a primary source of data for examining teaching and curriculum practices in their own countries. Such a transformation in personal agency involves developing diverse ways of thinking and new modes of consciousness.

Chapter 13. In this chapter, The Future of Meaning-Centered Education, Kovbasyuk and Blessinger describe the interdisciplinary and transdisciplinary nature of MCE-MCL. They explain and frame MCE-MCL at a micro-analytical level. They discuss MCE-MCL concepts and principles and how it relates to other prominent educational paradigms, and they discuss MCE-MCL classroom and curricular issues and strategies, and the meaning-centered learning environment and context.

Conclusion

In *Bread and Jam for Frances* (Hoban, 1964), the little badger's parents yield to her food fussiness and give her a steady diet of her favorite bread and jam. As time goes by, what Frances had longed for becomes dull and unappetizing. When Frances finally asks for some other food, her parents comment "naively" that they thought Frances did not like that other food. "How do you know what I'll like if you won't even ask me?" captures learners' need for a diversity of educational approaches in the classroom. In an MCE-MCL classroom, both teachers and students are learners, so all need to offer and to be open to new experiences as well as being supported in trying them out. The MCE-MCL experience may provide us with a chance to develop new likes, new interests, and new areas of competence, because it is centered on personal meaning, something we all seek throughout our lives. "How do I know what I like?" would be a good extension of Frances's question within the MCE-MCL domain, which supports learning about "self" and helps us to understand who we are and where we are heading.

References

Ausubel, D. P. (1963) *The Psychology of Meaningful Verbal Learning*. New York: Grune and Stratton.

Asmolov, A.G. (1990) *Psychology of Personality*. Moscow: Moscow State University.

Barnes, D. R., Todd, F. and Heinemann (Firm) (1995) *Communicating and Learning Revisited: Making Meaning through Talk*. Portsmouth, NH: Boynton Cook Publishers.

Chudnovsky, V.E. (2009) "Meaningful aspect of modern process of education." *Issues of Psychology* 2: 50–60.

Glover, M. (1997) *Making School by Hand: Developing a Meaning Centered Curriculum from Everyday Life*. Urbana, IL: National Council of Teachers of English.

Hoban, R. (1964) *Bread and Jam for Frances*. New York: Harper & Row.

Kronman, Antony (2007) *Education's End: Why Our Colleges and Universities Have Given Up on the Meaning of Life*. New Haven and London: Yale University Press.

Lobok, A. (2001) *Veroyatnostnyimir*. Ekaterinburg: Evrika.

Shuell, T. J. (1990) "Phases of meaningful learning." *Review of Educational Research* 60(4): 531.

Wulf, C. (2012) *Anthropology of Upbringing*. Moscow: Paxis.

Zepke, N. and Leach, L. (2002) "Contextualised meaning making: One way of rethinking experiential learning and self-directed learning?" *Studies in Continuing Education* 24(2): 205–217.

ACKNOWLEDGMENTS

In compiling this book, the editors have assembled some of the brightest and most innovative scholars from around the world to write on a topic that represents an educational philosophy (meaning-centered education) and learning theory (meaning-centered learning). In undertaking such an endeavor, we are especially grateful to the authors whose collegial efforts embody the spirit and ethos of the academy.

Next, we would like to give our word of gratitude to the teachers that we meet throughout the course of our life. They inspire us to seek learning, to stay relentless, and to be passionate and patient at the same time. Lydia Kulikova taught me to stay human under any circumstances and to presume goodness in people.

Our first teachers of life are our parents, so we would like to dedicate the book on teaching and learning to the ones who gave us the gift of life and learning.

Olga Kovbasyuk
President, 2011-2012
The HETL Association
E-mail: olga.kovbasyuk@gmail.com

PART I

Theory and Principles of Meaning-Centered Education

1

THE NATURE AND ORIGINS OF MEANING-CENTERED EDUCATION

Olga Kovbasyuk and Patrick Blessinger

Introduction

This book explores a vision of education where students and instructors engage in an open meaning-making process and where educational practices are not limited to preset curricular endpoints and standards. This book explores a vision of learning where learning is personally meaningful for learners and where communities of learners have rights and responsibilities on defining, exploring, and negotiating the themes and meanings of the teaching–learning process. Today's learners belong to a generation that is confronted with many challenges and changes brought about by the post-industrial age (Bell, 1999). As with prior generations, today's generation must re-examine the following perennial questions: What is the main purpose and aims of education? What are the proper roles for instructors and students? What is the meaning of learning in a post-industrial age? Why and how does personal meaning relate to human learning?

Only humans have the capacity for complex meaning making and higher order thinking (Goldberg, 2001), and educational institutions have been established to facilitate this meaning making through the teaching–learning process. One major difference between humans and the rest of the animal kingdom is the human ability to adapt, in very complex ways, the environment to themselves rather than simply adapting to the environment in a uni-directional way (Gredler, 2009). So, during the transition from the industrial era (1850–1950) to the post-industrial era (1950–present) we once again find ourselves asking these fundamental questions about the purpose, role, and meaning of education and learning (Kronman, 2008).

Globalization, Internet-based communication technologies, and other modern inventions have made us more inter-connected and inter-dependent and have altered the ways we communicate with and relate to each other and the world.

In essence, we have created many of the changes in the environment that we now find ourselves, in turn, having to adapt to. Thus, human adaption works in a bi-directional manner wherein we both adapt the environment to meet our own needs and also adapt to the environment that we helped create, thus creating a continuous cycle of complex change that we must learn to effectively manage in a sustainable way. Gredler (2009) notes that, "the relationship between knowledge and society has changed from the early centuries of civilization, in which knowledge was a privilege of the few, to the current open access to vast domains of knowledge" (p. 432).

Education, as a social institution, has been developed by modern nations to help maintain and sustain a well-functioning society. Education, and the learning that it produces, is important to both individuals and society. It is important for individuals because it equips them with the necessary knowledge, skills, abilities, attitudes, and values to adequately function in society as well as contribute to the development of a diverse lifestyle (Gredler, 2009). It is important for society because it allows the values, language, symbols, and developments of one generation to be "inherited" by the next generation (Vygotsky, 1978b). This, in turn, leads to progress of all kinds, without having to entirely re-discover or re-invent prior discoveries or inventions. Hence, education allows us to learn from prior generations in a more effective way.

Also, it follows that the more challenges and problems faced by societies, the more that educational institutions will be called upon to prepare current and future generations. Many groups, including policy makers, employers, the public, parents and school administrators, have an interest in making sure that higher education is relevant and meaningful to both instructors and students, and yet, how best to do this seems to remain elusive. Educational systems must be responsive to the changing needs of the current generation while at the same time laying the groundwork for future generations. The demands placed on educators as we enter the third millennium continue to challenge us to seek new and better ways to understand and improve the world we live in. So, educators around the world continue to seek new ways to improve and transform current educational systems to better address these needs. Educational philosophies and practices that were used for the industrial era are insufficient for meeting prevailing needs. With the development of a wide set of learning theories in the twentieth century, educators are now in a more informed position to develop new, improved philosophies and theories to explain human learning. The value of good theories is that they help us better explain and more reliably predict human behavior.

Evolution of Learning Theories

Early learning theories that evolved in the early part of the twentieth century include behaviorist theories (e.g. classical conditioning—Pavlov, 1927; connectionism—Thorndike, 1913), and cognitive theories (e.g., Gestalt—Wertheimer,

1928). While these two branches of theories have continued to evolve during the latter half of the twentieth century (e.g., operant conditioning theory—Skinner, 1953; information processing theory—Broadbent, 1958), a new branch of learning theories has evolved from an interactionist perspective which includes: developmental epistemology theory—Piaget (1963), cultural-historical theory—Vygotsky (1962), learning conditions theory—Gagne (1965), social-cognitive theory—Bandura (1986), and several recently developed academic motivation theories such as expectancy-value theory, goal orientation theory, and attribution theory. Also, these learning theories can be grouped according to learning process (e.g., Gagne, 1965; Skinner, 1953), cognitive development (e.g., Piaget, 1963; Vygotsky, 1962), and social context (e.g., Bandura, 1986; motivational theories). Finally, from a psychological view, these learning theories can be viewed from a behavioral perspective (e.g., Skinner, 1953; Thorndike, 1913; Watson, 1924), a cognitive perspective (e.g., Lewin, 1936; Tolman, 1932), or an interactionist perspective (e.g., Bandura, 1986; Gagne, 1965; Piaget, 1963; Vygotsky, 1962). The general trend in the last few decades has moved towards focusing on the complex nexus of personal, social, and cultural factors, at both the micro-analytical and macro-analytical levels, to help explain learning in a more holistic context (i.e., the totality of a person's life-world) and to better clarify the discrepancies within and the tensions between these theories (Gredler, 2009). Learning is a complex phenomenon due to the overlapping and intertwined nature of learning domains and the integrated nature of life experiences, which operate within a milieu of personal, social, and other factors.

The developments of these learning theories have been aided by developments in many fields, especially psychology, sociology, anthropology, brain research, and social science research methods. Also, the shift from animal and laboratory studies to real-life classrooms in order to study learning in its natural environment (e.g., formal learning in an organized classroom setting and informal life learning) has enriched our understanding of human learning and all its complexities. This shift has also been aided by moving from mechanistic models and metaphors (e.g., computers) to more naturalistic metaphors to better understand human learning. Some learning theories can be viewed as universal (e.g., Bandura, 1986; Piaget, 1963; Skinner, 1953; Weiner, 1985) because they presumably can be applied to any person in any setting and some learning theories can be viewed as particularistic (e.g., Vygotsky, 1962) where learning is particular to the signs and symbols of one's own language, history, and culture (Gredler, 2009).

Although these theories have differences in how they view and explain learning, each adds another piece to the puzzle of our understanding of the complex phenomenon of human learning. Although theory is necessary to our understanding of human learning, it is not, in and of itself, a sufficient condition for learning. Also needed is a sound educational philosophy that is consistent with the theory to help guide us in the proper use of the theory. The appropriate application of theory occurs within the broader context of the environment it operates within— the macro-level socio-cultural context (e.g., economic and social needs), the institutional context (e.g., the school's mission, vision, and value system, and its administrative policies), and down to the more micro-level professional context (e.g., code of ethics). Thus, although philosophy and theory are different, they can and should work together in a consistent and coherent manner in order to best fulfill the needs of society, the educational goals of the institution, and the learning outcomes of the students. To that end, sound philosophy is informed by sound theory, and vice versa, just as theory and praxis inform each other.

Educational Epistemologies

Educational constructivism is another recent development in learning, although its roots can be traced back to the work of Socrates, Aquinas, Kant, Heidegger, Dewey, and Foucault, among others. It is an educational philosophy that also has its roots in some of the previously mentioned learning theories. Constructivist philosophy holds that individuals construct their own knowledge from the personal or social milieu in which they live. There are several varieties of constructivism, including personal constructivism, which has its roots in Piaget, social constructivism, which has its roots in Dewey and Bentley (1949), Vygotsky (1978a, b) and Bandura (1986), and cognitive constructivism, which has its roots in Bruner (1990). Social constructivism, for instance, views learning in a technology saturated and highly mobile society as extending beyond the walls of the classroom and the school campus. Here, knowledge is a construct of a particular social setting and cognition is socially shared. The locus of learning extends beyond one's mind because learning is dispersed among a wider social community of learners. It is within this rich and diverse milieu of social interactions that personal meanings are continually reconstructed (Berger and Luckmann, 1967; Bredo, 1994; Hacking, 1999; Marshall, 1996). Another recent development known as critical constructivism integrates social constructivist with critical social theories (Kincheloe, 2004; Taylor, 1998). As noted by Taylor (this volume), the goal of this branch of constructivism is to build a democratic ethos of openness in the classroom using critical dialogue. For instance, the instructor guides the students to use multiple modes of inquiry and self-reflection (e.g., critical analysis, creative writing, role play) to develop higher order thinking skills and multiple perspectives.

Constructivist philosophy is held in contrast to objectivist philosophy, which has its roots in Aristotle, Locke, and others, and holds that knowledge and reality exists independent of the mind (Jonassen, 1991; Russel, 1945). These two main contrasting epistemologies (i.e., philosophy of knowledge and justified belief) have been debated for nearly 2,500 years and, broadly speaking, represent the rationalist (constructivist) and empiricist (objectivist) views (Steup, 2012; von Altendorf, 1993). We delve deeper into these epistemologies in Chapter 13 and offer a third view oriented around meaning-centered learning (MCL). Meaning making is a common thread that flows through these philosophies and theories but the challenge, however, is to conceptualize a meaning-centered education (MCE) philosophy that can be implemented in an educational setting in a coherent and evidence-based manner and to further develop the theoretical and practical foundations of MCE and to facilitate the development of a meaning-centered learning (MCL) theory. To help us move in that direction, we focus on the psychological character of MCE and we describe meaning-based principles of life and the fundamental ideas of personally meaningful education. We define meaning and meaning making from psychological, philosophical, and sociological perspectives to clarify the concept of meaning in relation to MCE. We also explain how MCE may be used to enhance student learning and professional development.

Philosophy and Theory

A philosophy is a structured, justified belief system that provides a consistent and unified view of the inner world of the individual and his/her external world and the relationship between the two worlds. A philosophy first defines the nature of reality (ontology) and then, using logic and reason, answers the relevant epistemological questions (what is knowledge?) and other questions that are coherent with that ontological definition (Gredler, 2009). Prior to the twentieth century, philosophy was greatly relied on to guide educational approaches and assumptions about learning. With the development of modern social sciences as academic disciplines (e.g., psychology, sociology, anthropology, neurology), and the refinement of various empirical research methods, we now have a much greater set of methods and methodologies upon which to assess the veracity of educational philosophies, teaching models, and learning theories. Theories, as opposed to philosophies, identify real-world events needed for learning to occur, they rely on research findings to substantiate the veracity of their claims, and they identify a specific set of principles that form the essence of the theory. Thus, in this sense, MCE can be viewed as an educational philosophy and MCL can be viewed as a proposed learning theory.

However, as Gredler (2009) notes, "the problem with a reliance on empirical research as the *sole* source of knowledge is that data collection does not necessarily clarify the nature of important events" (p. 7). Also, correlation does not equate to causation so one must be careful when interpreting quantitative data. Thus, the use of a wide array of both qualitative (e.g., ethnography, interviews, observations) and quantitative methods together with a sound educational philosophy and psychological principles can help us to better "triangulate" a more accurate and complete understanding of human learning that operates within a complex personal and social milieu. The power of theory is in its ability to predict human behavior but no single theory can account for all human learning. Each theory adds a piece of the puzzle to our understanding of human nature and human learning. The power of philosophy is to provide a broad value system upon which to guide educational development that is consistent with society's cultural values or a group's religious or ethical values. Although philosophy and theory are different, they need not necessarily be mutually exclusive and need not work in isolation of each other. For instance, as we discussed earlier, the development of an educational philosophy such as constructivism has been greatly influenced by the learning theories of Piaget, Vygotsky, Bruner, and Bandura, and learning theories are also informed by educational philosophies.

Hull (1935) identified three criteria for a theory and Gredler (2009) identified a fourth criteria related specifically to human learning theory. First, the theory must explicitly state the *underlying assumptions* upon which the theory is based. Second, the theory must explicitly define the *key terms* (e.g., concepts, ideas) upon which the theory is based. These two criteria then form the basic framework for the theory. Third, a *set of principles* must be defined and derived from the first two criteria and then tested and refined through appropriate research. Whereas the assumptions and terms form the foundation of the theory, the principles form the body of the theory. Fourth, the learning theory should adequately explain the core *psychological* mechanisms that impact learning, and in turn, help predict human behavior in a reliable way.

Meaning-Centered Learning

MCL, as a proposed learning theory, expands the following psychological and existential principles of the learning process: holism, self-regulation, and the self-creating experiential personal life-world. Holism in education corresponds to the humanitarian tradition (Gessen, 1998; Ventzel, 1993) as developing the humane in a human being and as the non-completeness of a human being who strives for completeness. Holism also corresponds to long-life sustainable learning and learning across all domains. These issues not only constitute the point of integration of MCL with philosophy, psychology, axiology, and other disciplines, but it also represents a challenge to set up criteria for testing the effectiveness of MCL.

The self-motivating and self-regulating character of MCL originates from the autonomous and self-strengthening nature of personality (Frank, 1992), which MCL seeks to support through a learner's efforts to self-evolve. The underlying mechanisms of personality development are freedom and responsibility, which are also considered as two major principles in personality existence and self-fulfillment (Leontiev, 2007). MCL aims to integrate these two major principles into the learning process, while providing diverse life contexts and developing meaningful relationships between learners and the world they live in. We hold that accepting freedom and responsibility as fundamental values of life and learning enables learners to create personal meaning from their own experiences in relation to prior experiences and supports them in developing their unique life-worlds.

Meaning-Based Principles of Life

All societies throughout history have maintained an interest in formal and informal educational systems as a way to equip citizens with needed knowledge and skills (Phillips, 2009). Dewey (1916) points out that education, in the broadest sense of the word, is also a means by which the social continuity and stability of life is maintained. So, education serves a variety of purposes and interests, at several levels and towards different groups. Education, as Dewey (1938) notes, should not be viewed from an either-or position, and educational philosophies and learning theories should not be viewed as completely mutually exclusive of each other. No single theory, by itself, can completely explain the whole phenomenon of human learning.

The changing world environment preconditions the newly emerging frameworks for education. Universities of the modern era should not only provide graduates with the knowledge and skills they need to function adequately within the modern world but they should also endeavor to create a supportive environment to help individuals develop mature personalities, able of taking full responsibility for their own life-worlds (Leontiev, 2007). This type of environment provides a setting where students are free to explore and develop diverse personal meanings within diverse life contexts that take place within the broad social milieu of life. The meaning-centered approach in education, as we view it, should bring more personal meaning into teaching and learning, more understanding of oneself in relation to the world, and a heightened awareness of multiple truths, multiple perspectives, and multiple modes of inquiry that exist in the world.

MCE-MCL aims to support the development of personality, which is in a constant state of evolving and maturing in order to participate in the variability of the world marked by enormous complexities, conflicts, and uncertainties. Modern societies will continue their evolution as long as education facilitates one's pursuit to evolve and to self-create (Berdyaev, 1999; Heidegger, 1962), thus allowing learners to achieve their personal authenticity and to act in accordance with self-sustaining meaning-based principles of life (Leontiev, 2007). The purpose of MCE-MCL is to facilitate the efforts to grow human potential within social groups, cultures, and people around the world.

Personally Meaningful Education and Learning

Education in the modern new era cannot only be concerned with just transmitting and acquiring factual knowledge, which Bloom (1956) described in his taxonomy of educational objectives to be a lower level of learning. Certainly, knowledge is a prerequisite stage but its value is most apparent when used together with higher order thinking skills such as synthesis, creativity, judgment, and moral reasoning. Thus, we cannot view students simply as passive recipients of factual knowledge (Ausubel, 1963; Bandura, 1986; Dewey, 1938; Freire, 1970; Novak, 2002; Shuell, 1990).

MCE-MCL aims at supporting the development of the self-determined personality, which possesses not just the cognitive abilities, but also the social and psychological abilities. Educators have an important role in facilitating the individual's pursuit to evolve and to self-create (Berdyaev, 1999; Heidegger, 1962). This facilitation allows the individual, as an authentic personality operating out of its own volitions, to be author of her/his life as she/he strives to make sense out of an often complex and confusing world and strives to find personal meaning in life experiences (Leontiev, 2007). There are several educational approaches related to personally meaningful education such as constructivist-based theories (Bredo, 2000; Dewey and Bentley, 1949; Lave, 1991; Marshall, 1996; Piaget, 1963; Vygotsky, 1989), learner-centered theories (McCombs and Whisler, 1997), and transformative theories (Brookfield, 1995; Cranton, 1994; Mezirow, 1991; Mezirow and Taylor, 2009), each complimentary to varying degrees. The complexity of human learning and the need for more effective and authentic ways to educate today's students is driving educational scholars and practitioners to search for more explanatory models that help bridge these learning theories and help provide more holistic and more personally meaningful and personalized learning environments. MCE-MCL includes the elements of dialogical and experiential learning, which support the uniqueness of each individual and strive to create a personalized learning environment.

Also, similarities with the cognitive-development theories of Piaget, Vygotsky, and Bruner stress the importance of inquiry learning and dialogue, instructor as facilitator, learning environments as open and collaborative places, and knowledge as relevant and personally meaningful. Thus, engaging students in personally meaningful activities and real-life experiences across all domains (cognitive, affective, social) is important. MCE-MCL places meaning making at the center of the teaching–learning process and thereby enriches the existent theories by the existential dimension of our being in the world and by viewing human life as a coherent whole, with a variety of possible contexts (preset biologically and culturally, as well as the contexts created autonomously).

For example, service learning is an educational approach that integrates community service activities with teaching and learning, thus supporting the diverse contexts of students' lives. Personally meaningful service learning allows students to answer the question: why is this important to me and to the world I live in? Personally meaningful service learning also allows students to learn more about themselves while solving real-life problems that are important to them. This can enhance learning by making it more authentic and more relevant to students' own value systems. The role of the instructor is also vitally important in MCE-MCL. The instructor is a facilitator and guide and should be in a dialogical relationship with students, capable of negotiating power boundaries, shared meanings, and transforming her/his personal perspectives along with her/his students.

Meaningful educational activities can also include global learning projects that are performed collaboratively by students and instructors from all around the world via modern communication technologies. Global learning favors collaboration and dialogue over power, control, and conflict (Belbin, 2001). MCE is anthropologically enriched because curricula (what to teach and learn) and process (how to teach and learn) and the context of meaning-centered teaching and learning (why teaching and learning is important) should orient around the human experience and become a discovery of "self" in relation to the world. According to Stepashko (2004), humankind, human being, and "self" constitute the axiological (value-related) essence of MCE.

Thus, the fundamental idea of MCE is to support authentic experiences that continually occur between "self" and people (interpersonal) and within each person (intrapersonal) and their life-worlds. The aim of MCE is to create a supportive, humane environment for students to self-develop their inner capabilities to become self-empowered and self-determined authors of their own life-worlds. In this book, we describe how MCE may help to serve as a bridge among current educational approaches, that is, a convergent educational philosophy, and how MCL may provide a theoretical framework for how higher education institutions can create supportive learning environments for individuals to explore multifaceted and flexible meanings in lives. In the next section, we look at meaning and meaning making through psychological, philosophical, and sociological lenses that help us further clarify the phenomenon of meaning, in relation to MCE-MCL.

Theoretical Framing of Meaning and Meaning Making

Meaning is a multidimensional phenomenon. For example, the cultural context includes meanings of language, symbols, etc., the personal context may include interpretations of human activity regulation (i.e., does it make sense for me to do this?) or deep philosophical instance (i.e., why is it morally important for me to do this?). Soloviev (1996) emphasizes the integrative instance of meaning for an individual this way: "Man should want something, celebrate something, and feel something—all this something is a starting point, a goal and credit of her/his internal power, life and spirit, this is exactly what is asked for, what is interesting, and what meaning is" (p. 134). Also, meaning making can be viewed from multiple dimensions, depending on the perspective of a researcher and/or a practitioner.

Meaning underlies all processes related to the human experience (e.g., subjective reality, objective reality) and is one of the key explanatory psychological principles of human behavior. Human behavior is driven by many factors beyond one's present situation; it concerns past events and future expectations and is not always purely rational or cognitive. In short, meaning involves the whole cluster of personal contexts (past, present, and future) that are personally important to an individual—the personal life-world that creates a web of meanings for an individual (Leontiev, 2005). MCE-MCL recognizes this as an important element in the learning process.

Meaning making is a uniquely human activity. The meaning-making process is not only of chief importance from a cognitive development and knowledge construction perspective but also because it allows us to intentionally link different contexts together and form a holistic web of meaning. The concept of meaning is one of the most important explanatory concepts of human life. Personal meaning helps to self-regulate human attitudes and behavior at all levels and in all contexts (Frankl, 1998). Dewey (1933) wrote, "Only when things about us have meaning for us, only when they signify consequences that can be reached by using them in certain ways, is any such thing as intentional, deliberate control of them possible" (p. 19). This implies that meaning has cognitive, affective, behavioral, and socio-cultural aspects to it. Thus, educators need to help learners link what they are learning to why it is important to them personally to how they can use it in their lives in a meaningful way.

So, MCE-MCL tries to address a fundamental question: how can we enhance the meaning-making process by making it more personally meaningful? Stated another way: how can we engage students and instructors to better develop their own life-worlds that will enable them to create more humane intentional contexts for the present and for the future? Answering the above question becomes increasingly important for higher education institutions as we move past the post-industrial era. We attempt to shed light on this question by exploring various perspectives of meaning and what it means to create a personally meaningful teaching–learning experience. These concerns are further investigated in this book within current teaching and learning practices and we hope the examples are thought provoking enough to spark further research and development on MCE and MCL.

The Meaning of Meaning: Dimensions of Meaning

Historically, the origin and relevance of our understanding of meaning is revealed through *hermeneutics*, which says that meaning is contextual and a word may have different meanings in different contexts (Gadamer, 1975). For example, educology as a science may represent the global dimension of education, which goes beyond the humanitarian sphere (Nikitenko, 2011). Thus, meaning operates at all levels (e.g., from the micro-level unique meanings to the macro-level life-encompassing meanings) and in all contexts. Meaning is constructed in a variety of ways and is presumably the underlying force behind our thoughts, feelings, and actions. It provides the framework through which we interpret the world relative to our beliefs, values, and motives, past experiences, future expectations, as well as any unconscious factors. New perspectives are brought about by our personal experiences and through the interaction with other perspectives. Knowledge and understanding of reality is therefore in an ongoing state of change where inquiry and personal reflection are of great importance to the learning process when it is grounded in thoughts, feelings, and actions that are personally meaningful to our lives.

The *phenomenological* dimension of meaning helps explain the way personal meanings occur and are fulfilled in educational settings. Thus, phenomenology makes the entire educational process more human-centered. In phenomenology, human consciousness is the source, which prescribes meaning to objects. "Meaning is not concrete, but the assumed or admitted idea of an object, which is perceived within the changeable characteristics, related to the context" (Husserl, 1999, p. 37). Human consciousness is intentional, so in education, it is critical to recognize the internal world of learners, which defines the trajectory of personality development and self-development. Cognizing unity through diversity of meanings also applies to the phenomenological constituency of MCE-MCL. For example, the traditional didactic approach of instructors differs from the phenomenological approach in the way learning is connected with the object of studies. Within the traditional approach, learners study the object itself, while the phenomenological approach considers the perception of the object by learners. Given that perceptions of learners are diverse, the object of study remains open for discovering new meanings, which continuously evolves, and diverse meanings may be applied to the same object, forming meaningful unities (Husserl, 1999).

The next relevant dimension of meaning, as related to MCE-MCL, is *philosophical* and is connected with the philosophy of existential meaning of the human being (Sartre, 1972; Tillich, 1995; Yaspers, 1991). "The human being can be the human being only due to her/his capacity to construct her/his own world in accordance with her/his meanings and values" (Tillich, 1995, p. 45). Human attitude to meanings, her/his striving to comprehend the deep contexts of things and events is directly connected with her/his uniqueness and creativity. Glasser (1975) states that, "the single basic need that people have is identity: the belief that we are someone in distinction to others, and that the someone is important and worthwhile" (p. 82). The belief that each person acquires a unique identity is critical in the philosophy of existential meaning of the human being, which supports the unique character of each individual to create and recreate self and reality (Bakhtin, 1990).

The *psychological* dimension of meaning, as related to MCE-MCL, is associated with existential psychology, which holds that meaning-based regulation of human behavior is viewed as a measure of humanity (Leontiev, 2005). Meaning-based regulation entails the logic of a life-world, the logic of free choice, the logic of responsibility to self and others, and the logic of justice, which are vital to the development of humanity. Humans are able to relate their activity to their entire life-world and their activity is determined by the world with all the relationships occurring within that life-world. This means that humans make decisions according to their own values, motivations, and preferences, taking into account the issues beyond the "here and now" situation. In MCE-MCL, personal reflection can become one of the major driving forces in developing the abilities of individuals to relate to their own inner worlds; it helps them make sense of the world events in the contexts of their own lives and to behave according to personal meaning (Kovbasyuk, 2010).

Another dimension of meaning, as related to MCE-MCL, is interpreted as the *sociological* dimension. Meaning of human action is manifested and thus can be explained through social interactions of individuals, as each action conveys subjective meaning. So, corresponding to one's own subjective meaning to others' subjective meanings, it is critical to be understood by others (Weber, 1990). Interpersonal relations also constitute important social and personal contexts of growth for an individual, since, "the human heart is woven of human relations to other people; what she/he is worthy of is fully determined by what human relations she/he aspires to and what human relations to other people she/he is capable to establish" (Rubenstein, 1957, p. 167). Consequently, developing value-based interpersonal relationships within a meaningful educational process, students and instructors will tend to explicate such value orientations towards the rest of the world (Vygotsky, 1989).

Taking into consideration all the different representations for meaning, represented in the arts, humanities, and sciences, the primacy of meaning is nonetheless very personal, contextual, relational, integrative, holistic, and dialogical (Mezirow and Taylor, 2009). Hegel (1927) noted that "Circumstances or urges dominate a person only to the extent to which he allows them to do so" (p. 45). People are constantly engaged in an analysis of their lives hoping to find personal meaning and purpose (Frankl, 1946; Rebore, 2001). One's life traverses the full range of emotions and lived experiences, from sorrow to happiness; from suffering to liberation; from oppression to emancipation; from alienation to belonging; from frustration to fulfillment; from humiliation to dignity. Along the way and in all experiences we attempt to find personal meaning in them; we even try to find personal meaning in the seemingly meaningless conditions of life (Frankl, 1946). Sharov (2005, p. 54) noted that humans are "doomed to explain themselves," and they naturally seek to explain their personal experiences in the world they live in.

Meaning Making as Sensemaking

According to theories on organizational sensemaking (Weick et al., 2005), meaning making involves peoples' attempt to not only understand the social environment they work in but also to try to shape that environment though their actions. Sensemaking is a social process that integrates meanings that people have acquired from past experiences and it is viewed from a group dynamics perspective (Weick, 1995). From this perspective, sensemaking as meaning making is considered more as a concept of a micro-sociological theory than a psychological one. Organizational sensemaking is influenced by several micro-sociological theories, including symbolic interactionism and ethnomethodology (Blumer, 1969; Garfinkel, 1967).

Organizational sensemaking is an iterative, interactive, contextual, interpretive, and retrospective process where the focus is on meaning making and the creation of group environments through social interactions (i.e., how sensemaking affects group behavior) rather than just on individual cognitive processes and behaviors. In this type of sensemaking, people co-construct the group environment (and group identity) they live in by interpreting the embedded meanings in their environment (e.g., group values, norms, symbols) and by creating new meanings by acting on that environment. Although the focus of sensemaking is at a group level, this micro-sociological view of sensemaking as meaning making may, nonetheless, serve as another starting point for studying meaning making at a personal level and from a psychological perspective (Dervin, 1992).

Meaning Making as Within Intentional Context

Adler (1992, p. 15) stated that "human beings live in the realm of meanings." Frankl (1967) believed meaning to be the central driving force that directs every human action. In spite of the different dimensions of the concept of *meaning*, it highlights the importance of the topic in both academia and the general public because meaning making is central and unique to the human experience (Leontiev, 2005). Regardless of what one studies and what one does, one cannot escape the relevance of meaning and the centrality of meaning making in the human experience.

A broad analysis of the various interpretations of meaning in psychology and the humanities explicates two common properties: (1) the meaning of something always exists within a definite context, and (2) meaning always relates to some intention or reason (Leontiev, 2007). This implies that meaning making is not just epistemological in nature but is also ontological, phenomenological, axiological, and existential in nature. Thus, meaning making is not a purely cognitive process and is, "why the problem of personal meaning escapes any positivistic approach (in the traditional sense of this word)" (Leontiev, 2005, p. 6). Making sense of the totality of our inner world (e.g., thoughts, feelings, beliefs, values, experiences, expectations) vis-à-vis the totality of the outer world we live in gives human experiences a unique quality not found in any other living creature.

Within the context of higher education, creating conditions for facilitating personally meaningful learning allows one to tap into that innate and unique human ability to transform both our inner worlds and the outer world in which we must all live. Thus, the role of the instructor is not just epistemological and pedagogical but is also value-based, ethics-based, and social action-oriented (Asmolov, 1990; Dewey, 1938; Freire, 1970).

Meaning Making as Critical Dialogue

Applied to education, the word 'dialogic' suggests a reinterpretation of the traditional mission of education to expand reason or 'λογοσ' ('logos'). On the monologic interpretation of λογοσ, education is understood as the transmission of correct thinking and true knowledge. The dialogic interpretation of λογοσ suggests education has to be understood as the continuous re-creation of meaning through engaging in dialogue (Wegerif, this volume).

MCE-MCL involves pedagogy where dialogue is not just a set of teaching methods but rather a holistic process for engaging both students and instructors in the co-creation of knowledge, skills, abilities, attitudes, and values. It is a collaborative and socially creative process of analyzing a problem or question through critical inquiry and personal reflection (Lowenthal and Muth, 2008; Searle, 1995). It is a pedagogy that is humane and value-based in its axiological approach, holistic and integrative in its epistemological approach, authentic and experiential in its phenomenological approach, and both objective and subjective in its ontological approach. This pedagogy is a communicative function that recognizes the importance of meaning making through dialogue and experience. Meaning itself is viewed as a dialogue by Buber (1993) and Bakhtin (1990).

In this way, education becomes more democratic in its ideals and begins to move away from a practice of domination, control, and passivity and towards a practice of self-determination, empowerment, and action where all people in the process are valued as critical thinkers and the focus of teaching is not merely on finding answers but on improving the quality of questions (Wegerif, this volume). So, MCE-MCL is concerned with the student as critical investigator as opposed to student as a mere receptacle to be filled with existent knowledge. In the latter case, the student is simply acted upon. In the former case, the student and instructor are both participants in the critical dialogue and are both co-creators in the learning process (Friere, 1993).

Meaning Making as Experiential Learning

The meaning-centered paradigm for education is related to experiential learning, as meaning making involves the integration of experiences into the multi-faceted context of one's life-world. Lewin, Dewey, Kolb, and others have asserted that experience is a widespread and effective means of learning. Experimental learning entails constructing and re-constructing life experiences in accordance with newly emerging meanings, where learning is meaning making (Potosky, this volume). Meaning making is the process of creating, reflecting, and assessing (Zull, 2002) and it is transformative by nature (Taylor, this volume). In the context of MCE-MCL, we view transformation not as a linear process but one full of zigzags and bifurcations, with confusion and chaos as a transitory state between one's prior state and one's new state.

According to Mezirow (1998), the process of learning is understood as a process of meaning making through reflection. The reflective experience becomes one of the major driving forces in transforming self and one's life-world. It widens the internal space in the individual, adding to her/his context of self-interpretation, self-identification, and personality development. Meaning making as experiential learning thus is a personalized process of self-transformation. Instructors can foster this process by allowing students to develop their own identity in a humane learning environment, respectful of their personal interpretations of objects, events, and experiences, which are rooted in their own values, motivations, and expectations. These voices and interpretations can be controversial as students take ownership of their individual reflection processes but educational settings should be places where students feel comfortable and safe enough to engage in these activities.

Students are more likely to engage in the learning process when they understand the purpose in what they are doing, and it is that authenticity and transparency which helps provide meaning (Kearsley and Shneiderman, 1998). Internal motivation to any activity occurs best when the causes for this activity germinate from inside an individual, according to her/his meanings and ultimate concerns (Emmons, 2004). To facilitate this motivation, education should become transformational and instructors should co-participate in explorations with students with caring, curiosity, discovery, and with the common struggle inherent in the human condition.

Meaning Making as Being and Evolving

Humans are in a continual state of evolving. An individual cannot help being in a state of self-formation as this is the only way for a person "to overcome her/his limits" (Berdyaev, 1999, p. 211) and to become free from externally imposed determination. This leads to the understanding that human self-becoming and the human aspiration for meaning in life may be viewed as a highly spiritual unity. The word spiritual, in this sense, stands for a human attitude that is characterized by sincere openness to the world (Kegan, 1982).

Each person acquires a unique identity and strives to overcome her/his insufficiencies through purposeful self-creation and individual empowerment (Kegan, 1982; Leontiev, 1975; Maysishev, 1989; Rubenstein, 1957; Zinchenko, 2004). Soloviev (1996) notes that "According to the moral foundations of life, we hold the process of human perfection as a collective process, which a collective person goes through, since the process of self-formation takes place in a family, among people, in mankind" (p. 77). This assertion emphasizes the importance of two critical issues: one holds that it is not only the individual efforts of people toward self-perfection that are valuable but also the general efforts of all people to perfect themselves and society. Thus, the pursuit of human potential cannot be carried out in isolation but only in cooperation between people. Within MCE-MCL, the value of collaboration among participants in co-creating new knowledge and meaning is one of the major prerequisites of creating meaningful learning environments.

Authors' Meaning Making Perspectives

The book authors define the various aspects of MCE-MCL from a variety of disciplinary perspectives, such as psychology, philosophy, pedagogy, instructor education, sociology, linguistics, and cultural studies.

Leontiev elaborates on why human education cannot be but meaning-centered, providing an analysis of the anthropological essence of human education.

Wegerif reminds us of the importance of critical dialogue and self-agency and explains why dialogism serves as a type of model for human meaning making.

Potosky, Spaulding, and Juzbasich stress the importance of reflection and intra-personal communication that are at the core of the meaning making process.

O'Brien and Kovbasyuk explain the importance of holistic self-development in meaning making.

Cañado holds that creating a learner-centered educational environment helps to develop learners' critical thinking skills as a necessary component in meaning making.

Shenkman stresses the importance of a learner-centered view of teaching and learning where the focus is on meaning making derived by the student.

Tolman and Lee explain why power sharing and student empowerment helps create a more effective meaning-making environment.

Hunt views meaning-making as a social process by placing meaning as a verb, rather than a noun, at the center of teaching and learning.

Geller illustrates how the meaning-making process facilitates personal growth by allowing individuals to discover who they are and who they will become.

Lee explains why inquiry guided learning is important in creating one's personal search for meaning and purpose in life.

Taylor reminds us that the social responsibility aspect of meaning-centered education is to create a democratic and open ethos in the classroom that fosters multiple modes of thinking.

Meaning-Centered Learning

MCL is human centered and is oriented around holistic human development because a human being represents the means, the aim, the subject, the result and the criteria of the MCL learning process. MCL provides diverse authentic life contexts for learning and for creating one's own life-world. Based on the broad concepts of MCE as an educational philosophy, MCL can be viewed as a human centered approach to learning that facilitates the holistic integration of all learning domains and (affective, cognitive, social) through diverse life contexts, which motivates learners to apply meaning-based principles into their own life-world. MCL is learning from life, in all its complexity and variety, through all meaning-making processes inherent in human consciousness.

Based on the suppositions presented in this book, we define MCL as a type of self-motivated and self-regulated learning through building personal meaning in one's life-world through diverse meaningful activities, including reflective, critical, and inquiry-based activities. Thus, the learner learns how to create personal meaning from personal experiences and their relationship to prior experiences on the basis of their own value system and motivations. The basic underpinnings for MCL were laid out by Kovbasyuk (2009, 2010, 2011) and will be explained further in Chapter 13 (Kovbasyuk and Blessinger, this volume).

Conclusion

In this chapter, we have explicated several salient ideas of meaning and meaning making from relevant educational philosophies and learning theories, and from this, we have identified the following set of characteristics that comprise the essence of MCE-MCL that may, in turn, provide a start to an ongoing critical dialogue and examination of the topic. Thus, MCE-MCL:

- enables learners to better learn and share from each other in a more authentic way because of its dialogic and social nature
- appeals to each student's personal experiences, meanings, values, and personal life-world because of its experiential nature
- encourages learners to actively seek, define, and express meanings through reflection, inquiry, and engagement with multiple dialogues and perspectives
- involves creating self and global awareness through multiple cultural and disciplinary perspectives about who we are, how we relate to the world, and what it means to be human in a post-industrial world
- minimizes unnecessary and arbitrary power distance between students and instructors because it rests on validity and merit claims, not on unquestioned power and privilege claims
- through its open meaning-making process:
  - o fosters higher levels of consciousness through the development of self-awareness, self-reflection, and self-actualization
  - o fosters higher levels of autonomy though the development of self-motivation, self-regulation, self-efficacy, and self-determination
  - o fosters creativity, imagination, and innovative thinking
  - o fosters critical dialogue, critical thinking, and problem solving
  - o supports and involves pedagogical pluralism and holistic learning
  - o supports and involves interdisciplinary and transdisciplinary practices and thinking.

Analysis of the philosophical and psychological foundations of MCE-MCL shows that a number of dimensions of meaningful approaches to education have been developed and pursued by many thinkers and educators around the world for the last two-and-a-half thousand years and it continues to evolve. Continuing to explore emergent educational philosophies like MCE is important as we enter the post-industrial age with all its complexities and interdependencies. Thus, based on the findings presented in this book, we define MCE to be an educational approach that facilitates the conscious integration of new learning with prior learning across all domains based on personal meanings about oneself in relation to the world. MCE aims to create an authentic learning environment that supports a self-regulating and autonomous personality who operates out of her/his own volition and strives to achieve self-fulfillment and self-determination as an indicator of his/her existential worldview.

However, it remains an ongoing challenge to implement an MCE philosophy and an MCL theory because of their interdisciplinary and transdisciplinary roots. Nonetheless, MCE as a guiding philosophy can serve as a useful guide to help shape educators' thoughts, attitudes, and behavior relative to teaching and learning. Because the nature of knowledge is fluid and the nature of the world and human consciousness is multidimensional, it is important, through research and evidence-based practices, to continually improve our understanding and application of MCE and MCL relative to the scholarship and practice of meaning-centered teaching and learning.

References

Adler, A. (1992) *What Life Could Mean to You* (C. Brett, Trans.). Oxford: Oneworld. (Original work published in 1931).

Asmolov, A. G. (1990) *Psychology of Personality*. Moscow: Moscow State University.

Ausubel, D. P. (1963) *The Psychology of Meaningful Verbal Learning*. New York: Grune and Stratton.

Bakhtin, M. M. (1990) *To the Philosophy of the Action*. Moscow: Nauka.

Bandura, A. (1986) *Social Foundations of Thought and Action: A Social-Cognitive Theory*. Upper Saddle River, NJ: Prentice Hall.

Barnes, D. R., Todd, F. and Heinemann (Firm) (1995) *Communicating and Learning Revisited: Making Meaning Through Talk*. Portsmouth, NH: Boynton Cook.

Belbin, R. M. (2001) *Managing without Power: Gender Relationships in the Story of Human Evolution*. Oxford: Butterworth Heinemann.

Bell, D. (1999) *The Coming of Post-Industrial Society*. New York: Basic Books.

Berdyaev, N. A. (1999) *Man, His Freedom and Spirituality*. Moscow: Flinta.

Berger and Luckmann (1967) *The Social Construction of Reality: A Treatise in the Sociology of Knowledge*. Garden City, NY: Anchor Books.

Bloom, B. and Krathwohl, D. (1956) *Taxonomy of Educational Objectives: The Classification of Educational Goals, by a Committee of College and University Examiners. Handbook 1: Cognitive Domain*. New York: Longmans.

Blumer, H. (1969) *Symbolic Interactionism: Perspective and Method*. Englewood Cliffs, NJ: Prentice Hall.

Bredo, E. (1994) "Reconstructing educational psychology: Situated cognition and Deweyan pragmatism." *Educational Psychologist* 29(1): 23–25.

Bredo, E. (2000) "Reconstructing social constructivism." In D. C. Phillips (Ed.), *Constructivism in Education. Ninety-ninth Yearbook of the Society for the Study of Education* (pp. 127–157).

Broadbent, D. E. (1958) *Perception and Communication*. London: Pergamon.

Brookfield, S. (1995) *The Critically Reflective Teacher*. San Francisco, CA: Jossey-Bass.

Bruner, J. (1990) *Acts of Meaning*. Cambridge, MA: Harvard University Press.

Buber, M. (1993) *I and YOU*. Moscow: Respublika.

Chudnovsky, V. E. (2009) "Meaningful aspect of modern process of education." *Journal Issues of psychology,* 2009(2): 50–60.

Cranton, P. (1994) *Understanding and Promoting Transformative Learning*. San Francisco, CA: Jossey-Bass.

Dervin, B. (1992) "From the mind's eye of the user: The sense-making qualitative-quantitative methodology." In J. D. Glazier and R. R. Powell (Eds), *Qualitative Research in Information Management* (pp. 61–84). Englewood, CO: Libraries Unlimited.

Dewey, J. (1916) *Democracy and Education: An Introduction to the Philosophy of Education*. New York: Macmillan.

Dewey, J. (1933) *How we think*. New York: Heath Books.

Dewey, J. (1938) *Experience and Education*. New York: Touchstone.

Dewey, J. and Bentley. A. (1949) *Knowing and the Known*. Boston, MA: Beach Press.

Emmons, R. (2004) *Psychology of Ultimate Concerns*. Moscow: Smysl.

Frank, S. (1992) *Moral Foundations of Society*. Moscow: Respublika.

Frankl, V. (1946) *Man's Search For Meaning*. Boston, MA: Beacon.

Frankl, V. (1967) *Psychotherapy and Existentialism*. New York: Simon and Schuster.

Frankl, V. (1998) *The Unheard Cry for Meaning*. New York: Basic Books.

Freire, P. (1970) *Pedagogy of the Oppressed*. New York: Continuum.

Freire, P. (1993) *Pedagogy of the Oppressed*. London and New York: Penguin.

Gadamer, H.-G. (1975) *Truth and Method*. New York: The Seabury Press.

Gagne, R. M. (1965) *The Conditions of Learning*. New York: Holt, Rinehart & Winston.

Garfinkel, H. (1967) *Studies in Ethnomethodology*. Englewood Cliffs, NJ: Prentice Hall.

Gessen, S. (1998) *Theory of Pedagogy: Introduction into the Applied Philosophy*. Moscow: Nauka.

Glasser, W. (1975) *Schools without Failure*. New York: Harper & Row.

Glover, M. (1997) *Making School by Hand: Developing a Meaning Centered Curriculum from Everyday Life*. Urbana, IL: National Council of Teachers of English.

Goldberg, E. (2001) *The Executive Brain: Frontal Lobes and the Civilized Mind*. New York: Oxford University Press.

Gredler, M. (2009) *Learning and Instruction: Theory into Practice*. Upper Saddle River, NJ: Merrill Pearson.

Hacking (1999) *The Social Construction of What?* Cambridge, MA: Harvard University Press.

Hegel, G. W. F. (1927) "Philosophische Propadeutik" [Philosophical prevention]. *In Samtliche Werke [Collected Works]* (Vol. 3). Stuttgart, Germany: Frommann.

Heidegger, M. (1962) *Being and Time*. New York: Harper & Row.

Hull, C. L. (1935) "Conflicting psychologies of learning: A way out." *Psychological Review* 42: 491–516.

Husserl, E. (1999) Идеи к чистой феноменологии [*Ideas Towards Pure Phenomenology*]. Moscow: Дом интеллектуальной книги [House of Intellectual Books].

Jonassen, D. H. (1991) "Objectivism versus constructivism: Do we need a new philosophical paradigm?" *Educational Technology Research and Development* 39(3): 5–14.

Kearsley, G. and Shneiderman, B. (1998) "Engagement theory: A framework for technology-based teaching and learning." *Educational Technology* 38(5): 20–23.

Kegan, Robert (1982) *The Evolving Self*. Cambridge, MA: Harvard University Press.

Kincheloe, J. (2004) *Critical Constructivism*. New York: Peter Lang.

Kovbasyuk, O. V. (2009) "The role of meaning in raising personality." *Selected Scholarly Publications on Timely Issues of Communication and Culture.* Moscow, Pyatigorsk: Pyatigorsk State Linguistic University, pp. 254–267.

Kovbasyuk, O. (2010) "Meaningful education as a resource of global learning." In M. Alagic, G. Rimmington, F. Liu and K. Gibson (Eds), *Locating Intercultures: Educating for Global Collaboration* (pp. 119–140). India: Macmillan.

Kovbasyuk, O. (2011) "Meaning centered global learning in the far east of Russia." *Regional Problems.* Russia: Academy of Science, Birobidjan, pp. 12–16.

Kronman, A. (2008) *Education's End. Why Our Colleges and Universities Have Given Up on the Meaning of Life.* New Haven and London: Yale University Press.

Lave, J. (1991) "Situated learning in communities of practice." In L. Resnick, J. Levine and S. Teasley (Eds), *Perspectives on Socially Shared Cognition* (pp. 63–82). Washington, DC: APA.

Leontiev, A. N. (1975) *Activity. Consciousness. Personality.* Moscow: Politizdat.

Leontiev, D. (2005) "The phenomenon of meaning: How psychology can make sense of it." *International Journal of Existential Psychology & Psychotherapy* 1(2).

Leontiev, D. (2007) *Psychology of Meaning.* Moscow: Smysl.

Lewin, K. (1936) *Principles of Topological Psychology.* New York: McGraw-Hill.

Lowenthal, P. and Muth, R. (2008) "Constructivism." In E. F. Provenzo, Jr. (Ed.), *Encyclopedia of the Social and Cultural Foundations of Education* (pp. 177–179). Thousand Oaks, CA: Sage.

McCombs and Whisler (1997) *The Learner-Centered Classroom and School.* San Francisco, CA: Jossey-Bass.

Marshall, H. (1996) "Clarifying and implementing contemporary psychological processes." *Educational Psychologist* 31(1): 29–34.

Maysishev, V. N. (1989) *Psychology of Relationships.* Voronezh: Institute of Applied Psychology.

Mezirow, J. (1991) *Transformative Dimensions of Adult Learning.* San Francisco, CA: Jossey-Bass.

Mezirow, J. (1998) *Learning as Transformation: Critical Perspectives on a Theory in Progress.* San Francisco, CA: Jossey-Bass.

Mezirow, J. and Taylor, E. W. (Eds) (2009) *Transformative Learning in Practice: Insights from Community, Workplace, and Higher Education.* San Francisco, CA: Jossey-Bass.

Nikitenko, V. N. (2011) "Mission of education from the global perspective." *Regional Problems.* Russia: Academy of Science, Birobidjan, pp. 23–26.

Novak, J. D. (2002) "Meaningful learning: The essential factor for conceptual change in limited or appropriate propositional hierarchies leading to empowerment of learners." *Science Education* 86(4): 548–571.

Pavlov, I. P. (1927) *Conditioned Reflexes: An Investigation of the Physiological Activity of the Cerebral Cortex* (G. V. Anrep, Trans.). New York: Dover.

Phillips, D. C. (2009) "Philosophy of education." In E. N. Zalta (Ed.), *The Stanford Encyclopedia of Philosophy* (Spring 2009 Edition). Available online from: http://plato.stanford.edu/archives/spr2009/entries/education-philosophy/ (accessed December 6, 2012).

Piaget, J. (1963) *The Origins of Intelligence in Children.* New York: Norton.

Rebore, R. (2001) *The Ethics of Educational Leadership.* Englewood Cliffs, NJ: Prentice-Hall.

Rubenstein, S. L. (1957) *Personality's Self-Consciousness and the Life Way.* Moscow: Nauka.

Russel, B. (1945) *A History of Western Philosophy*. New York: Simon & Schuster.

Sartre, J. P. (1972) *The Psychology of Imagination*. London: Methuen.

Searle, J. (1995) *The Construction of Social Reality*. New York: Free Press.

Sharov, M. (2005) *Personality in Modern Philosophy*. Moscow: Mysl.

Shuell, T. J. (1990) "Phases of meaningful learning." *Review of Educational Research* 60(4): 531.

Skinner, B. F. (1953) *Science and Human Behavior*. New York: Macmillan.

Soloviev, V. S. (1996) *Moral Philosophy*. Moscow: Mysl.

Stepashko, L. (2004) *Philosophy of Education*. Khabarovsk: KhGPU.

Steup, Matthias (2012) "Epistemology." In E. N. Zalta (Ed.), *The Stanford Encyclopedia of Philosophy* (Fall 2012 Edition). Available online from: http://plato.stanford.edu/archives/fall2012/entries/epistemology/ (accessed December 6, 2012).

Taylor, P. C. (1998) "Constructivism: Value added." In B. J. Fraser and K. G. Tobin (Eds), *The International Handbook of Science Education* (pp. 1111–1123). Dordrecht, The Netherlands: Kluwer Academic.

Thorndike, E. L. (1913) *Educational Psychology: Vol. II. The Psychology of Learning*. New York: Teacher's College Press.

Tillich, P. (1995) *Theology of Culture*. Moscow: Moscow State University.

Tolman, E. C. (1932) *Purposive Behavior in Animals and Men*. New York: Appleton-Century-Crofts.

Ventzel, K. (1993) *Free Upbringing: Selected Works*. Moscow: Pedagogika.

von Altendorf, A. and von Altendorf, T. (1993) *ISMs: A Compendium of Concepts, Doctrines, Traits, and Beliefs from Ableism to Zygodactylism*. Memphis, TN: Mustang Publishing.

Vygotsky, L. S. (1962) *Thought and Language*. Cambridge, MA: MIT Press. (Original work published in 1934).

Vygotsky, L. S. (1978a) *Mind in Society: The Development of Higher Psychological Process*. Cambridge, MA: Harvard University Press.

Vygotsky, L. S. (1978b) "Consciousness as a problem in the psychology of behavior." *Soviet Psychology* 176(4): 3–35. (Original work published in 1924).

Vygotsky, L. S. (1989) *Pedagogical Psychology*. Moscow: Nauka.

Watson, J. B. (1924) *Behaviorism*. New York: Norton.

Weber, M. (1990) *Selected Works*. Moscow: Progress.

Weick, K. E. (1995) *Sensemaking in Organizations*. Thousand Oaks, CA: Sage.

Weick, K. E., Sutcliffe, K. M. and Obstfeld, D. (2005) "Organizing and the process of sensemaking." *Organization Science* 16(4): 409–421.

Weiner, B. (1985) *Human Motivation*. New York: Springer-Verlag.

Wertheimer, M. (1928) "Laws of organization in perceptual forms." In W. Ellis (Ed.), *A Source Book of Gestalt Psychology* (pp. 71–88). New York: Harcourt Brace.

Yaspers, K. (1991) *Meaning and the Purpose of History*. Moscow: Izdatelstvo Politicheskoi Literaturi.

Zepke, N. and Leach, L. (2002) "Contextualised meaning making: One way of rethinking experiential learning and self-directed learning?" *Studies in Continuing Education* 24(2): 205–217.

Zinchenko, V. P. (2004) *Man Self-Developing*. Moscow: Trivola.

Zull, J. E. (2002) *The Art of Changing the Brain*. Sterling, VA: Stylus.

2

EMERGING CONTEXTS AND MEANINGS OF HUMAN EDUCATION

Dmitry Leontiev

Introduction

Education is one of the cornerstones of human civilization. It was only in the last century that it was recognized as a social, rather than personal, concern, as something that brings critical benefits for the whole of society and humanity at large, above and beyond individuals. Indeed, it was only at the beginning of the twentieth century that free time and some money for making use of it emerged in some economically advanced countries as a societal phenomenon rather than a privilege of "the idle classes," giving birth to "the revolt of the masses" (Ortega y Gassett, 1929). Now education is one of the main domains of public policy in most countries. At the individual level education has always been recognized as one of the main paths to social success; however, if in the past it has been a privilege for the few and the object of envy for many, now it is a *sine qua non* condition for a decent social position in many technologically advanced societies. On the other hand, it is not always a matter of well-being and financial success; what is influenced most by educational level is the style of life, rather than its quality.

Nowadays, despite broad experimentation with educational methods in advanced schools—mostly private ones—mass education in most societies has turned into an assembly line and is broadly criticized for its incapacity to solve the problems of personality development, rather than simply competence. The increasing role of technologies—including social and psychological technologies such as democratic elections, career development or vocational choice—shifted the focus of education to those technologies, establishing the level of their mastery necessary for every member of society. The same refers to basic knowledge, the traditional focus of education. This aspect of education is relatively easy to formalize and standardize. The more emphasis is put on it, however, the less attention is paid to the other, less formal aspects that are harder to put into algorithms. Bertrand Russell, a truly profound thinker, paid attention to this as early as 1930, detecting as one of the defects of modern higher education its having become too much "a training in the acquisition of certain kinds of skill, and too little an enlargement of the mind and heart" (Russell, 1930, pp. 173–174). More recently Krasko (2004) put it this way:

> However, only recently this awareness has become the issue of public concern. Education in our society has given way to *training*, which focuses on providing a person with specific knowledge, called *skills*, useful in getting a good or better job, rather than enlarging that person's connection with the world of humanitarian culture, and enhancing one's sense of identity with our civilization. Unwittingly, our educational system, rather than helping to develop strong personalities, in fact prevents people from acquiring *maturity*. Hence, the loss of direction in people's lives.
>
> *(p. xxi)*

This loss of direction can be seen in the growing number of serious problems with adolescent addictions, abortions, suicides, violence, etc. They are rooted in a vacuum of meaning. Having learned the adult technologies of dealing with people and things in the world, many adolescents did not learn the reasons to apply these technologies. Simply speaking, they received no sense of meaning from their education.

In this chapter I shall try, starting from the analysis of the anthropological essence of human education, to prove the inevitability of its being person-centered, or meaning-centered. Then I will briefly present two views in present-day Russian philosophy of education that give due value to the living, informal, personalized aspects of this lifelong enterprise. Finally, I will dwell on subtler distinctions within what is usually called meaning, distinguishing between the dynamics of cultural and personal meanings, and draw some conclusions for the educational domain.

Education as Human Enterprise

Referring again to Krasko (2004):

> *Education* is an aspect of human civilization that is of a fundamentally individual character, although an effort by the whole society is necessary for its successful development. Education is also of a fundamental *existential* character simply because it is the opening of a window on the world. It allows us to see *who* we are, *where* we came from, and *where* we are heading. It gives us a gulp of fresh air, even if we feel there is no air left to breathe. It tells us something about ourselves that we did not know before. It helps

us to mature—building up our souls and filling them with meaning. Education helps us to become members of the family called humankind and thus have a share in its inheritance. It leads us to feel responsible not only for our loved ones and ourselves, but also for the whole world—its destiny.

(pp. xix–xx)

In other words, education in many ways connects us to each other and to the world in which we live, helping us to transcend the boundaries of our individual experience. The place of education in the global evolutionary process, as well as its specifics in humans, can be deduced from the structure of autoregulation processes (Leontiev, 2012b). Autoregulation as the basis of development of all living creatures means the capacity to improve performance based on feedback signals about the discrepancy between the desired and the actual state of affairs (Bernstein, 1967; Carver and Scheier, 1998). The structure of this process includes a few necessary elements: a criterion of the desired; motor activity implementation mechanisms; an "acceptor" of the incoming feedback information on actual activity results; a unit of comparison between the desired and the factual; and a unit of motor corrections upon the results of the comparison. This is the universal basis of all learning, all survival, all natural selection; adjustment requires constant corrections and survival presupposes constant improvement: improve or die. All animal and human learning is based on these mechanisms; however, in animals, what is being improved through lifelong training is, first, activity implementation mechanisms, and second, cognitive mechanisms of getting the feedback information from the environment. The invariable criteria of the desirable are preset biological imperatives of survival and procreation.

Human beings are the only creatures in which criteria of the desirable vary. Over and above the biological imperatives, new dimensions of human existence, the social and personal ones, emerge, and new imperatives of what is good and desirable enter the stage (Leontiev, 2012a). Not only different persons but even one person at different times may give different answers to the question about the ultimate meaning of his or her life that would serve as the criterion for evaluating and correcting all current activities. Hence, human lifelong learning includes not only training in the most efficient ways to achieve the preset goals and desired outcomes, but also learning meanings and goals, choosing and prioritizing what is to be desired, where to direct one's activity and what is worth efforts of this or that scale.

These meaning-making criteria and contexts vary across cultures and across individuals and may change—or not change—with individual maturation or historical dynamics. In all societies, growing individuals learn cultural norms and expectations that regulate social behavior. This is a technological knowledge. However, they also learn the meaning—the reason why they should conform to the norms even if they don't like them. This meaning can be different. Some patriarchal cultures and societies refer to these norms as divine gifts. Some authoritarian societies state that an individual should sacrifice his or her individual convenience in favor of the common interest and order. Democratic cultures explain it as a mechanism of respecting your fellows who have the same rights as you.

Seventy years ago Bronislaw Malinowski, one of the founders of cultural anthropology, listed new imperatives stemming from the social way of life inherent in humans, which are distinct from biological imperatives. Education is a human response to one of them, that of intergenerational transmission of collective experiences and competencies (Malinowski, 1944). I would deem it more appropriate to speak of education as a human cultural institution accounting for individual development.

Three aspects can be separated in human development: maturation of organs and functional systems aimed at successful biological functioning (Development 1), socialization through the appropriation of accumulated collective experience aimed at adjusted social functioning (Development 2) and optional self-determination and choice of personal developmental trajectory aimed at fulfilling personal existence (Development 3) (Leontiev, in press). Education as a cultural institution is designed mostly for supporting Development 2; however, the three aspects cannot be fully isolated from each other except as a theoretical speculation. Educational systems are not committed to considering what is going on with personality development in educational systems, and usually they don't take over the responsibility for this.

Person-Centered Alternatives to Technological Education

What has been stated above makes clear the gap between the actual technological emphasis in the curricula of mass school education worldwide and the actual demands of a more personalized approach. It is evident now that education cannot be reduced to the transfer of skills and information but must be relevant to varied life contexts and value problems, to the issues of the important and unimportant, the good and the evil. Martin Seligman (2011, p. 78) proposed that readers compare what they most want for their children to what schools are actually teaching. The most important things are lacking in what is being taught at schools. Though, indeed, a large part of human education goes implicitly and outside the classroom (Gardner, 1999), this does not mean that schools are to deny this responsibility at all.

There is more than one conception of what particularly should be the focus of an appropriate education. The authors of the person-centered approach to education (Rogers and Freiberg, 1994) put the emphasis on the process of interaction in the class and on the role of the teacher as a facilitator of learning. Howard Gardner (1999), in his "education for understanding" model, on the contrary, emphasized educational contents and formulated the major goals of education as "the modeling of adult roles and the transmission of cultural values" (p. 28). Seligman (2011) stated that positive education implies not only teaching the skills of achievement, but also those of well-being (p. 78); in fact, his general theoretical model treats achievement as one of the components of well-being (ibid., p. 18). Krasko (2004, p. xx) stressed the importance of education "for restoring meaning in our lives."

Asmolov (2011), one of the leading theoreticians and practitioners of the educational system in Russia, defined education as

> the leading sociocultural activity, contributing to the generation of social and mental systemic effects in the social life like emergence of the civil, ethnocultural and universal identity, dynamics of the social differentiation and stratification, appropriation of varied traditions, values, norms, and behavioral attitudes of large and small social groups, acquisition of a repertory of personal, social, and professional competencies, providing a person's individualization, socialization and professionalization in the world of human beings and professions, the growth of human potential as the critical condition of the competitiveness of the country.
>
> *(p. 2)*

Asmolov stated that the expectation that education would compensate for the defects of socialization emerging in the family, under the influence of mass media and other institutes of socialization, is groundless (ibid., p. 31). His views on education are based on three main principles: the culture of dignity, meaning-centeredness and a variational worldview. The culture of dignity is treated as being in opposition to the culture of utility; the mosaic of human cultures can be roughly arranged along this polarity. As Asmolov (1996) has noted, that utility-oriented culture

> is always concerned with survival rather than with living . . . As long as a culture is oriented at the relationships of utility, rather than dignity, the time for childhood is cut in it, old age is deprived of value, and education is given the role of a social orphan to be endured only inasmuch as some time should be granted for training, a person's preparation for the fulfillment of useful service functions.
>
> Another case is a culture based on the relationships of dignity. The leading value in such a culture is that of a human person, independently of whether something can be gained from that person for some business or not. In a culture of dignity children, old people and people with deviations are sacred. They are under protection of public charity. And a culture of dignity is more ready than a culture of utility for overcoming social disasters, resolution of crises in the dramatic process of human history.
>
> *(p. 589)*

Modern education cannot be rationalistic, merely information-oriented. "Education must be meaning-centered, must bring an understanding, help a person to construe the meaning of events he or she faces in the world" (Asmolov, 1996, p. 688). What such an education gives to a person is a worldview, personal meanings of the world and of human actions. Changing the person's life relationships with the world and other people is necessary for any changes in the person's mind (ibid., p. 637).

However, a worldview is not equivalent to an unambiguous picture of what the world "truly is." The modern mind has left far behind the patriarchal illusion of the sole truth that merely needs to be revealed; on the contrary, an awareness of multiple paths and multiple truths as well as personal responsibility for reasonable and responsible choosing and accepting one's values at one's own risk is critically important for living in the world of the twenty-first century. Correspondingly, meaning-centered education must be variational, must strive to prepare a person to accept, understand and work with the variability of the world.

Variational education may be defined as "exploratory education, probing different uncommon paths from various indeterminate situations in culture and providing to a person a fan of possibilities for choosing one's destiny" (ibid., p. 604). Variability accounts for the extension of a person's possibilities in situations of increasing variation (Asmolov, 2011, p. 34).

Closely related to variational education is another approach with a similar name, namely probabilistic education, as proposed by the Russian philosopher, psychologist and pedagogue Alexander Lobok, who departs from the philosophical ideas of the essence of human beings and human culture. Lobok notes that the human being is the only creature that transcends the evolutionary "logics of living," steps beyond biological determinism of the species, creating a universal intentional relation to the world. There is nothing like an *a priori* biological scale for a person's making a multifactor choice in the world of culture created by him/herself (see Lobok, 2001, p. 143). More than this,

> genuine culture always suggests a risk, unpredictability, boldness, deviation from rules, canon violation and at the same time work with huge amounts of optional materials . . . This means that the authentic being of a culture is beyond curriculum, beyond classes and beyond control. To put it in school language, this means to be "beyond education."
>
> *(ibid., p. 127)*

As Lobok states, a profound change in school ontology is required—"the transition from the culture of education, oriented at the type of an educated person (the one capable of successfully following one or another's position) to the totally new type of culture—the educational culture, oriented at the type of person capable of having one's own position" (Lobok, 2001, p. 101). Needless to say, the technical, instrumental side of education is in no way sufficient. "A person who, formally speaking, has learned reading, but *the need to read* has not developed in him/her, and he/she cannot enjoy reading, is the person for whom the activity of reading is essentially unavailable, and we are to confess that *in fact this person has not learned reading*" [emphasis added] (Lobok, 2001, p. 219).

Cultural and Personal Meanings in Educational Processes

The most controversial issue stems from the ambiguity in the concept of the word "meaning" that is characteristic of the English language. In the human sciences, "meaning" has always been an intriguing and at the same time a very fuzzy concept, its protean nature turning different sides to us in different situations.

First, in the English word *meaning*, two somewhat different things are melded: common cultural meaning (German *Bedeutung*, Russian *Znachenie*), unambiguously decoded by those who share the cultural code (e.g., language meanings, traffic signs, or church rites), and personal meaning (German *Sinn*, Russian *Smysl*), private and idiosyncratic, shared with no one. Second, over 20 theories of personal meaning in psychology through the twentieth century define it in quite different ways (see Leontiev, 1996). Meaning is conceived either as the integrating instance of personality (the Meaning), or as an element of the all-encompassing mechanism of activity regulation (meanings); either as something objectively existing out there in the world, as something existing only in our mind, or as something emerging in the communication, in the conversational space between individuals.

The common denominator for all these conceptions of meaning seems to be the following: meaning is a link, a tie, a connection, a reference linking a person to something or someone beyond him/herself (Leontiev, 2006, 2007). Cultural meanings create horizontal ties, the possibility of common languages that provide mutual understanding and coordination between fellow humans; personal meanings make vertical ties, linking the acting person to broader contexts. Cultural meanings are fixed semantic units that require the appropriate cultural code to be unambiguously comprehended. Personal meanings, on the contrary, are not something to be learned, they are not defined and cannot be decoded. As Mikhail Bakhtin stated, personal meaning is defined by a context rather than by a code; the latter is just a reduced, deliberately established, amortized context, while the true context cannot be completed and frozen (Bakhtin, 2002, p. 431). Personal meaning thus cannot be transmitted in a fixed form; any personal meaning is to be revealed anew in every individual life, defined by its unique contexts.

Cultural meanings account for the possibility of understanding each other and adjusting to the culture at large or special social groups. Cultural meanings are generated by many overlapping cultural contexts, each of which is a source of special meanings. These meanings reflect all kinds of differences in social class, religious traditions, family history, educational and professional background, regional specificity, etc.; they account for variations in understanding the same obstacles and details of habitual living that unite the members of the given culture or subculture as distinct from other cultures.

By learning cultural meanings (knowledge, skills, technologies, theories, etc.), a growing person learns what is taken for granted in the given culture. An understanding of culture based on the theory of sociocultural myth as the field of cultural meanings, and cultural memory accumulated through the millennia of existence of the given culture, has been proposed by Alexander Lobok (1997):

> Human being is inborn in a given culture, in one or another cultural whole, in one or another cultural reality, and hence, inborn in some meaning field permeating this cultural whole, cultural reality. Meaning benchmarks of the culture in which he or she is born and resides, are transmitted through trans-actions with parents, friends, teachers at school, works of literature and arts, etc., and every person becomes to some degree merged with the sum-total of these implicit meaning settings of the culture, without being aware of it. These implicit settings and benchmarks of culture create a distinctive mean-ing dimension of human life, put the meaning scale onto the human life.
>
> *(pp. 82–83)*

Lobok speaks of myth in this context to stress the point that what is self-evident for those inborn in a given culture is incomprehensible to those who grew up and were educated in other meaning fields. Every myth at the same time unites a group that shares it and marks the boundaries of this group as distinct from other groups immersed in other myths.

Personal meanings, unlike cultural ones, are construed (G. Kelly), or discov-ered (V. Frankl), in the course of one's attempts to make sense of one's living as a unique experience. They are related to personal obstacles and choices and fulfill a very important function of making one's life a coherent whole rather than a set of fragmented self-sufficient episodes. A meaningful action, a meaningful life, a meaningful person, unlike meaningless ones, are, first, internally coherent rather than fragmented and, second, are tied to superordinate contexts rather than being self-sufficient. Personal meaning is thus the answer to the question "What for?" If it were for nothing, the action (or the entire life) would seem meaningless. Personal meanings of all the elements of individual experience link them together and serve as regulators of one's actions (Leontiev, 2007, 2012b).

Two important consequences follow from the above distinction. First, tra-ditional scholastic technological education can rightly claim to be meaning-centered, but only if we have in mind the realm of cultural meanings, objectified in cultural texts, artifacts and codes. The present-day challenge is that of putting the emphasis on personal rather than cultural meanings, relevant to the "changing person in the changing world" (Asmolov, 1990, p.365), rather than to the person well adjusted to the fixed world.

Second, since personal meanings do not exist in fixed, objectified forms, they can and should be the outcomes of education, but cannot be its object. They are not something to be taught but rather something emerging in the pupils' worldview in the course of getting acquainted with the infinite variety of individual worlds and individual paths in the world we populate. In no way does it devalue the slogan of meaning-centered education; it merely stresses that to be meaning-centered, education must be centered on more than just meanings. It should be centered on manifold possible contexts of our lives, preset by our biological organization, the givens of the world in which we live, and the culture in which each of us has grown on the one hand, and on the other the contexts we create ourselves to make sense of our experiences and actions. This can be seen as an essential contradiction inherent in the idea of meaning-centered education; it is, however, a creative one giving an impulse for development.

Conclusion

In summary, I will repeat that in the twenty-first century education must pay much more attention to the personal dimension of human development, to the one relevant to the realm of personal meanings of our being-in-the-world. What I am trying to substantiate is, first, that meaning-centeredness must be treated as person-centeredness rather than just culture-centeredness, and, second, that the emphasis on personal meanings implies the variational, or probabilistic, view of the world to be developed in non-traditional ways that are still to be elaborated.

Russell (1930) puts it this way:

> If I had the power to organize higher education as I should wish it to be . . . I should seek to make young people vividly aware of the past, vividly realizing that the future of man will in all likelihood be immeasurably longer than his past, profoundly conscious of the minuteness of the planet upon which we live and of the fact that life on this planet is only a temporary incident; and at the same time with these facts which tend to emphasize the insignificance of the individual, I should present quite another set of facts designed to impress upon the mind of the young the greatness of which the individual is capable, and the knowledge that throughout all the depths of stellar space nothing of equal value is known to us.
>
> *(p. 175)*

The problem is that, although in fact every school does open a window on the world, often this is a narrow window only looking onto a dirty backyard, or, in contrast, onto a non-stop glamorous party. It always conveys some ideas about who we are, where we came from and where we are heading, but very often these ideas are uncritical, prejudiced and one-sided. It helps us to grow up, but not always toward personal maturity—often it is towards a rigid adjustment to external reality considered as ultimate and unchangeable. And the soul is often filled up with rigid, distorted meanings rather than with comprehensive and flexible ones. Instead of feeling like members of humankind, many feel abandoned and alienated, or see themselves as members of a small group struggling against the whole of society, not to mention other rival groups. And, finally, many learn lack of responsibility even for themselves, indifference, or even learned helplessness. In other words, schools do in fact implicitly teach pupils many existential aspects of their being-in-the-world, but usually incidentally, without explicit planning or defined goals. What is being taught this way is definitely not what we would want for our children. Unfortunately, schools that don't teach humanity, positive meaning, or well-being, do teach something opposite to this, though they may believe they do not attend to such matters at all.

And the point is not just to elaborate special positive or meaning-centered practices and apply them to the blank space. The challenge is much more difficult even than transforming effective undesirable practices into more helpful ones. All educational practices can be seen as successful when their authors can plan the precise desired effect of their efforts, and the point is merely to plot a course toward it. The model of education badly needed at the beginning of the twenty-first century, however, is one of a common journey, shared exploration of unknown shores; and the most valuable result of this journey is not the maps and trophies, but rather the mature traveler. Meaning-centered education cannot but be activity-centered. Personal meanings, activity structures and skills, tolerance for ambiguity and risk, and relationships of dignity and support are equally important aspects of such an education.

References

Asmolov, A. G. (1990) *Psikhologiyalichnosti [Psychology of personality]*. Moscow: Moscow University Press.

Asmolov, A.G. (1996) *Kulturno-istoricheskaya psikhologiya i konstruirovanie mirov [Cultural-Historical Psychology and Construing Worlds]*. Moscow: Institute for Practical Psychology.

Asmolov, A.G. (2011) *Strategiya i metodologiya sotsiokulturnoi modernizatsii obrazovaniya [Strategy and Methodology of the Sociocultural Modernization of Education]*. Moscow: Federal Institute for the Development of Education.

Bakhtin, M.M. (2002) "Rabochjie zapisi 60-kh—nachala 70-kh godov [Working notes of the 1960s–early 1970s]. In Bakhtin M.M. *Sobranie Sochinenii [Collected Works], vol. 6* (pp. 371–439). Moscow: Russkie slovari; Yazyki slavyanskoi kultury.

Bernstein, N.A. (1967) *The Co-ordination and Regulation of Movements*. Oxford: Pergamon Press.

Carver, C. and Scheier, M. (1998) *On the Self-Regulation of Behavior*. New York: Cambridge University Press.

Gardner, H. (1999) *The Disciplined Mind: What All Students Should Understand*. New York: Simon & Schuster.

Krasko, G.L. (2004) *This Unbearable Boredom of Being: A Crisis of Meaning in America*. New York: iUniverse, Inc.

Leontiev, D. (1996) "Dimensions of the meaning/sense concept in the psychological context." In C. Tolman, F. Cherry, R. Van Hezewijk and I. Lubek (Eds), *Problems of Theoretical Psychology* (pp. 130–142). York: Captus University Publications.

Leontiev, D. (2006) "Meaningful living and the worlds of art." In A. Delle Fave (Ed.), *Dimensions of Well-Being: Research and Intervention* (pp. 529–537). Milan: Franco Angeli.

Leontiev, D. (2007) "The phenomenon of meaning: How psychology can make sense of it?" In P.T.P. Wong, L. Wong, M. J. McDonald and D. K. Klaassen (Eds), *The Positive Psychology of Meaning and Spirituality* (pp. 33–44). Abbotsford, BC: INPM Press.

Leontiev, D. (2012a) "From drive to need and further: What is human motivation about?" In D. Leontiev (Ed.), *Motivation, Consciousness, and Self-regulation* (pp. 9–25). New York: Nova Science Publishers.

Leontiev, D. (2012b) "Why we do what we do: The variety of human regulations." In D. Leontiev (Ed.), *Motivation, Consciousness, and Self-regulation* (pp. 93–103). New York: Nova Science Publishers.

Leontiev, D. (in press) "Lichnostnoe izmerenie razvitiya" ["The personality dimension of human development"]. *Voprosy psikhologii.*

Lobok, A. (1997) *Antropologiya Mifa [Anthropology of Myth].* Yekaterinburg, Russia: Oktyabrsky District Administration.

Lobok, A. (2001) *Veroyatnistnyi Mir [Probabilistic World].* Yekaterinburg, Russia: AMB Press.

Malinowski, B. (1944) *A Scientific Theory of Culture.* Chapel Hill, NC: University of North Carolina Press.

Ortega y Gasset, J. (1932) *The Revolt of the Masses.* London: George Allen and Unwin; New York: Norton.

Rogers, C.R. and Freiberg, H.J. (1994) *Freedom to Learn* (3rd edn). New York: Maxwell Macmillan International.

Russell, B. (1930) *The Conquest of Happiness.* New York/London: Liveright.

Seligman, M. (2011) *Flourish: A Visionary New Understanding of Happiness and Well-Being.* New York: Free Press.

3

DIALOGIC EDUCATION IN THE AGE OF THE INTERNET

Rupert Wegerif

Introduction

Theory is important in education because it shapes people's actions from the inside. The default assumption of most people most of the time seems to be that education is about the transmission of knowledge. When facing a class for the first time and asked to teach a subject most people fall back on their inbuilt theory of education as transmission and get out a textbook, reach for a work sheet, or put on the PowerPoint. However, this default theory is misleading. In reality knowledge only has meaning for us in the context of our participation in relationships and dialogues that are larger than us and can take us beyond ourselves. If teachers realize that their job is mainly to draw students into dialogues, and support them as they engage in those dialogues, then education is likely to have more personal meaning for students. In other words I would like to see a future when a new teacher standing in front of the classroom for the first time thinks: "What should I do? I know, this is education, so I will draw them into dialogue."

Dialogic Theory

Dialogic theory begins with the claim that meaning is always internal to dialogues and so should not be thought of on the model of fixed external things like objects that we might encounter in the world. If meaning is a kind of thing then you can transmit it. If meaning is a dialogue then you have to participate in it.

The meaning of any word can never be fixed since at any time a participant in the dialogue might interpret previously spoken words in a new way. This is true not only of small local dialogues but also of the larger dialogues of culture, such as the long-term dialogues of science and philosophy, which are often global in reach and can last for thousands of years. The meanings of Socrates' words, for example, which I will refer to in this chapter since they are relevant to understanding dialogic, have evolved over centuries of interpretation and each new reading by a student freshly introduced to Socrates may add to or change this meaning.

What has generally been called "logic" in modern times turns out to be "monologic," implying the ideal of a single true, fixed perspective on the world. The prefix, "dia," from the Greek, suggests "through or across difference." Using the term "dialogic" therefore implies a critique of the assumption of monologic that there is ever a single fixed meaning or truth. The term "dialogic" can be interpreted as the idea that meaning always involves a dialogue across difference.

Applied to education the word "dialogic" suggests a radical reinterpretation of the traditional mission of education to expand reason or "λογοσ" ("logos"). On the monologic interpretation of λογοσ education is understood as the transmission of correct thinking and true knowledge. The dialogic interpretation of λογοσ suggests education has to be understood as the continuous re-creation of meaning through engaging in dialogue.

Main Argument

In the rest of this chapter I will outline a dialogic theory of education. According to this theory education should be understood as opening, sustaining, widening and deepening those dialogues that generate meaning. I argue that dialogic education offers a way forward in the context of our increasingly global and networked society. To help make this argument I introduce some of the main themes of this dialogic theory of education with illustrations from the affordances of the Internet rather than simply from more traditional face-to-face dialogues. The assumption of policy makers that education should serve as a tool for the production of value in the knowledge economy carries with it the threat that the living meaning found in dialogues will be reduced to commodities that can be traded. However, the same Internet that supports the global knowledge economy can also support participation in global dialogues where shared meanings are generated.

Wikipedia and Dialogic Theory

I still sometimes overhear my university colleagues warning students against using Wikipedia because it is "not reliable" since "anyone can change anything." This is true, of course, but what they neglect to mention is that Wikipedia represents a new approach to knowledge quite different from the idea of the authority of the great print encyclopedias of the past. In fact, a recent study found that Wikipedia, the main collaboratively constructed encyclopedia on the Internet, is not only more up to date than *Encyclopedia Britannica*, which one would expect, but is also more accurate when it comes to checkable factual errors (Giles, 2005). But such comparisons miss the point. Wikipedia is an altogether different kind of text than a print encyclopedia. Print is a one-to-many medium with the authority, the authorship, very much controlled by the center. Wikis are, by their nature, collaborative and participatory. This means that the reader of a wiki needs to be critically aware that they are reading in a context and so might need to cross-check with other sources. Using Wikipedia effectively requires a shift in attitude from being a passive consumer of other people's knowledge to becoming an active participant in the construction of knowledge.

Those who compare Wikipedia to print encyclopedias and find it wanting are often revealing an underlying assumption about knowledge. The same assumption can be seen behind the consternation expressed by newspapers and politicians when websites and email trails reveal that scientists have different views on matters such as whether global warming is man-made or the harmful side effects of vaccinations. The Print Age encouraged the illusion revealed by Socrates as the danger inherent in writing. This danger is the false idea of unsituated Truth that is not part of any dialogue and so "cannot answer back when questioned" as Socrates put it (Plato, 2006b). The Internet Age brings back to prominence the everyday experience that truth is constructed through real dialogues in which there are real differences of perspective. Print texts are often seen as representations of the Truth. The Internet, by contrast, simply carries the dialogues between voices that construct knowledge. According to the logic of the Print Age, education is the transmission of true knowledge through reading the right books (Hirsch, 1987). The logic of the Internet Age returns us to Socrates' original insight that intelligence lies in dialogues and not in books. The essence of Wikipedia knowledge is not the passive representation of true knowledge but the active participation in dialogues that construct knowledge. At its best Wikipedia consists of the intelligent words that Socrates valued, words that can be questioned, that answer back, and that participate in the endless project of shared inquiry.

Some Sources for a Dialogic Theory of Education

Socrates

Socrates is often referred to as the father of dialogic education. This attribution probably stems from the way in which he practiced philosophy as the pursuit of truth through dialogues in which all claims are tested and his own ignorance is discovered along with the ignorance of his interlocutors. He claimed to be the wisest man in Athens not because he knew more than others but because he alone knew his own ignorance whereas others all believed in their claims to knowledge. His method was often to question others in a way that brought to light the contradictions in their beliefs and so made them reflect. His aim or teaching goal was not the transmission of knowledge, nor even collaborative knowledge construction, so much as teaching critical thinking and so expanding awareness. To put this same point in another way, the focus of his teaching was not on finding answers so much as on improving the quality of questions (Plato, 2006b).

However, reading the dialogues gives the impression that Socrates' educational practice was often very different from his educational theory. It is hard, for example, to read the dialogue between Socrates and the slave boy in *Meno* as anything other than intellectual bullying. Matuzov (2009) has conducted a detailed analysis of all Socrates' dialogues as reported by Plato and he concluded that, "I did not find any evidence of Socrates seeking truth and learning something new himself from participation in these dialogues. Rather he tried to bring other participants to something he already knew" (p. 46).

Socrates often argues by examining the claims that others make in order to draw out a contradiction. This may or may not lead to a new and better understanding but at least it leads to their awareness of their own ignorance. This approach is often called dialectic and it lies behind the more codified dialectic of Hegel in which an initially too abstract claim is tested and challenged by its opposite or its negation in order to develop a more complete or concrete understanding. Clearly this kind of dialectical reasoning, or reasoning through oppositions, emerges out of dialogues in which different voices confront each other but dialectic is only one possibility of the larger concept of dialogic.

Bakhtin claims that dialectic is trying to make the argument too abstract and so forgets the embodied nature of dialogues (Bakhtin, 1986, p. 147). Hegel's dialectic and also the kind of dialectical reasoning often practiced by Socrates, seems to assume that the correct answer or "synthesis" is given in advance and so will inevitably emerge from the dialogue. Hegel calls this "the cunning of reason" whereas Socrates in *Meno* refers to the way that reasoning helps us recall the truth that we know from the beginning. In real dialogues, however, it is not possible to know what the outcome will be in advance. If dialectic implies assuming a larger perspective in which the apparent differences in dialogue with each other are revealed as mere stages in a story of progress towards the Truth then dialectic is not dialogic but a disguised form of monologic.

Freire

In the second half of the twentieth century Paulo Freire, a Brazilian-born educator, explicitly argued for the need for dialogic education in the context of what he called a "pedagogy of the oppressed." Conventional education, Freire claimed, followed what he called a "banking model" in which knowledge is treated as something to be deposited in the heads of students. Education on the banking model is a way of oppressing people through manipulation in which the words and meanings of the oppressors are inserted into the heads of the oppressed. Dialogic education, by contrast, is about empowering the oppressed to speak their own words and so to name the world in their own way. Freire offers three key elements that can contribute to an understanding of dialogic education: first, the importance of starting with the lived experience of students; second, the idea that dialogic education is about making a real difference in the world through empowerment or giving voices to those initially without a voice; and finally, the importance of genuine respect and collaboration between educator and student so that meaning can be co-constructed rather than imposed. Freire (1972) made an explicit link between a dialogic approach and education for meaning:

> If it is in speaking their word that people, by naming the world, transform it, dialogue imposes itself as the way by which they achieve significance as human beings. [. . .] And since dialogue is the encounter in which the united reflection and action of the dialoguers are addressed to the world which is to be transformed and humanized, this dialogue cannot be reduced to the act of one person's "depositing" ideas in another; nor can it become a simple exchange of ideas to be "consumed" by the discussants. [. . .] Because dialogue is an encounter among women and men who name the world, it must not be a situation where some name on behalf of others. It is an act of creation; it must not serve as a crafty instrument for the domination of one person by another.
>
> *(p. 69)*

Freire argued clearly for a kind of dialogic education that did not impose meanings on people. However, he has been accused of doing precisely what he argued against, that is manipulating people into meanings prepared in advance. Freire made it clear in his writings and actions that he was committed to a socialist vision of liberation. This can be seen in his location of education within the dichotomy of oppressor and oppressed. Those who have examined his methods in practice and tried to implement them tend to converge on the conclusion articulated by Mark Smith (2002) that

> what is claimed as liberatory practice may, on close inspection, be rather closer to banking than we would wish. In other words, the practice of Freirian education can involve smuggling in all sorts of ideas and values under the guise of problem-posing.

Matusov argues that Freire's commitment to dialogue as a means to bring social justice overwhelmed his concern with dialogue as a shared inquiry into truth (Matusov, 2009, p. 109). In a way this is a particular version of the dialectic as opposed to dialogic problem that emerged also from examining Socrates' educational practice. The main problem with dialectical thinking is the illicit assumption of a master viewpoint outside of any dialogue from which one can know in advance how the dialogue should turn out. Freire appeared to accept a broadly Marxist dialectical understanding of history in which the oppressed needed to become conscious of their oppressed state and overthrow it in order to bring about a better world. The opening of dialogue was seen by Freire as a necessary moment within this larger dialectical vision. As with Socrates, Freire's practice was not really as dialogic as his rhetoric.

Bakhtin Against Vygotsky

Vygotsky's well-known "zone of proximal development" or ZPD brings dialogic relations into educational theory. In the ZPD the teacher has to engage with the perspective of the student and vice-versa in order to connect the development of ideas in the student to pre-existing culture (Vygotsky, 1986). The dialogic relation, which is well characterized as "attunement to the attunement of the other" (Rommetveit, 1992), is certainly implicit in the idea of the ZPD but it is invoked as a temporary tool or scaffold to help in a direction of individual development known in advance.

Dialectic and dialogic sound similar and often look similar in practice. However, making a distinction between them is important for a theoretical understanding of the distinctive basis of dialogic thinking. For those postmodernists influenced by Lévinas's critique of monological reason, including Derrida and Lyotard, dialectic was seen as monologic dressed up to look like dialogic. The argument is that the "other," which often appears in the dialectic algorithm, is not genuinely other at all but merely a prop for the development and expansion of the "self," in the form of a totalizing system of explanation and control. "Difference," Lévinas claims, is posited by dialectical thinking only to be appropriated and reduced to "equivalence" in systems of "representation" (Lévinas, 1989, p. 77). Lévinas contrasted the "egology" of western rationalism to the "wisdom" of responding to the "infinite" call of "the Other," an infinite call that, he claimed, disrupts all totalizing systems of thought.

In some ways Bakhtin prefigured the importance given to the concept of difference by some so-called post-modern thinkers such as Derrida. He was clear in his own writings about the significance of the important distinction to be made between dialectic and dialogic. He describes Hegel's account of the development of the personality in the Phenomenology of Spirit, the account explicitly adopted and applied to psychology by Vygotsky, as "a monologism" (Bakhtin, 1986, p. 162). Bakhtin (1986) writes of dialectic:

> Take a dialogue and remove the voices (the partitioning of voices), remove the intonations (emotional and individualizing ones), carve out abstract concepts and judgments from living words and responses, cram everything into one abstract consciousness—and that's how you get dialectics.
>
> (p. 147)

Bakhtin's main point seems to be that dialectic, at least in its Hegelian form, is a dynamic form of logic leading all apparent differences to be subsumed into identity in the form of a more complexly integrated synthesis; it is not dialogic since dialogic refers to the interanimation of real voices where there is no necessary "overcoming" or "synthesis." Vygotsky of Thinking and Speech is not really a dialogic thinker, and never claimed to be, but he is a dialectical thinker who gives dialogue a role in his theory of development.

Oakeshott

Writing in a very similar period to Freire, the English philosopher Michael Oakeshott articulated an essentially dialogic theory of education that is interesting because it does not share Freire's socialist political assumptions (Oakeshott, 1989). Oakeshott did not explicitly use the term dialogic but he applied the metaphor of conversation to education and he linked education to his idea of what he called the conversation of Mankind. Oakeshott (1962) elaborates on what he means by the conversation of Mankind:

> In conversation, "facts" appear only to be resolved once more into the possibilities from which they were made; "certainties" are shown to be combustible, not by being brought in contact with other "certainties" or with doubts, but by being kindled by the presence of ideas of another order; approximations are revealed between notions normally remote from one another. Thoughts of different species take wing and play round one another, responding to each other's movements and provoking one another to fresh exertions. Nobody asks where they have come from or on what authority they are present; nobody cares what will become of them when they have played their part. There is no symposiarch or arbiter, not even a doorkeeper to examine credentials. Every entrant is taken at its face-value and everything is permitted which can get itself accepted into the flow of speculation. And voices which speak in conversation do not compose a hierarchy. Conversation is not an enterprise designed to yield an extrinsic profit, a contest where a winner gets a prize, nor is it an activity of exegesis; it is an unrehearsed intellectual adventure. It is with conversation as with gambling, its significance lies neither in winning nor in losing, but in wagering. Properly speaking, it is impossible in the absence of a diversity of voices: in it different universes of discourse meet, acknowledge each other and enjoy an oblique relationship which neither requires nor forecasts their being assimilated to one another.
>
> [. . .] As civilized human beings, we are the inheritors, neither of an inquiry about ourselves and the world, nor of an accumulating body of information, but of a conversation, begun in the primeval forests and extended and made more articulate in the course of centuries. It is a conversation which goes on both in public and within each of ourselves.
>
> *(p. 198)*

I quote this passage at length because it offers a clear expression of several key dialogic themes. Facts are never fixed and final but constructed and deconstructed within dialogues. A diversity of voices is essential for meaning. There is no privileged outside standpoint offering a "correct" view. Dialogue is an end in itself and not a means to an outside end such as profit or adaptation to the environment. This account of the importance of the "conversation of Mankind" implies a particular understanding of education as initiating newcomers into this conversation. This is an account of education that Oakeshott developed in several papers that explicitly opposed policies that tried to make education subservient to the needs of the larger society or what he referred to as the end of "socialization." In a way he shared Freire's concern to preserve education from the banking model and a concern that education served the end of intellectual emancipation rather than an economic or productive end. But he would have rejected Freire's assertion that dialogic education should be about transforming society towards greater social justice. For Oakeshott education needed a space separate from practical concerns where the freedom to imagine alternatives was protected from social projects of every kind (Oakeshott, 1989, p. 133).

Oakeshott presented his conversational account of education in conservative terms focusing on the need to teach students their inheritance of culture from the past. However, it is clear that the goal of education for Oakeshott is a person who is able not only to participate in the conversation of humanity but also to take it forward. In other words, the aim of education is not only an educated person but also a better quality of conversation. Although it is clear that teachers are needed to induct students into the conversations from the past, the role of these teachers is also to empower and liberate students to acquire their own voice and be able to speak in order to help shape the shared human world of meaning in the future. Oakeshott is useful in showing us that dialogic education is not intrinsically progressive or intrinsically conservative but that it is, above all, intrinsically educational. Education involves preserving and deepening our dialogue with the voices of the past as much as it requires engaging in a dialogue with possible futures. For Oakeshott education can only liberate students and help to create a better future, through first engaging them within their inherited traditions of thought. We can learn from Oakeshott that the dialogue in dialogic education should not be treated only as a means to the end of more knowledge or more productivity or more social justice but that it needs to be respected as an end in itself.

So What Does "Dialogic" Mean?

Below I outline some of the key axioms of dialogic theory that emerge from reading and reflecting on the literature on dialogic as a way of understanding education.

Dialogic Education Is Education for Dialogue

To be dialogic implies that dialogue is not only the means of education but is also an end. In the brief survey above of approaches to education that have been called dialogic, the approaches of Socrates, Freire and Oakeshott, it has emerged that the key factor in distinguishing dialogic education from other kinds is that one important aim of dialogic education is dialogue itself.

The Dialogic Gap or Difference Between Voices Is Constitutive for Meaning

Voice is a term in dialogic theory for a unique perspective on the world that is the unit of analysis of a dialogue. Individual humans can have many voices. Things can be given voice. Nations and abstract conceptual entities can take on voice. The gap between voices is what constitutes them. There is a dialogue between voices only if they are different. If they merge then the dialogue ceases and so the meaning ceases.

Progress Occurs by Augmentation, Not by Superseding or Replacing

Bakhtin gives the example of how, for him, reading the texts of ancient Greece gave him an extra perspective from which to see his situation in twentieth-century Russia in a way that opens up the possibilities of thought in general (Bakhtin, 1986, p. 7). Many theories of development and educational progress are monologic, assuming that understanding progresses in a linear way from A to B, replacing old theories with better theories. For dialogic, however, the past is always preserved and so progress is always from A to "A and B." For example, the voice of the child is still available to adults and allowing that voice to speak can expand and enrich the experience of the adult. Bakhtin (1986) hinted at an idea of progress from the narrow time and space of small dialogues concerned with local issues to the great time and space of the dialogue between all voices from all cultures and all times (p. 192).

The Inside-Outside Outside-Inside Nature of Dialogic Relations

In any dialogue the person you are speaking to, the "addressee," is always already there at the beginning of the utterance just as you are there already on the inside when they frame their reply to you. In any dialogue we do not just address ourselves to the other as a physical object but we address them from within a relationship in which the words are often as much theirs as ours (Rommetveit, 1992; Linell, 2009).

This inside-out and outside-in nature of dialogues explains why education is possible at all. Bakhtin points out that there is a difference between an authoritative voice and a persuasive voice. The authoritative voice remains outside of me and orders me to do something in a way that forces me to accept or reject it without engaging with it, whereas the words of the persuasive voice enter into the realm of my own words and change them from within (Bakhtin, 1981, p. 343). Education, as opposed to training or dressage, always requires this persuasive or dialogic voice that speaks to the student from the inside. The addressee enters into the very beginning of an utterance and how in a true dialogue it is no longer possible to say who is thinking (Merleau-Ponty, 1968, p. 15, 113; Merleau-Ponty, 1964, p. 29, 159).

Dialogues Always Project Virtual Super-Addressee Positions

As well as having perhaps a physically situated addressee and cultural voices, according to Bakhtin utterances in dialogues also always address a "super-addressee" (Bakhtin, 1986, p. 126). This super-addressee is described by Bakhtin as the "witness" or "third" that is an inevitable part of any dialogue. Bakhtin does not spell this out but the "third" addressee in a dialogue is inevitably present in all dialogues simply because I can hear myself speaking. When I talk and hear my own words it is as if I am another person listening to them and then I naturally assume the position of a witness or "third" to myself. Bakhtin makes the point that, as well as seeking to persuade you, my immediate addressee, I also seek to engage in dialogue with an ideal listener who could make sense of what I am saying even if you cannot. I think this could be seen as stemming from a projection of the self as another who listens to the words of the self but can understand and judge them as if from an outside position. He points out that in different times this super-addressee is imagined differently, sometimes being God and sometimes "the future community of scientists," but in every age there is such an ideal as it is an essential part of the nature of dialogue. This elaborated cultural image of the super-addressee is an extension, I would argue, of the witness position in every dialogue that comes from listening to myself speaking as if I was other to myself.

Dialogic Space Is Real

Dialogues in education are often discussed in terms of epistemology as a form of "shared inquiry" and a way of helping in the "collaborative construction of knowledge" (Linell, 2009). I propose that it is also useful to think of dialogues in terms of ontology. By using the term ontology I am suggesting that the concept of Dialogic Space is not just an idea constructed within dialogues but is pointing to something real that makes dialogues possible in the first place, a kind of real lack of foundation and inter-connectedness of all with all in a way which is unbounded and so intrinsically undetermined and undeterminable. I am not sure if this idea should count as ontology because it is not the idea of a foundation outside of dialogue but more the idea of a real lack of foundation outside of dialogue that makes dialogue possible in the first place. Another way to think about Dialogic Space is to think about the space of the Internet. What is it, where is it, and how is it possible in the first place?

A second way in which the term ontology is useful is to suggest that the aim of education is not simply knowledge or ways of knowing but also ways of being. Dialogic is not simply a way for a subject to know about a world out there beyond the subject but it is also about a way of being in the world. Referring to an onto-logical interpretation of dialogic is another way of saying that dialogic education is education *for* dialogue as well as *through* dialogue, in which dialogue is not only treated as a means to an end but also treated as an end in itself (see also Matusov, 2009, and Sidorkin, 1999). I think it is useful to be able to talk about "opening dialogic space," through interrupting an activity with a reflective question, for example, or "widening dialogic space" through bringing in new voices, or "deep-ening dialogic space" through reflection on assumptions.

A Dialogic Theory of Education in the Internet Age

Outlining some of the implications of what I mean by the term dialogic has already sketched the outlines of a dialogic theory of education for the Internet Age. Education can be understood as a dialogue carried both through culture and through individual thoughts. This dialogue is an end in itself but is also a shared inquiry making sense of the world and learning from the past how best to act in the future. Although ultimately this is one dialogue it has many branches or eddies where more or less specialist dialogues work out responses to particular challenges or understandings in specific domains of experience.

The answer to the question "What should we teach?" is to teach participation in educational dialogue both as an end in itself and as a means to understanding and knowledge construction in different areas. To teach participation in dialogue we must teach knowledge of what is being talked about, communicative skills for talking about it and, most importantly, we need to teach in a way that empowers new learners to find their own voice so that they can respond to other voices and contribute to the ongoing development of the collective dialogue. But in analyz-ing the parts of dialogue in order to teach them there is no need to slip into the illusion that these parts are really separate from the main thing that is being taught: dialogue itself.

This vision of education offers a clear direction for progress away from identi-fication with narrow and parochial concerns and towards identification with the unbounded and infinite space of collective dialogue in which all voices can be heard. This expansion in awareness is achieved not through increasing abstrac-tion and generalization so much as through engagement in dialogue with multi-ple voices including disembodied cultural voices of the past and super-addressee voices that call us to the future. Ultimately what is being taught here is an expansion not of knowledge so much as of a capacity to respond to otherness and newness in the moment.

The answer to the question "How should we teach?" is also dialogue. It is the "inside-out: outside-in" nature of the dialogic relation that makes teaching and learning possible. In order to teach at all this relationship needs first to be established and then all teaching needs to be responsive to and build on the voices of learners. Education into dialogue is therefore ethical and emotional before it is cognitive. While dialogic education can involve scaffolding to enable participation in dialogues for beginners it can also require education through challenge in which the teacher withdraws and the learner is left to find their own voice in a new and unfamiliar situation. Many techniques for dialogic education, that is to say, education for dialogue as well as through dialogue, have been developed for particular kinds of teaching in particular contexts. But however "tried and tested" a technique is, this cannot take away responsibility for judgment from teachers (including the teacher voice in self-directed learners or within learning communities) because contingent responsiveness in the moment is of the essence in a dialogic relationship.

The answer to the question "Why should we teach like this?" returns us to the context of the Internet Age. Much of what has been said above about a dialogic theory of education could have been said before the Internet Age and probably has been said before by dialogic educational thinkers including Oakeshott, generally seen as a conservative voice, and Freire, generally seen as a progressive voice. Writing in the 1960s and 1970s, both Oakeshott and Freire presented their ideas as a protest about what they saw as the dominant trend in education in their time, the subordination of education to economic concerns. This is still a threat of course, perhaps still the main threat to education, but the advent of the Internet changes everything and makes a dialogic approach to education both more relevant and more possible than ever before.

In a very real sense the Internet has given a concrete form to Oakeshott's abstraction "the conversation of Mankind" (where Mankind would be translated now as humanity). The most influential works of culture from all over the world are now being digitized and made available online in many ongoing projects. Many thinkers from the last 50 years are available in video form explaining and defending their ideas. Education as induction into participation in the dialogue of humanity no longer takes place only through face-to-face conversations in elite universities or in the long time cycle of book or article writing and publishing but can be engaged live through multiple media via the Internet.

The Internet obviously offers the opportunity for education into global dialogue. More than that, the Internet Age has created a necessity for such education. A global space of interaction in which there are multiple voices and no certainties is already the reality of life for everyone on the Internet. Not all are comfortable with this and it has led to reactionary responses as people retreat from the challenge of global dialogue into local certainties. Education for the Internet Age has a crucial role to play if people are to be able to thrive not only economically but also psychologically in this new context. The Internet makes global constructive dialogue a possibility, but it is the job of education to make this a reality.

References

Bakhtin, M. M. (1981) "Discourse in the novel." In M. M. Bakhtin, *The Dialogic Imagination: Four Essays by M. M. Bakhtin.* Austin, TX: University of Texas Press.

Bakhtin, M. M. (1986) *Speech Genres and Other Late Essays.* Austin, TX: University of Texas Press.

Freire, P. (1972) *Pedagogy of the Oppressed.* Harmondsworth: Penguin.

Giles, J. (2005). "Special Report Internet Encyclopaedias go head to head." *Nature* 438: 900–901 (15 December 2005). doi:10.1038/438900a; Available online at: http://www.nature.com/nature/journal/v438/n7070/full/438900a.html (accessed 1 December 2011).

Hirsch, E. D. (1987) *Cultural Literacy: What Every American Should Know.* Boston, MA: Houghton Mifflin.

Lévinas, E. (1989) "Substitution" (trans. A. Lingis). In S. Hand (Ed.), *The Lévinas Reader.* Oxford: Blackwell.

Linell, P. (2009) *Rethinking Language, Mind and World Dialogically: Interactional and Contextual Theories of Human Sense-Making.* Charlotte, NC: Information Age Publishing.

Matusov, E. (2009) "Journey into dialogic pedagogy." *Hauppauge.* New York: Nova Publishers.

Merleau-Ponty, M. (1964) *Le Visible et L'Invisible.* Paris: Gallimard.

Merleau-Ponty, M. (1968) *The Visible and the Invisible* (Notes translated and edited by Claude Lefort).

Oakeshott, M. (1962) *The Voice of Poetry in the Conversation of Mankind, Rationalism in Politics and Other Essays.* London: Methuen, pp. 197–247.

Oakeshott, M. (1989) *The Voice of Liberal Learning: Michael Oakeshott on Education* (Ed. T. Fuller). New Haven and London: Yale University Press.

Plato (380 BCE/2006a) *Phaedrus* (trans. B. Jowett). Available online at: http://ebooks.adelaide.edu.au/p/plato/p71phs/ (accessed 1 December 2011).

Plato (380 BCE/2006b) *Meno* (trans. B. Jowett). Available online at: http://ebooks.adelaide.edu.au/p/plato/p71phs/ (accessed 1 December 2011).

Rommetveit, R. (1992) "Outlines of a dialogically based social-cognitive approach to human cognition and communication." In A. Wold (Ed.), *The Dialogical Alternative: Towards a Theory of Language and Mind.* Oslo: Scandanavian Press.

Sidorkin, A. M. (1999). *Beyond Discourse: Education, the Self and Dialogue.* New York: State University of New York Press.

Smith, M. K. (1997, 2002) "Paulo Freire and informal education, the encyclopaedia of informal education." Available online at: www.infed.org/thinkers/et-freir.htm (accessed 1 December 2011).

Vygotsky, L. (1986) *Thought and Language* (trans. Kozulin). Cambridge, MA: MIT Press.

Vygotsky, L. (1991) "The genesis of higher mental functions." In P. Light, S. Sheldon and B. Woodhead (Eds), *Learning to Think.* London: Routledge.

Wegerif, R. (2007) *Dialogic Education and Technology: Expanding the Space of Learning.* New York and Berlin: Springer.

Wegerif, R. (2008) "Dialogic or dialectic? The significance of ontological assumptions in research on educational dialogue." *British Educational Research Journal* 34(3): 347–361.

4

MEANING-CENTERED EXPERIENTIAL LEARNING

Learning as an Outcome of Reconstructed Experiences

Denise Potosky, Jim Spaulding, and John Juzbasich

> Unfortunately, it is not that simple to deposit ideas in another mind.
>
> *(Barnlund, 1962, p. 199)*

Meaning-making is a constructive process that organizes our experiences. The meaning-centered paradigm for education is logically related to experiential learning, whereby meaning-making represents a methodology for actively incorporating experiences into schemas, or "something learned." As Rupert Wegerif explained (this volume), education is not the transmission of knowledge but the process of engaging learners in dialogues, which are constructed and reconstructed such that learners create personal meanings. Hence, learners cognitively reconstruct experiences, including dialogues, in ways that are meaningful to them. Learning, broadly understood as acquiring new facts and information (Barnlund, 1962) and incorporating experiences into one's own thoughts and behaviors (Zull, 2002), can be viewed as an outcome of the meaning-making process. Learners represent the subject, not the receiver, of educational activities. By this logic, instructors do not disseminate knowledge or transmit information, but co-create experiences with learners and for learners to process.

Experiential learning (EL) is an important area of scholarship in education, and examination of EL has expanded our understanding of learning processes, influenced important changes in pedagogic practices, and enriched theories of the nature of experience and knowledge (Fenwick, 2003). According to Merriam and Brockett (1997) "what we know and the meanings we attach to what we know are socially constructed. Thus, learning and knowing are intimately linked to real-life situations" (p. 156). Bandura (1977) argued that people learn from observing role models, which then serves as a blueprint for the behavior. Lave (1988) suggested learning is naturally tied to authentic activity, context, and culture. In each case, the learning process is initiated by experiential activities. Meaning-making is the constructive process of reflecting, creating, and testing (Zull, 2002); learning is the result.

This chapter examines the relationship between experiential learning and meaning-centered education, and is organized as follows: First, we describe the meaning-centered paradigm as a process used to construct and organize our experiences. We also point out the important role of reflection, or intrapersonal communication, in the meaning-centered paradigm. Second, we summarize experiential learning theory and articulate three types of learning experiences (direct, observed, and imagined) that the meaning-centered educational paradigm robustly accommodates. Finally, we explain how experiential learning theory and the meaning-centered paradigm fit together to extend their theoretical boundaries. We also suggest some considerations for practice where a meaning-centered perspective is applied to experiential learning activities.

Meaning-Centered Education

From a human communication perspective, meanings reside in people, or the message-users, not in the messages themselves (Berlo, 1960). Meaning-centered communication (Barnlund, 1962; Fairhurst, 2001) focuses on the co-creation of understanding. Barnlund (1962) proposed that communication is a dynamic, nonlinear process in which meanings are actively assigned, not passively received. This communication perspective is particularly relevant to educational contexts, as the meaning-centered perspective clearly includes teacher-learner interactions where the teacher does not impart knowledge on students, but students co-create understanding (to varying degrees) with their instructors and often with each other. As Freire (2007) notes, "Knowledge emerges only through invention and re-invention, through the restless, impatient, continuing, hopeful inquiry human beings pursue in the world, with the world, and with each other" (p. 72). From the perspective of social construction (Berger and Luckmann, 1966) and sense-making (Weick, 1969, 1995), reality is perceived and negotiated within social systems. The social construction of meaning implies that dialogic view in which meanings are co-constructed through communication (Cooperrider *et al.*, 1995; Gergen, 1985).

The constructive nature of meaning-centered communication is evident in its assumptions about what communication is, and what it is not. For example, as suggested by the opening quote for this chapter, Barnlund (1962) effectively argued that communication is not the transmission of messages or the transfer of a speaker's ideas, but the creation of meaning, "generated from within" (p. 200). Indeed, because the meaning-centered perspective uniquely includes intrapersonal communication, it can robustly address the process by which individual learners interpret and reflect upon their experiences to construct meanings from them. For example, Wegerif (this volume) observed that thinking can be dialogic, such that one can be engaged in a dialogue with oneself. More specifically, Barnlund (1962) explained that an individual comprises a "communication system unto himself" whenever he or she discovers and interprets an occurrence in nature or derives meaning from his or her own reflections. As such, reflection or "consummatory communication" (Festinger, 1957) is integral to Barnlund's meaning-centered communication process model, as the "mind of the interpreter" is the most critical aspect of meaning-making. It is worth noting that this conceptualization of intrapersonal communication does not negate a dialogic view of meaning-centered education, but rather adds that learning must include conversations with oneself as well as with others. This perspective differs somewhat from Bakhtin's (1981) proposition that meanings are created in processes of reflection *between* people, as it argues that meaning-making is a process that involves multiple concurrent dialogues. Some of these dialogues are externally or interpersonally focused, and one or more must be self-reflective, or intrapersonal (Zull, 2002).

The notion of reflection as a critical component in the learning process is supported by several theories of adult learning. Kolb (1984) described his learning cycle theory as a set of four stages: concrete experience, reflective observation, abstract conceptualization, and active experimentation. Kolb points out that experience alone is insufficient for learning to take place; some transformation of the experience is required through the reflective observation process, which is a central tenant of his definition of learning: "Learning is the process whereby knowledge is created through the transformation of experience" (p. 38). The individual must make meaning from their experiences (Dewey, 1938; Schon, 1991), and as Taylor (2006) points out, "we must make meaning before it becomes our own. We are inevitably meaning-making, not meaning-taking, organisms" (p. 74). According to Mezirow (1996), the process of learning is understood as a process of meaning-making through reflection. Some life experiences cause an individual to reflect and reorganize existing meaning schemas in order to include the new information. Schema theory (Anderson, 1977) explains that an individual's knowledge is organized as a network of abstract mental structures, or schemata. From this perspective, experiences are not "reflected upon" or analyzed by learners; experiences are cognitively reconstructed by learners through intrapersonal reflection dialogues.

As suggested by schema theory, schemata change as new information is acquired, and may be cognitively reorganized if there is a perceived need to restructure a conceptualization. Mezirow observed that learning can be normative or transformative. In normative learning, a change occurs in the learner's way of thinking. For example, a disorienting dilemma is fitted into an existing meaning perspective (or frame of reference). New information is interpreted through the lens of existing schemas. Other life experiences may challenge a person's most basic notions, which lead to fundamental changes in perspective in which new schemata are created. This type of learning is transformative, as it produces a paradigm shift in the student's frame of reference; old events are no longer perceived in the same way, but take on different meanings. Individualized transformative learning (Mezirow, 1978) occurs as the result of critical self-reflection by the individual on an experience and the manifestation of the learning in some form of action taken by the learner (Dirkx, 1998; Merriam *et al.*, 2007). The learner becomes, "aware of a need to change . . . through critically reflecting on assumptions and biases . . . learn[s] what actions are appropriate in particular situations to implement change" (Merriam *et al.*, 2007, p. 135), and executes the change.

It is interesting to note that contemporary neuroscientific research also supports the central role of reflection in the learning process from a biological perspective. Zull notes that during the learning process the brain changes physically, forming more synapses between active neurons; "reflection is searching for connections— literally" (Zull, 2002, p. 164). His four fundamental pillars of the learning process (i.e., gathering, reflecting, creating, and testing) are very similar to Kolb's (1984) learning cycle. First, one gathers data through one's senses; however, the process of data collection does not create understanding or meaning. Second, one reflects on the data, combines it in different ways to produce more meaningful images, and associates the data with existent memories and knowledge. The "assembly and association of bits of data, memories, and images might be considered the slowest part of learning. It takes time and involves rerunning our data over and over. It takes reflection" (p. 6). Once meaning has been created in the brain the third phase of learning begins, where one creates plans, theories, and abstractions, which are then used in the fourth phase, testing. "They [tests] are physical acts that produce signals from the motor brain, which the body then senses. This changes a mental idea to a physical event; it changes an abstraction once again into a concrete experience, thus continuing the learning cycle" (p. 7).

In summary, relying primarily on research and theory from the interpersonal communication discipline, we have described some of the origins of the meaning-centered paradigm. Meaning-centered communication is a constructive process by which meanings are created and maintained within people. We also explained that reflection, as intrapersonal communication, is at the core of the dialogic meaning-centered process.

Experiential Learning

Dewey (1938) suggested that we learn by doing, confirming what Plato, Aristotle, Aquinas, Locke, and others have asserted about experience as a widespread and effective means of learning. The word *experience* may be used as a noun: a catalogued, objectified, and reflected-upon resource, but it can also be understood as a process of learning. Experiential learning (EL) is usually associated with a constructivist approach, which argues that humans construct meaning from current knowledge structures. Current conceptualizations of experiential learning theory also build on Dewey's pragmatism and focus on education, Lewin's social psychology and group dynamics, and Piaget's model of learning and development. In essence, experiential learning requires meaning-making: "Experiential Learning is the sense-making process of active engagement between the inner world of the person and the outer world of the environment" (Wilson and Beard, 2006, p. 2). Kolb (1984) claimed, "learning is the process whereby knowledge is created through the transformation of experience" (p. 38). Boud *et al.* (1993) argued that it is "meaningless to talk about learning in isolation from experience. Experience cannot be bypassed; it is the central consideration of all learning" (p. 8).

Although a distinction can be made between experiential education and experiential learning, the two theoretical frames are related. Experiential education is understood as a philosophy that links teachers and learners through the learners' experiences (Dewey, 1938). In particular, experiential education argues against the "delivery" of knowledge in favor of the construction of experiences that meet learners' internal needs and goals. Dewey (1938) labeled experiences void of reflection as "non-educative." Whereas experiential education focuses on the process by which teachers engage learners, experiential learning focuses on how individuals learn from their experiences, even without a teacher. Kolb and Fry (1975) described their experiential learning model in terms of the individual learner such that experiential learning is the process of making meaning. From an experiential learning perspective, teachers can facilitate the learning process, but learning is a personalized process in which learners gain knowledge from their peers and from their environment as they pursue what they want and what they need. Both the experiential education philosophy and the experiential learning model rebuff a transmission perspective on experiential learning in which activities, simulations, and exercise are "done to" students as receivers of instruction (cf., Potosky, 2006). Experiential learning is less about instructional design than about the personally interpreted experience of each learner.

Experiential learning involves affective, cognitive, and metacognitive processes that are set into motion by interpretation, reflection, interaction, and iteration. Rather than focus on learners' direct experience with a specific environment, we propose that experience can be broadly defined to include not only direct contact with a learning environment, but also observed environments experienced by others as well as imagined environments. We explain below how the meaning-centered perspective effectively accommodates all three learning environments.

Learning Through Direct Experience

Experiential education was originally proposed as both a philosophy as well as a methodology "in which educators purposefully engage with learners in direct experience and focused reflection in order to increase knowledge, develop skills, and clarify values" (Association for Experiential Education, n.d.). These direct experiences include games, simulations, and activities that directly engage students in ways that enable them to experience and construct information first hand. In direct experiences, learning is guided by what we do with our bodies and learning objects. Widely accepted types of learning objects include Design and Construction, Conceptual Manipulation, and Reality Role Play. These concepts have shifted into the digital world in a similar classification scheme. Even though the physicality is different, the cognitive effects of virtual objects can be similar to real objects, and they provide insights into the process of abstraction and imagination in learning (van Joolingen, 1999; Zuckerman, 2006). With reflection as a mechanism, students may learn skills, tactics, or stratagems from different activities with the same objects.

The philosophy of experiential education, which posits that experience provides the foundation for learning, is attributed to the work of John Dewey (1938). An implicit assumption of this philosophy is that direct contact in a learning environment will evoke reactions that become part of a symbolic, internalized learning experience. An instructor may focus a learner's attention and structure the learning environment, but ultimately it is the learner's experience that creates the learning content. "Student perceptions and responses are central, not tangential, content for learning" (Savicki, 2008, p. 75).

Active learning through direct experience includes case-oriented methods such as problem-based learning (PBL), in which students collaboratively solve problems and reflect on experiences. Teachers may act as facilitators in a staged self-directed learning activity (Altman, 1986). This process of inquiry begins with an experience of not knowing what to do next, and leads to finding answers through collaborative inquiry with fellow learners. This activity is a profound shift from dependence on available expertise and pride in self-learning to learning with and from others, disclosing doubts and admitting ignorance. Darvin (2006) says "When teachers provide opportunities for students to apply their cognitive skills to a personal issue or problem, learning is enhanced and the students experience an affirming sense of accomplishment" (p. 398).

One critique of Kolb's ideas is the lack of attention to the body as a site of learning and knowledge construction (i.e., somatic or embodied learning). Fenwick (2003) argued that, "Experience exceeds language and rationality, because it reiterates the crucial locatedness of bodies in material reality that cannot be dismissed as a solely linguistic construction" (p. 6). As Iacucci *et al.* (2004) observed, "Meaning is created in use of shared objects and social interaction is related to how we engage in spaces and artifacts. In this interplay the body has a central role, in many ways the body can be seen as the medium for having a world" (p. 7). According to Goodwin and Goodwin (2000), learning is tightly connected with the objects and materials around us: "Cognition is not lodged exclusively within the head of an isolated actor, but instead within a distributed system, one that includes both other participants and meaningful artifacts" (p. 8). This notion that learners, acting within a setting, are key components of a system of learners engaged in an experience is consistent with our argument that meaning-centered learning entails multiple, concurrent dialogues that include each learner's personal reflection (meaning-making) process. Experiential learning incorporates embodied learning based on situated cognition, in which context is key to understanding. According to Merriam and Brockett (1997) "what we know and the meanings we attach to what we know are socially constructed. Thus, learning and knowing are intimately linked to real-life situations" (p. 156).

Experiential learning is not a simple hit-and-miss proposition. Not all activity results in experience and painful experiences may discourage learning. Wlodkowski (1999) noted that experience can even lead to *mis-educative experiences*, in which experiences do not produce learning, or in which students learn the wrong thing from an experience. Kolb (1984) goes further, and suggests that experiential learning is also not simply incidental learning. We consciously or subconsciously engage with the experience and reflect on what happened, how it happened and what it means. He suggests a conscious choice is involved in learning, along with an extensive set of skills needed to exploit the experience, including observational, analytical, reflective, decision making and problem solving skills, as well as a commitment to invest in that learning process. This suggests a clear role for instructors as they encourage reflection and propose and discuss appropriate frames for interpreting students' experiences. Also, the design of some direct experiences may incorporate feedback and iterative challenges that encourage students to refine their understanding of their experience and the knowledge gained from the activity. For example, Gee (2007) examined the detailed interactions of humans and machines in a game environment and highlighted the cyclical nature of experiential learning in the design of games:

> Good games offer players a set of challenging problems and then let them practice these until they have routinized their mastery. Then the game throws a new class of problems at the player, requiring them to rethink their taken-for-granted mastery, only to be challenged again. This cycle of consolidation and challenge is the basis for the development of expertise in any domain.
>
> *(Gee, 2007, p. 217)*

In sum, experiential education and EL theory propose that an individual's direct experience creates an opportunity for reflection and, ultimately, learning. Activities designed by an instructor to engage students as well as the direct experience of an object or an event encountered by individuals themselves provide the stimulus for knowledge construction. We pointed out, however, that the meaning-making cognitive process does not guarantee learning as defined by an instructor. Students own their individual reflection processes. Hence, there is an important role for the instructor as a guide to aid students as they interpret (or "frame") and debrief their experiences.

Experience as Observation

In Kolb's (1984) model, experiential learning is a cycle that begins with a concrete experience, which is then processed by observation and reflection. Observation and reflection lead to new understandings, skills, and affective responses, which are applied and tested in new situations. These applications create new concrete experiences, and the cycle is repeated. We argue, however, that observation can *be* the experience that is reflected upon. That is, although Kolb's model emphasized the role of learners' direct experience, other theoretical frameworks and empirical studies have suggested that learners can also re-create symbolic experiences for their own learning by observing others (Lave, 1988). For example, Bandura's (1977) social learning theory posits that individuals learn from observing and imitating others. Individuals observe models encountered in social interaction and/or listen to stories of others' experiences, and those individuals can learn from these observations as well. Observing and listening are understood as interpersonal actions or behaviors, which comprise experiences. Hence, a learner can experience a film or a lecture or a story in a book. As with other experiential learning models, perception and reflection play key roles in this framework.

Experiential learning and meaning-making are not a "once and done" process. Our memories and the learning we accumulate in our lives are in a constant state of reinterpretation, as Huxley (2004/1954) notes: "The past is not something fixed and unalterable. Its facts are re-discovered by every succeeding generation, its values re-assessed, its meanings re-defined in the context of present tastes and preoccupations" (p. 132). This process continues as individuals try to make meaning from all of their experiences in light of current information and recent experiences. Experience as observation implies that individuals are neither restricted to a single event (i.e., they can revisit, re-enact, and reinterpret events) nor limited to reflect only on their own direct experience in order to construct meanings.

Experience as Imagination

A third type of experience that can be considered here resides within the intrapersonal realm, namely, imagination and projection. Imagination plays a key role in the learning process and helps people make sense of the world by assisting in the process of creating understanding of knowledge and bringing meaning to experience (Norman, 2000; Sutton-Smith, 1988; Egan, 1992). Imagination can be evoked by play and expressed through stories such as fairy tales or fantasies. Imagination seems to be an effort of the mind to develop a discourse of what was previously known, or a development of a pre-existing concept, which may yield new thinking.

The essence of experiential learning may be in the stories individuals create in their cognitions, which can be reviewed, retold, and adapted as different situations may demand. Some research has suggested that real-world decision making is guided by internalized stories that direct our goals, judgments, and actions (Bruner, 1986; Cole, 1997; Crites, 1986; Sarbin, 1986). The use of internalized stories provides an imagined experience that frames one's understanding of current circumstances. Stories also provide new ways to re-examine past experiences. Further, stories enable a learner to project goals and envision scenarios for the future. By rephrasing a story in language with conceptual, verbal, and physical elements, it becomes useful to the individual and can even be shared within a community. Shared stories can be represented as staged plays, dances, music, drawings, and carvings, enhancing the narrative recreation and social acceptability. Stories, reflecting imagined experiences, become the basis for art and culture (Caillois, 2001; Huizinga, 1950).

There may be aspects of the eternal child in all of us, especially in the sense of the imagination. Children often use narratives or pretend play to exercise imagination. Such fantasy play happens at two levels: Children use role playing to act out what they have developed with their imagination, and then they play again with their make-believe situation by acting as if what they have developed is an actual reality that already exists in narrative myth (Goldman, 1998). Although imagination might imply that something "new" is being conjured, Pascoli claimed that imagination is a tool of a "true poet, who is not an inventor but a discoverer" (Horne, 1983, p. 12). Educators can empower learners to discover "the new in the unfamiliar and to uncover the essence of things under their outward appearance" (Horne, 1983, p. 12). As an ability that can be learned and refined, imagination can develop by listening to stories or narratives (Norman, 2000) in which words may "evoke worlds" (Horne, 1983, p. 12). Evoking imagination through stories may create a sense of enchantment and playfulness:

> We were all enchanted . . . The more we listened, the more gaily Mr. Skimpole talked. And what with his fine hilarious manner, and his engaging candour, and his genial way of lightly tossing his own weaknesses about, as if he had said, "I am a child, you know! You are designing people compared with me;" (he really made me consider myself in that light;) "but I am gay and innocent; forget your worldly arts and play with me!"—the effect was absolutely dazzling.
>
> *(Charles Dickens,* Bleak House*, Chapter 6)*

McCarthy *et al.* (2006) described enchantment as an experience of "being caught up and carried away . . . perception and attention are heightened . . . we are awakened to wonder and imagine" (p. 370). They point out that enchantment is induced when there is the potential for the unexpected or for new discoveries, and when a range of possibilities is apparent. Enchantment enables the mind to adjust the rules of reality to fit desired reality. In this sense, enchantment is a form of imagined experience that prompts cognitive playfulness. Theories and research associated with playfulness (e.g., Barnett, 1990, 1991; Csikszentmihalyi,

1990; Glynn and Webster, 1992, 1993; Lieberman, 1977; Miller, 1973) have suggested that individuals differ in their intellectual curiosity and capacity for cognitive spontaneity. Contextual stimuli, however, can prompt spontaneous, inventive, and imaginative responses in individuals inclined, to varying degrees, toward playfulness.

Learners can engage in creative play or metacognitive fantasy, aided or unaided by games or manipulatives. Such activities present learners with challenges that engage them in what Csikszentmihalyi (1990) referred to as flow. According to this work, flow happens when individuals are engaged in the optimal experience of playfulness and learning, in which individuals are appropriately challenged but not exceedingly frustrated. Vygotsky (1978) described how a learner may solve problems and perform above their abilities with a coach, teacher, or mentor tapping into the learner's imagination, awakening his or her capacity for play, through various means, for example, leading questions from a mentor, the teacher initiating a solution and the learner completes it, or collaborative problem solving with peers. In this zone of proximal development (ZPD) the learner reaches beyond their existent knowledge base and navigates through uncharted territory. Johnson (2006) noted that "the ZPD can thus be seen as an incubator of abstract thinking or creativity" (p. 68) in phase 3 of Zull's (2002) brain learning process. It is here that the mind manipulates, re-arranges, and reflects upon the information to form connections (literally), make meaning of the experience, and develop deep understanding.

Piaget (1967) observed that perceptions depend on a person's worldview, which is the result of arranging perceptions into existing imagery by imagination. He gave an example of a child saying that the moon is following her when she walks around the village at night. After much observation, consideration, and research this basic perception becomes a meaningful piece of knowledge about the mechanics of distance and perception. Piaget demonstrated that perceptions are integrated into the worldview to make sense, and that imagination is needed to make sense of perceptions (Piaget, 1967).

Kolb's (1984) experiential learning model suggests that knowledge is created through grasping and transforming experiences, which form the basis for observation and reflection. Learners assimilate and distill their reflections into abstract concepts from which implications for action and experiences are drawn. As powerful as this model is, it focuses on the rational processes of the mind and diminishes the impact that imagination, emotion, and social meaning play in adult learning. The process of making meanings may be less like a rational adult walking on a well-trod lane and more like a group of playful children exploring a primeval forest. In such a metaphorical forest, we can assume that many paths can be carved through the woods. In some cases, sections of the paths may be equivalent, with similar results no matter which path is followed, but in others, minor deviations can lead to radically different outcomes. This image seems more consistent with real-world learning and meaning-making scenarios than the basic Kolb model.

Meanings are constructed by and filtered through both the rational expectations and the cognitive playfulness of each learner.

Meaning-Centered Experiential Learning

Engagement, understood as the experience of something, elicits learning, retention, and transfer to the real world. Kearsley and Shneiderman (1998, p. 1) claim that "students are intrinsically motivated to learn due to the meaningful nature of the learning environment and activities," and they emphasize the importance of providing an authentic (i.e. meaningful) setting for learning. Students are engaged when they see meaning and purpose in what they are doing, and that authenticity provides meaning and purpose (Kearsley and Shneiderman, 1998). As described above, engagement can be achieved not only through direct experience, but also through observation of others' experiences and through play and imagined experiences.

The process of gainful learning or meaning-making begins when learners are provided the opportunity to experience something. The model of "Informal and Incidental Learning" is a suitable model to examine learner-centered activities and important elements in the learning cycle (Marsick and Watkins, 2001). In this model, learning begins with some kind of a trigger, that is, an internal or external stimulus that frames what there is to experience. Experiences are the basis for reflections. Reflections are assimilated and distilled into abstract concepts, or schemata, from which implications and intentions for action are created. These implications can be actively tested and serve as guides in creating new experiences (Boyatzis and Mainemelis, 2000; Kolb, 1984). It is important to note, however, that the meaning-centered approach to experiential learning does not assume a linear process whereby one event at a time is experienced and interpreted. As noted earlier, meaning-centered theory assumes multiple concurrent conversations at any one point in time. Some of these conversations may construct the event itself, and some may be reflective in order to interpret the event, and still others may create new events or experiences. These new experiences may be linked to the initial experience as episodes within an ongoing story, or they may be offspring of the initial event that prompt new meanings, or they may be "turns of events," that is, distinct new experiences that emerge for any number of reasons.

A constructivist explanation of experiential learning as an outcome of a meaning-making process challenges traditional educational paradigms that assume the transfer of information and knowledge from teachers to learners. Although experiential learning can be approached from a transmission perspective in which an educator designs an activity and attempts to predetermine learning outcomes, this approach is inherently flawed because it ignores the learners' own reflection processes. Reflection can move through a byzantine path dominated by stories and imagined or past experiences, can be misdirected by rumor and belief systems, and is driven by emotions and social norms. A meaning-centered approach to experiential learning disputes the transmission view of communication and suggests that learning is not a direct outcome of teaching, but of students' meaning-making activities. These activities include conversations that students have with instructors, with other students, with themselves, and with imagined and real others. These activities can be proposed, guided, and framed by educators. Ultimately, though, they must be constructed (and reconstructed) by learners.

The nature of experience, direct, borrowed, or imagined, begins the construction process by which lessons may be learned. Teachers can influence the meaning-making process through the design of direct, observed, and imagined experiences and also through the framing and debriefing process by which students reflect on their experiences. Instructional design must focus on the learners (not the instructors) as the meaning makers, and should address the broad array of emotional and social opportunities and obstacles that are likely to prompt reflection on the path to effective learning. Educators must make allowances for these challenges in the form of better preparation for and perhaps reframing of the learning context as well as better post-analysis, discussion, and guided reflection. A meaning-centered perspective on EL not only places greater demands on the facilitator for sensitivity and exploration as learners make sense of each experience, but it also demands that the learners themselves be prepared to reflect on their experiences at some point. With regard to practice in higher education, both educators and students need to understand the meaning-centered perspective, including interpersonal considerations, in order to anticipate the experiential learning process.

In summary, learning is the outcome of meaning-making processes, which in turn can be initiated by experiential activities. Specifically, learning can be constructed from what learners experience directly, from what learners observe, and from what learners imagine. Reflection by the learner is required if these environments of experience lead to learning. We equated reflection with meaning-making, specifically intrapersonal communication processes. Learners communicate with others and interact with their environment, but they also, concurrently, engage in reflective dialogues with themselves in order to make sense of their experiences. Although learning, like meanings, resides in the learners and therefore cannot be guaranteed across individually constructed and maintained schemas, the meaning-centered paradigm for education offers a robust and realistic perspective on how students' experiences facilitate learning.

References

Altman, B. (1986) "Working with play." *The Child Care Worker* 4(8): 10–12. Available online from: http://www.cyc-net.org/cyc-online/cycol-0102-altman.html (accessed December 6, 2012).

Anderson, R. C. (1977) "The notion of schemata and the educational enterprise." In R. C. Anderson, R. J. Spiro, and W. E. Montague (Eds), *Schooling and the Acquisition of Knowledge* (pp. 415–431). Hillsdale, NJ: Erlbaum.

Association for Experiential Education, n.d., *What Is Experiential Education?* http://www. aee.org/about/what IsEE (accessed December 1, 2011).

Bakhtin, M. (1981) *The Dialogic Imagination: Four Essays.* Austin, TX: University of Texas Press.

Bandura, A. (1977) *Social Learning Theory.* New York: General Learning Press.

Barnett, L. A. (1990) "Playfulness: definition, design, and measurement." *Play and Culture* 3: 319–336.

Barnett, L. A. (1991) "The playful child: measurement of a disposition to play." *Play and Culture* 4: 51–74.

Barnlund, D. C. (1962) "Toward a meaning-centered philosophy of communication." *Journal of Communication* 12(4): 197–211.

Berger, P. L. and Luckmann, T. (1966) *The Social Construction of Reality: A Treatise in the Sociology of Knowledge.* Garden City, NY: Anchor Books.

Berlo, D. (1960) *The Process of Communication.* New York: Holt, Rinehart, & Winston.

Boud, D., Cohen, R., and Walker, D. (1993) *Using Experience for Learning.* Buckingham: Open University Press.

Boyatzis, R. and Mainemelis, C. (2000) An empirical study of the pluralism of learning and adaptive styles in an MBA program. Department of Organizational Behavior, Case Western Reserve University, Cleveland, OH. Working Paper, WP 00-1.

Bruner, J. (1986) "Two modes of thought." In *Actual Minds, Possible Worlds* (pp. 11–43). Cambridge, MA: Harvard University Press.

Caillois, R. (2001) *Man, Play and Games.* (M. Barash, Trans.). Urbana-Champaign, IL: University of Illinois Press. (Original work published in 1958).

Cole, H. (1997) "Stories to live by: A narrative approach to health-behavior research and injury prevention." In D. S. Gochman (Ed.), *Handbook of Health Behavior Research IV: Relevance for Professionals and Issues for the Future* (pp. 325–349). New York: Plenum.

Cooperrider, D., Barrett, F., and Srivasta, S. (1995) "Social construction and appreciative inquiry: A journey in organizational theory." In D. Hoskin, P. Dachler, and K. Gergen (Eds), *Management and Organization: Relational Alternatives to Individualism* (pp. 157–200). Aldershot, UK: Avebury.

Crites, S. (1986) "Storytelling: Recollecting the past and projecting the future." In T. R. Sarbin (Ed.), *Narrative Psychology: The Storied Nature of Human Conduct* (pp. 152–173). New York: Praeger.

Csikszentmihalyi, M. (1990) *The Psychology of Optimal Experience.* New York: Harper & Row.

Darvin, J. (2006) "Real-world cognition doesn't end when the bell rings: Literacy instruction strategies derived from situated cognition research." *Journal of Adolescent and Adult Literacy* 49: 398–407. International Reading Association.

Dewey, J. (1938) *Experience and Education.* New York: Collier Books.

Dirkx, J. M. (1998) "Transformative learning theory in the practice of adult education: An overview." *PAACE Journal of Lifelong Learning* 7: 1–14. Available online from http://www.coe.iup.edu/ace/PAACE%20Journal%20PDF/PDF1998/Dirkx1998.pdf (accessed March 12, 2009).

Egan, K. (1992) *Imagination in Teaching and Learning.* Chicago, IL: University of Chicago Press.

Fairhurst, G. T. (2001) "Dualisms in leadership research." In F. M. Jablin and L. L. Putnam (Eds), *The New Handbook of Organizational Communication* (pp. 379–439). Thousand Oaks, CA: Sage.

Fenwick, T. (2003) "Reclaiming and re-embodying experiential learning through complexity science." *Studies in the Education of Adults* 35(2): 123–141.

Festinger, L. (1957) *A Theory of Cognitive Dissonance*. Evanston, IL: Row, Peterson.

Freire, P. (2007) *Pedagogy of the Oppressed (30th anniversary ed.)*. New York: Continuum.

Gee, J. P. (2007) *What Video Games Have to Teach Us about Learning and Literacy* (VGLL). New York: Palgrave Macmillan.

Gergen, K. J. (1985) The social constructionist movement in modern psychology. *American Psychologist*, 40: 266–275.

Glynn, M. A. and Webster, J. (1992) "The Adult Playfulness Scale: An initial assessment." *Psychological Reports* 71: 83–103.

Glynn, M. A. and Webster, J. (1993) "Refining the nomological net of the Adult Playfulness Scale: Personality, motivational, and attitudinal correlates for highly intelligent adults." *Psychological Reports* 72: 1023–1026.

Goldman, L. (1998) *Child's Play: Myth, Mimesis and Make-Believe*. Oxford; New York: Berg Publishers.

Goodwin, M. and Goodwin, C. (2000) "Emotion within situated activity." In A. Duranti (Ed.), *Linguistic Anthropology: A Reader* (pp. 239–257). Malden, MA; Oxford: Blackwell.

Horne, P. (1983) *Pascoli, Selected Poems*. Manchester: Manchester University Press.

Huizinga, J. (1950) *homo ludens* (playful man). Roy Publishers.

Huxley, A. (2004/1954) *The Doors of Perception and Heaven and Hell*. New York: Harper Collins.

Iacucci, G., Linde, P., and Wagner, I. (2004) "Exploring relationships between learning, artifacts, physical space, and computing." In *CADE2004 Web Proceedings of Computers in Art and Design Education Conference, Sweden*. Available online from: asp.cbs.dk/cade2004/proceedings/ (accessed December 6, 2012).

Johnson, S. (2006) "The neuroscience of the mentor-learner relationship." *New Directions for Adult and Continuing Education*, 110: 63–69. doi: 10.1002/ace.220.

Kearsley, G. and Shneiderman, B. (1998) "Engagement theory: A framework for technology-based teaching and learning." *Educational Technology* 38(5): 20–23.

Kolb, D. (1984) *Experiential Learning: Experience as the Source of Learning and Development*. Englewood Cliffs, NJ: Prentice-Hall.

Kolb, D. A. and Fry, R. (1975) "Toward an applied theory of experiential learning." In C. Cooper (Ed.), *Theories of Group Process*. London: John Wiley & Sons.

Lave, J. (1988) *Cognition in Practice: Mind, Mathematics and Culture in Everyday Life*. Cambridge: Cambridge University Press.

Lieberman, J. N. (1977) *Playfulness*. New York: Academic Press.

McCarthy, J., Wright, P., Wallace, J., and Dearden, A. (2006) "The experience of enchantment in human–computer interaction." *Pers Ubiquit Comput* 2006(10): 369–378.

Marsick, V. and Watkins, K. (2001) "Informal and incidental learning." *New Directions for Adult and Continuing Education*, 89: 25–34.

Merriam, S. and Brockett, R. (1997) *The Profession and Practice of Adult Education. Perspectives on the Past*. San Francisco, CA: Jossey-Bass.

Merriam, S. B., Caffarella, R. S., and Baumgartner, L. M. (2007) *Learning in Adulthood: A Comprehensive Guide* (3rd ed.). San Francisco, CA: Jossey-Bass.

Mezirow, J. (1978) "Perspective transformation." *Adult Education* 28: 100–110.

Mezirow, J. (1996) "Contemporary paradigms of learning." *Adult Education Quarterly* 46(3): 158–172.

Miller, S. (1973) "Ends, means, and galumphing: Some leitmotifs of play." *American Anthropologist* 75: 87–98.

Norman, R. (2000) *Cultivating Imagination in Adult Education.* Proceedings of the 41st Annual Adult Education Research Conference.

Piaget, J. (1967) *The Child's Conception of the World.* (J. and A. Tomlinson, Trans.). London: Routledge & Kegan Paul.

Potosky, D. (2006) "The instructor's toolbox: A meaning centered framework for the social construction of experiential learning." *Association for Business Simulation and Experiential Learning (ABSEL), Developments in Business Simulation and Experiential Learning* (CD), 7th Edition.

Sarbin, T. (Ed.) (1986) *Narrative Psychology: The Storied Nature of Human Conduct.* New York: Praeger.

Savicki, V. (2008) "Experiential and affective education for international educators." In V. Savicki (Ed.), *Developing Intercultural Competence and Transformation* (pp. 74–91). Sterling, VA: Stylus Publishing.

Schon, D. A. (1991) *Educating the Reflective Practitioner: Toward a New Design for Teaching and Learning in the Professions.* Hoboken, NJ: John Wiley & Sons, Inc.

Sutton-Smith, B. (1988) "In search of the imagination." In K. Egan and D. Nadaner (Eds), *Imagination and Education.* New York: Teachers College Press.

Taylor, K. (2006) "Brain function and adult learning: Implications for practice." In S. Johnson and K. Taylor (Eds), *The neuroscience of adult learning* (pp. 3–9). San Francisco, CA: Jossey-Bass.

van Joolingen, W. (1999) "Cognitive tools for discovery learning." *International Journal of Artificial Intelligence in Education* 10: 385–397.

Vygotsky, L. (1978) *Mind in Society: The Development of Higher Psychological Processes.* Cambridge, MA: Harvard University Press.

Vygotsky, L. S. (1924/1978) "Consciousness as a problem in the psychology of behavior." *Soviet Psychology* 176(4): 3–35. (Original work published in 1924).

Weick, K. (1969) *The Social Psychology of Organizing.* Reading, MA: Addison-Wesley.

Weick, K. E. (1995) *Sensemaking in Organizations.* Thousand Oaks, CA: Sage.

Wilson, J. and Beard, C. (2006) *Experiential Learning: A Best Practice Handbook for Educators and Trainers* (2nd ed.). London and Philadelphia: Kogan Page.

Wlodkowski, R. (1999) *Enhancing Adult Motivation to Learn: A Comprehensive Guide for Teaching All Adults.* San Francisco, CA: Jossey-Bass.

Zuckerman, O. (2006) *Historical Overview and Classification of Traditional and Digital Learning Objects.* Cambridge, MA: MIT Press.

Zull, J. E. (2002) *The Art of Changing the Brain.* Sterling, VA: Stylus.

Zull, J. E. (2006) "Key aspects of how the brain learns." In S. Johnson and K. Taylor (Eds), *The Neuroscience of Adult Learning* (pp. 3–9). San Francisco, CA: Jossey-Bass.

PART II

Worldwide Successful Practices

Voices of Experience

5

FOSTERING INTERCULTURAL DIALOGUE VIA COMMUNICATION TECHNOLOGIES

Alyssa J. O'Brien and Olga Kovbasyuk

US-Russia Dialogues: A Praxis of Intercultural Education

In *Pedagogy of the Oppressed*, Paulo Freire defines praxis as "reflection and action upon the world in order to transform it." Aristotle named praxis as one of the three activities of humanity, in addition to theory and poetry, and he divided practical knowledge or praxis into ethics, economics, and politics. In scholarly circles today the term praxis evokes an emphasis on repeated experimentation or lived experience as a way towards developing theory, or what Aristotle would call truth.

In this chapter, we begin with praxis and move to theory, with the aim of offering insights into meaning-centered education (MCE) that derive from empirical research and collaborative classroom practices. Specifically, we describe a series of dialogic encounters between students at Khabarovsk State Academy of Economics and Law, in Russia, and students at Stanford University, in the USA. In characterizing these encounters, we refer to Wegerif's (this volume) articulation of the "dialogic" as "the continuous re-creation of meaning through engaging in dialogue." Such dialogues were made possible through the communication technologies of video conferencing and blogging over the course of three years. By presenting the design, implementation, and outcomes of these dialogues, we hope to offer a concrete model for how other educators might integrate intercultural dialogic activities into classes and curricula. At the same time, by analyzing these encounters through the lens of MCE, we hope to enrich the theory with our reflections on the efficacy of such intercultural exchanges in university settings.

Our central argument is that active collaboration, through exchanging questions and perspectives, as well as through working on shared projects, can enrich students' experiences in higher education and open their minds to alternative ways of thinking and making meaning out of the world. To that end, we delineate the process by which we brought together our students in a shared virtual space for the purpose of exchanging intercultural perspectives on leadership, economics, politics, and ethics, particularly in the realm of dialogic communication through social media. Our main claim is that such hands-on, interactive meaning-centered educational practices are essential for developing intercultural competencies and skills, which are vital for twenty-first century graduates, given the demands of a global economy in which all countries are interconnected and students need to learn effective strategies for communicating and collaborating with others from around the world. From our case study, we contend that meaning derives from negotiations and collaborations which resonate with the internal experience of the participants, and that such negotiations are premised upon trust and equality in human relationships, which can be fostered by educators/facilitators in a safe virtual environment, created with the help of communication technologies, across great geographic and ideological differences.

Designing International Encounters: The Pedagogical Process

The official collaboration between Khabarovsk State Academy of Economics and Law and Stanford University began in January of 2009, when we committed to connect our classes through digital technologies for the purpose of helping students develop intercultural competencies and practical strategies for cross-cultural communication. Over the past three years, our collaboration has evolved towards meaning-centered education as a result of the rich and personal experiences of the students during the connections, and the evolution of the pedagogical strategies of the facilitators. By meaning-centered education, we concur with Potosky's (this volume) emphasis on the "constructive process by which meanings are created and maintained within people." We have made intercultural dialogue the focus of our collaboration, and in this section we describe our objectives, methodology, implementation choices, and results.

From the beginning, our aim in bringing together our students in a shared virtual space was to promote discussion among them, foster analysis of cultural and political perspectives, and to make possible the acquisition of "intercultural competencies" (Lovitt and Goswami, 1999), or the increasingly important skill of approaching others with consideration for and sensitivity towards diverse cultural contexts. At the core of intercultural competence is the ability to communicate effectively and appropriately (Spitzberg and Cupach, 1984) across cultural or intercultural situations. An often contested term in the literature, intercultural communication competence (ICC) might be best understood through Arasaratnam's (2009) three dimensions, as cognitive, affective, and behavioral (Cui and Van den Berg, 1991; Sercu, 2004; Spitzberg, 1991). Our objective was to foster ICCs in our students by giving them an opportunity for visual, audio, and textual collaboration made possible by information communication technologies (ICTs). As facilitators, we initiated our discussions about the technological and pedagogical possibilities available for our connections through video conference and email communication. Strong models preceded us, such as the Cross-Cultural Rhetoric project's work in connecting students between Örebro, Sweden, and Stanford, USA (O'Brien and Eriksson, 2010). We decided to use the technological platforms of blogging and video conferences through Polycom technology as the means to connect the students for several meetings in the course of one academic term. We would initiate a dialogic feedback loop between student writing on the blog and student conversations through video conferences, such that deeper relations could be facilitated and more meaningful insights could be exchanged.

In the first year of implementation, students in Carolyn Ross's Stanford course on Environmental Rhetoric connected with students in Olga Kovbasyuk's Khabarovsk course on Intercultural Communication. At this point, we had not yet designed our collaboration through the lens of MCE. Attention to meaning, dialogue, and experience would emerge from the results of the praxis. Specifically, in blog posts, students articulated their perspectives through words and images about topics such as the environment and future professions available to both Russian and American students. In generating hybrid texts on the blog, they initiated a dialogue in which the English word did not necessarily dominate; they used a visual language to connect with each other and exchange world views. The blog posts were followed by a class-to-class video conference, in which students had the opportunity to introduce themselves, share their perspectives on the issues presented in the blog posts, and engage in meaningful dialogue about their differing views as a means to develop their intercultural competencies.

Subsequently, in the second and third years of implementation, we brought together students in Alyssa O'Brien's Stanford course on Rhetoric and Global Leadership and Olga Kovbasyuk's Khabarovsk course on Intercultural Communication. The focus of conversation and analysis migrated from issues in the environment to questions about leadership styles across countries, rhetorical skills in speaking and communicating across media, and international security policies. Building upon on our earlier experiences, our methodology was to deliberately structure the video conference as a series of dialogic encounters, based upon the opportunity for students to ask questions of each other and inquire as to academic interests and practices, career options, and views on contemporary issues, including politics. The blog posts both preceded the initial video conference conversation and served as a follow-up on the material covered during the connection; in this way, the blog posts extended the dialogue into an asynchronous learning environment. This praxis of dialogic intercultural engagement, occurring across media, time, and technology, would lead us to see the emergence of an MCE mode of pedagogy.

In terms of technologies, we used a Wordpress blog hosted by Stanford's Cross-Cultural Rhetoric project, along with the video conference technology

Polycom, the use of which allows for the exchange of video, audio, as well as computer screen capture. Moreover, Polycom as a technology offers advanced features such as zooming in on a speaker, and in this way we were able to approximate physical closeness between students, enhance eye contact, and match audio to a specific speaker. These technological aspects of the research implementation are worth mentioning since they contributed to the overall positive experience of the students and the way in which the students were able to make meaning out of these educational exercises.

Most recently, we decided to structure the video conferences as a series of conversations between globally-distributed teams consisting of members of both countries, and these teams remained consistent over the course of the academic term. We picked as the subject the Presidents Medvedev and Obama, and we invited students to choose among a focus on leadership strategies, a focus on communication skills, or a focus on international policy stances. Each team's disparate and designated intellectual focus allowed for an in-depth analysis of character and communication across diverse cultural contexts. The result was that students learned about culturally appropriate modes of discourse and ways of being in both cultures, while also transforming how they viewed themselves and communicated as global citizens.

Importantly, we designed a recursive pedagogical process in which both informed dialogue and personal reflections could co-exist. The first step was for students to read and analyze a number of critical texts on their focus area. These materials included an analysis of leadership styles in Russia and the US, an assessment of the social media communication strategies of both Medvedev and Obama, and articles concerning contemporary international "hot topics" such as the assassination of Osama Bin Laden. The student teams then each composed a blog entry in which they introduced themselves and articulated their initial responses to the reading material. Next, we held the first video conference, during which time students had a chance to make the acquaintance of their other team members, comment on each other's initial reading response, and, most importantly, ask questions of each other concerning the subject area or anything else that they might wish to discuss. What we found, consistently, was that students began with an academic focus on the topics of the readings but then soon migrated to asking each other more interpersonal questions, which in turn led to the students co-creating meaning out of these new relationships. After the first video-connection, we captured students' experiential and intellectual responses through asking them to post again on the blog.

The subsequent phase in the encounter was for students to work as globally distributed teams, constructing a PPT presentation with new knowledge and research on their topic areas. We planned for a second video conference connection, during which time each team would showcase its work in a collaborative cross-cultural presentation, using both script and slides. To accomplish this, the students had to meet independently, and they set up Skype meetings as well as chat sessions to discuss their collaborative projects. They also exchanged emails, posted on the CCR blog, and shared their ideas with educational facilitators on both sides.

During the final video conference, each team worked together to deliver an argument about presidential strategies appropriate for the team's focus area. They decided on an order of speaking, alternated explaining the slides and presenting evidence, and articulated conclusive findings on their subject. The pedagogical process of collaborative presentation-making fostered the students' intercultural communication competencies through engaging their cognitive abilities (to organize, synthesize, and make an argument about research), their affective abilities (to make decisions on how best to engage the audience, show interest, demonstrate positive team unity), and their behavioral abilities (to learn best practices for communicating through electronic media, by attending to the time lag, compensating for the approximated or compromised visual field, and accommodating the technical limitations of Polycom in terms of a low-volume speaker and moving image). In these ways, the pedagogical process made possible deep learning of intercultural communication competencies by accessing the three dimensions through the international, technologically mediated encounter.

However, while in our observations as facilitators we noted that students showed increased measures of the five qualities of competent intercultural communication—empathy, intercultural experience, motivation, global attitude, and ability to listen well (Arasaratnam and Doerfel, 2005)—we wanted to substantiate our professional observations with qualitative and quantitative evidence from students about such a transformation.

Developing a Research Questionnaire

In order to generate empirical data, we sought to administer both pre-connection and exit surveys on intercultural communication competence, which was our anticipated outcome. Intercultural competence has received widely differing attempts to measure and assess it. Efforts at arriving at definitive ICC assessment measures remain problematic and fragmented, with little cross-cutting about agreed-upon methodology. Indeed, over decades of research on intercultural competence, a variety of approaches have been applied to assess it (Deardorff, 2006). Many scholars and practitioners have tried to implement methods for assessing intercultural competencies in their teaching. First of all, there are *standard cultural tests* which consist of multiple-choice questions that are easy to administer and correct (Hashem, 1995), but which cannot provide information or evidence on somebody's intercultural competence because they only test factual knowledge, which is sometimes generalized and stereotypical. Assessment tools, such as diagnostic scales (Fantini, 2006) that are composed of Likert-type items, have also been largely criticized. Ruben casts doubts on these tests, stating that "the validity of data of this type rests fundamentally on the presumption that respondents have the desire and ability to engage in valid self assessment" (Ruben, 1989, p. 231). All in all, many criticisms have been targeted at these attempts. In place of these methods, we concur with combining quantitative and qualitative methods of assessment, such as "case studies, interviews, analysis of narrative diaries, self report instruments, observations by others/host culture, judgment by self and others" (Deardoff, 2006), as well as "surveys, evaluation forms, reflective diary entries, critical incident reports, individual and group interviews" (Jackson, 2005). Byram suggests working from a portfolio that he calls an "autobiography of intercultural experiences," which he describes in the following manner: it is problem focused, it only deals with experiences which reflect difference and there may be a tendency to focus on difficulties rather than pleasurable experiences, but "key experiences" are not necessarily difficult or problematic (2005, p. 14). Such a portfolio entails significant additional writing and reflections, which we were not able to make space for given our curricular obligations at both institutions. Nevertheless, we recognize the value of including some form of intercultural autobiographical reflection on key experiences within our own assessment framework.

Having studied previous assessment models, and taken into account all the criticism of the validity of assessing intercultural competence, we found no one single model appropriate for gauging the outcomes of our work. Therefore, we resolved to craft our own survey in order to meet the criteria we set forth in our collaborative project. To that end, we included both quantitative and qualitative assessment measures, including surveys, evaluation forms, self-report instruments, reflective blog posts, open response questions, individual and group interviews, and judgment or observation by outsiders. The survey consisted of quantitative and qualitative questions in the form of self-report answers, which we felt confident using given Arasaratnam's (2009) claim that "if effectiveness is one's ability to accomplish one's communication goal, then it can be reasonably evaluated through self-reported data." Specifically, we constructed six scenarios in which students would need to engage in dialogue with people from another cultural or geographic context. Students addressed these scenarios through an online writing questionnaire.

The second part of the survey was aimed at capturing quantitative data. It asked students to rate themselves on a Likert scale of six possible answers with regard to their aptitude in the following core concepts:

- Collaboration skills that will help future interactions with those from different cultures.
- Strategies of cross-cultural communication.
- How to approach cross-cultural situations with sensitivity to and consideration for others.
- Skills for technology-mediated communication.
- Understanding of how people from different cultural contexts perceive,

analyze, and produce knowledge (in the form of visual, written, or spoken texts).

Following the video conference connections and blog exchanges, we asked students to complete the survey again as a post-test, and we compared the scores. In addition, we collected qualitative data in the form of interviews and reflection letters regarding the student experience, the learning achieved, and the development of intercultural competencies.

Student Responses to Intercultural Conversations and Collaboration

The student response in exit surveys was largely positive, with the strongest positive change in self-report scores appearing for the question concerning, "how to approach cross-cultural situations with more sensitivity to and consideration for others." These scores went from 6.3 percent (strongly agree) and 37.5 percent (agree) before the dialogic connections, up to 33.3 percent (strongly agree) and 16.7 percent (agree). This increase in sensitivity and consideration shows effective development of intercultural communication competencies, and we will analyze it through the lens of meaning-centered education below.

With regard to the question concerning a student's "understanding of how people from different cultural contexts perceive, analyze, and produce knowledge (in the form of visual, written, or spoken texts)," there was also an increase in scores. Before the connections, these scores landed as shown in Table 5.1.

After the connections, students rated themselves higher in this key domain, with scores shown in Table 5.2.

Also positive were responses in the qualitative fields on the survey, in which students articulated their learning in specific and tangible phrases. One major theme was that students acknowledged becoming more interculturally competent and attending to specifics of cross-cultural communication. As one student on the Khabarovsk side wrote, he/she learned "to be more culturally sensitive" and noted that the exchange "helped me to develop analytical thinking." Another commented

TABLE 5.1

12.1%	42.4%	33.3%	12.1%
(strongly agree)	(agree)	(somewhat agree)	(somewhat disagree)

TABLE 5.2

33.3%	66.7%	0.0%	0.0%
(strongly agree)	(agree)	(somewhat agree)	(somewhat disagree)

that the US-Russia dialogues "helped me to improve public speaking skills and to become more sensitive to the diversity of cultures." A third reflected, "It did help me improve my understanding of some aspects of cross-cultural business communication." A few other comments revealed that the cross-cultural collaboration "is a way of learning more about 'self,'" and "thinking and reflecting on ourselves and our worldview," which helped students "change perspectives on leadership and human relationships." These statements indicate that the shift in thinking and sensitivity towards others occurred as a result of bringing together students in a shared virtual space for the purpose of developing intercultural competencies.

In qualitative comments on the Stanford side, students expressed an appreciation for the chance to interact and learn from peers across the globe concerning issues such as leadership and cultural experience. One student wrote, "What I enjoyed most was engaging in interesting dialogue and just having fun with other young people from across the world. Although I learned a lot about the different rhetorical strategies used by foreign leaders in different cultural contexts, what was most intriguing was how similar we were." This statement testifies to the deep human relationships made possible through the video conference connections. Another student voiced the view of many when he/she emphasized the value of dialogic exchange and meaningful conversation: "I liked most how I was able to talk frankly and openly with people from across the globe of similar age. That opportunity is something special and I wouldn't trade it for anything. I also value this experience because I realized just how similar the other participants were to me." The meta-cognitive realization of commonality across difference indicates an instance of self-transformation as a result of the video conference dialogic communication. Such learning often happened when students went off topic, as one responded, "The best part was being able to ask questions of students from other countries [and] be asked questions. I think we learned most from the offhand comments that weren't scripted by either side." In this case, students identified a desire for even more meaningful conversations and an interest in self-determined dialogue with others from different cultural contexts.

In addition to valuing dialogue, especially unscripted conversation, the students also voiced a strong recognition of the value of multiple viewpoints and perspectives. As one student explained in terms of learning core intercultural communication competencies: "[I learned most] how to effectively communicate with somebody from a different culture and how valuable it can be to have a different culture's perspective on the same issue and how they can have a view that varies so much from one's own." Another phrased this learning in terms of the value of international dialogue: "I received some first-hand experience in communicating with international students—people with absolutely different backgrounds. I think that is the most valuable thing I've learned yet." A third brought in the gain in cultural sensitivity as an outcome achieved by the connection: "Most importantly, I learned to be culturally sensitive. It was great seeing how other people's perspectives were shaped by their culture."

A third major result of this collaboration to emerge in the survey results con-cerns the fact that cross-cultural video conferences and blogging activities make possible a meta-cognitive reflection on intercultural communication. One student noted, "I would recommend continuing the [connections]. They created a great opportunity to discuss current leaders with students from different cultural and national perspectives and to compare our reactions to them. I also think they offer an important opportunity to practice our ability to communicate across cultures and to challenge our assumptions about that communication." In this reflection, the student points to the value of the pedagogical focus on leadership, politics, and ethics from a situated position, yet also identifies the need for dialogue to bring into question "assumptions about that communication." This comment indicates intellectual and emotional growth, since the student does not end her/his state-ment of learning at the point of comparing differences; she/he offers insight that such dialogues can challenge assumptions, disrupting or validating world views, and leading to self-developmental growth.

Taken together, these reflections demonstrate recognition of self-transformation and a prioritizing of affective learning, which used to be subordinated by the scientific discourse of education. The attitudes generated in the participating student body made us re-evaluate our project through the lens of MCE. In other words, we recognized that we had designed and implemented a pedagogical encounter that could be fruitfully assessed through the perspective of MCE and which might also help support, clarify, or extend our theoretical understanding of meaning-centered learning.

Meaning-Centered Education as an Interpretative Lens

In assessing our collaboration through the lens of meaning-centered education, we discovered that the intercultural dialogue via communication technologies was perceived by the majority of participants as novel learning due to the follow-ing factors which are essential in an MCE setting: a safe and respectful environ-ment; the motivating role of teachers; students' active and critical learning; "here and now" educational ecology, appealing to the discourse of students' personal experiences; future orientation of learning; self-defining strategy and goals of learning; self-evaluation of results; and reflection and co-reflection.

Each of these constituencies makes the learning process meaning-centered, thus innovative, and "probabilistic" (Lobok, 2001). At times students experienced hardships (Russian students needed to translate some of the TV programs and papers into English for Stanford students; some teams could not find a mutual time to meet through Skype for independent work); at times classes were filled with excitement and joy, and with the challenges of taking responsibility. But overall the learning was always full of life, which strengthens the "meaning-ful vertical" (Brutus, 1993) of a personality. Being invisible, this vertical helps individuals become different and value the difference. Dialogic relationships between "self" and others in meaning-centered learning entail reflection on the way we exist in the world with which and in which we find ourselves; reflection enables us to see the world not as a static reality, but as a reality in transformation. It is our perception of ourselves which determines to a large extent our behavior and attitudes towards what we do and how we do things. Self-reflection often triggers self-efficacy, if students find themselves in a safe and supportive environment. We concur with Bandura, who holds that a person who does not believe in personal capability to be efficient in new life-settings is likely to disengage after experiencing failures (Bandura, 1986). Meaning-centered intercultural dialogue provided more possibilities for students to succeed rather than to fail, although discovering and exploring often entails failures along with successes.

The success of incrementally building students' confidence toward intercultural interaction occurs when we, as facilitators, widen and deepen the dialogue with a new culture. For example, the earliest video conferences were not regular; nor were they imbedded within classes of intercultural communication, so the students did not initially sound confident when they met virtually across cultures. As we all proceeded through a series of video conferences, we gradually gained more interest, trust, and thus more confidence. We also gained more emotional satisfaction, sense of self-worth, and motivation to continue the intercultural dialogue. Although each video conference session involved uncertainties and complexities, the attitude of how to deal with these perspectives gradually changed to a more positive one. This influenced the level of self-satisfaction, which was confirmed by improved results in the surveys.

The reflective experience becomes one of the major driving forces in transforming self and the world; it enhances self-awareness and world-awareness and motivates people to act accordingly. Meaning-centered education is dialogic in nature: it encourages learners to actively seek, express, and negotiate meanings. The dialogue of meanings takes place when students explore their "telling moments" within the conference and/or after the conference. In this way they take experience from their inner world, give it a form and make it accessible to those in the outer world. Thus, students develop an authentic voice which enables them to make choices based on their values and experiences.

As educators, we consider that like every transformation in general, personal transformation entails not linear progress, but some points of regression and even stagnation as we progress. In fact, students learn how to deal with uncertainty, confusion, and chaos as a transitory state between their prior convictions and their new perspectives. It can also be viewed as a reversible process of quantitative and qualitative transformations of psychological attributes and states which add to one another in timely reformations (Maralov, 2003). Through participation in video conferences with a meaning-centered approach, students adopt an integrative multisensory holistic approach to learning. They are encouraged to utilize the physical, emotional, sensory, and cognitive processes to experience deep learning;

improve self-knowledge and cognition; acquire an enhanced understanding of the feelings and motivation of others; and bolster self-efficacy.

In the meaning-centered classroom, the teacher is an author of her/his own teaching strategy. No teaching technique will help if teachers are not "authoring their own words, their own actions, their own lives" (Palmer, 1998, p. 33). We are the ones to whom the learners address their concerns and questions, their ways of becoming different. Moreover, in meaning-centered education, dialogue entails partnerships between learners and teachers. "Through dialogue, the teacher-of-the-students, and the students-of-the-teacher cease to exist and a new term emerges: teacher-student with students-teachers" (Freire, 1970, p. 80). The dialogic position of learners and teachers constitutes their independence, freedom, and responsibility. True dialogue requires developing "efforts towards others" (Bakhtin, 1999) in order to understand. An understanding is a transfer of meanings, but not a transfer of knowledge. "I can't teach you, but I can only hope you understand me" (Mamardashvili, 2007). Understanding cannot be predicted, but may occur as a result of transfer and re-construction of meanings. A true dialogue is open ended; interlocutors may be unaware of conclusions they reach at the end. In the process of a truly dialogic interaction, it requires courage from those engaged in a dialogue to admit the possibility of change and re-construction of one's views and perspectives.

According to Buber and Bakhtin, dialogue entails such quality relationships between interlocutors as mutuality, responsibility, engagement, and acceptance. The existential interpretation of dialogue holds that it is only in true dialogic relationships that an individual is able to unfold and experience self as personality. True dialogic interaction cannot exist without deep human relationship, characterized by care, trust, commitment, humility, and faith: the values which constitute the fabric of human life. "The human heart is woven of human relations to other people; what she/he is worthy of is fully determined by what human relations she/he aspires to and what human relations to other people she/he is capable to establish" (Rubenstein, 2008). The kind of relations students and teachers develop in the classroom are often internalized by people (Vygotsky, 1999) and thus influence their behavioral patterns and attitudes.

What is unique and resourceful about meaningful education is that it facilitates people's capability for constant self-developmental growth, which is innate to being human. It is holistic because it embraces all aspects of personal growth. The subjective power of an individual is recognized by a number of scholars (Leontiev, 1975; Zinchenko, 2004; Lobok, 2001) as one of the major driving forces in the process of personality self-development. According to Leontiev's psychological theory of individual development, personality self-creation can be viewed as the process of human nature unfolding its potential, initially under the strong influence of such external factors, such as heredity, environment, and education/nurturing. Self-creation progresses with individual self-transformation and is conditioned by subjective power and self-creating activity, which can only come from an individual her/himself. This major outcome of self-transformation is hardly assessable in a traditional way. We concur with Nagata that self-creation "involves experiencing a deep structural shift in the basic premises of thought, feelings, and actions. It is a shift of consciousness that dramatically alters the way of being in the world" (Nagata, 2006).

To confirm these conclusions, we share the analysis and reflection of Margaret Williams, a Fulbright Teacher in Khabarovsk from 2011 to 2012, who served as an external observer and wrote about the Russia-US intercultural dialogues as a strong instance of meaning-centered learning:

> Having been a student in the US and Russia as well as teacher at Khabarovsk State Academy of Economics and Law, I have had the opportunity to experience first-hand how the differences between the two systems impact one's experiences. The participants of video conferences share meaningful discussions and evaluate what new cultural insights they gain. Throughout the video conferences there is minimal teacher involvement and the discussions are almost entirely student driven.
>
> The program is founded upon the principles of meaningful and autonomous learning which helps engender leadership skills and self-confidence among participants. Throughout the entire program students are held responsible for initiating dialogue, asking questions, and evaluating the knowledge they gain. The results of this are increased ownership of the learning process and an increased desire to control the future direction of their education.
>
> *(Williams, 2011, n.p.)*

Williams points to the cognitive, affective, and behavioral benefits of intercultural dialogues in a way which highlights the importance of *meaning* through responsibility, ownership, and even desire. Her report concludes with a statement regarding the significance of this work for fostering global-ready graduates:

> Cultivating and developing these leadership and communication skills are the ultimate long-term objectives of the Intercultural Dialogue program. Today's local and global communities are in desperate need of leaders who possess confidence, and who are willing to look at a problem from multiple perspectives to find new and creative solutions. It is our responsibility as educators to use all available resource[s] to help students prepare for these roles and the bright future they might bring.
>
> *(ibid.)*

Emphasizing the need to cultivate in students the aptitudes of confidence, multiple perspectives, and creative problem solving, Williams concludes with a strong statement about the responsibility of educators to work towards these outcomes.

That was our mission with the Russia–US intercultural dialogues and shared project presentations. An external observer and researcher at Stanford noticed the accomplishment of these goals in her report on the connections; Rachel Lambert (2010) wrote her assessment as follows:

> For this exchange, Stanford students conversed with students from Russia as an entire class rather than in small groups. The conference format allowed for students to exchange questions about their research and how it relates to culture and leadership. [. . .] Everybody seemed very excited about the exchange at the beginning and the enthusiasm carried on through the end.
>
> *(Lambert, 2010, n.p.)*

Lambert's observation analysis highlights the prominent role of questions and dialogue in the pedagogical design of the intercultural encounter, and she notices the strong positive affect of the participants. Lambert (2010) also concludes her report with a statement of significance in terms of the application of these dialogues for substantial research-based writing projects:

> Overall, I think this conference demonstrated excellent progress in terms of achieving the CCR project's goals. Students from both schools exemplified basic, but solid cultural understanding and applied this learning to their individual research and the theme of leadership. The question–answer format may have precluded some individuals from speaking more than once, but the format allowed for lots of intriguingly diverse dialogue which centered around cultural leadership.
>
> *(ibid.)*

While Lambert makes an important claim in her observation notes that the entire class format may have inhibited or reduced the amount of participation on a per person basis, the structure of the connection did nonetheless allow "for lots of intriguingly diverse dialogue." In the process of recognizing what worked well in the exchange, however, we must turn next to places where the collaboration failed or undermined our objectives.

Challenges and Impediments to Successful MCE

We now identify some of the problems we encountered, in order that our work might help others avoid the pitfalls we experienced. To that end, we find the data from our quantitative and qualitative survey to be especially enlightening. Specifically, in terms of challenges, we have realized that intercultural learning in the virtual space is optimized when there is frequency of dialogic contact. As one student reflected in the exit survey, "I think the blogging would be more meaningful for students if there was more of a response and reply format. Although groups from both universities shared blog posts, it might have been possible to structure the posts in more of a conversation format." This student's suggestion indicates the value of dialogic work when connecting students across cultures. The students wanted a more extensive and rigorous iterative process of writing and responding on the blog, which would facilitate increased ownership, exchange of ideas and perspectives, and even encourage affective bonds.

Similarly, the students made a strong case for more video conference connections, more collaboration, and more structured assignments. We have found that only one or two connections within a project are not sufficient to foster deep meaning-centered learning; it is better to structure a series of collaborative activities on which the students could work together as globally distributed teams throughout the academic term. Lambert (2010) noted additional areas for further study or consideration, including the presence of the instructor in the room on student body posture, engagement, and affective display; the impact of audio technologies on the stance and voice of participants; and the focus on formal questions over personal conversation in the large group format. Our ongoing collaboration in Russian-US video connected pedagogy continues to research and investigate these areas.

Finally, from our own reflections as facilitators, we recommend that educators seeking to establish intercultural dialogue through similar technologies work together to devise structured lesson plans with iterative feedback loops on student communication; to establish accountability and parity in workload across institutions; and to give credit for work accomplished located within each course's evaluative rubric; and to minimize the interference of technology on body, voice, and emotional engagement. Thus, despite its failings—and as Aristotle noted in the *Nichomachean Ethics*, "It is possible to fail in many ways,"—we nevertheless find this method of fostering intercultural dialogue through communication technologies to offer a beneficial means of realizing the aims of meaning-centered education while also promoting global intercultural communication competencies.

Praxis Informs Theory and Constructs a New Subjectivity

Now that we have seen how this study in pedagogical collaboration across borders, with the aim of fostering intercultural communication competencies, can be fruitfully interpreted through the lens of meaning-centered education, what possible implications might we identify in terms of how praxis informs theory? Perhaps one answer is that such practices encourage and even make possible a fundamental re-construction of subjectivity on the part of the learned. As Nagata observes, self-creation "involves experiencing a deep structural shift in the basic premises of thought, feeling, and actions." These transformations in cognition, affect, and behavior may be linked to the process of negotiated meaning-making that must take place in the dialogic structure of the encounter. Consequently, the internal experience of participants changes just as knowledge is shared and questions are exchanged and answered. The praxis suggests an active role for educators/facilitators in meaning-centered education, and the strategic integration of communication technologies as a means to meet more theoretical ends. In this way, we can help our students bridge great geographic and ideological differences. Moreover, we conclude from our teaching practice that a focus on constructions of leadership, in particular, can generate meaning-centered learning growth in participants, as they begin to reassess their own subjectivities in the mirror of those under cross-cultural examination. That is, a focus on leadership can serve as a means to interrogate static constructions of subjectivity and can in turn lead to self-assessment and eventually self-transformation.

This is crucial work to be doing right now. We are experiencing a fundamental shift in the ways people from various countries and cultures interact with each other. It changes the environment of education, and a new spectrum of challenges and opportunities for students and teachers appears. We as educators should open our minds to new perspectives so that we can learn from one another and successfully cooperate across cultures. Intercultural dialogue via modern communication technologies is one of these new approaches, with a strong emphasis on open meaning-making process and self-organizing educational practice. Dialogic space allows the communities of learners with all participants, including the instructor, to have equal rights on exploring and negotiating the themes and meanings of teaching/learning discourse.

A meaning-centered approach to cross-cultural collaboration projects facilitates the formation of "the vector of subjectivity," which, according to Lobok, navigates a human being to the maximum development of her/his individuality. Meaning-centered pedagogy aimed at fostering intercultural competencies prioritizes: thinking over knowledge, questions over answers, creativity and initiative over formal task performance, educational needs/interests of an individual over the educational standards, holistic over intellectual, internal attitudes over external requirements, and self-education over the trajectory exposed by someone externally.

We view this as an innovative educational ecology with collaborative and dialogic pedagogy, aimed at supporting the innate capacity of an individual to create an authentic project of his/her life activity, which proves to make learning more meaningful, responsive, relevant, and rewarding for the students and faculty. The shift—which we believe to be of special significance in the time of globally changing environments and economic challenges—needs special attention: while many countries around the globe have been attempting to reform educational systems aimed at promoting higher educational standards, we strongly believe that education should provide active, hands-on learning experiences that students feel ownership over. Such ownership not only motivates them to further expand their human capacities, but it also helps develop confidence, responsibility, and important leadership skills that will be of great value to them in their future endeavors.

References

Arasaratnam, L. A. (2009) "The development of a new instrument of intercultural communication competence." *Journal of Intercultural Communication* 20.

Arasaratnam, L. A. and Doerfel, M. L. (2005) "Intercultural communication competence: Identifying key components from multicultural perspectives." *International Journal of Intercultural Relations* 29: 137–163.

Bakhtin, M. M. (1999) *To the Philosophy of the Action.* Moscow: Nauka.

Bandura, A. (1986) *Social Foundations of Thoughts and Actions: A Social Cognitive Theory.* Englewood Cliffs, NJ: Prentice-Hall.

Bratus, B. S. (1993) *Moral Consciousness of a Personality.* Moscow: Znanie.

Byram, M. (2005) *European Language Portfolio: Theoretical Model and Proposed Template for an Autobiography of "Key Intercultural Experiences."* Strasbourg: Council of Europe, Language Policy Division.

Cui, G. and van den Berg, S. (1991) "Testing the construct validity of intercultural effectiveness." *International Journal of Intercultural Relations* 15: 227–241.

Deardorff, D. (2006) "Identification and assessment of intercultural competence as a student outcome of internationalization." *Journal of Studies in International Education* 10(3): 241–266.

Fantini, A. E. (2006) *Exploring and Assessing Intercultural Competence.* Available online from: http://www.sit.edu/publications/docs/feil_research_report.pdf (accessed May 3, 2010).

Freire, P. (1970) *Pedagogy of the Oppressed.* New York: Continuum.

Hashem, M. E. (1995) Assessing student learning outcome in teaching intercultural communication. Speech Communication Association Convention, San Antonio, Texas. Available online from: http://eric.ed.gov/ERICDocs/data/ericdocs2/content_storage_01/000000b/80/26/04/92.pdf (accessed December 6, 2012).

Jackson, J. (2005) "Assessing intercultural learning though introspective accounts." *Frontiers*, XI: 165–186.

Lambert, R. (2010) Analysis of Khabarovsk-Stanford Video Conference: Global Leadership and Intercultural Communication. White paper. Stanford, CA.

Leontiev, A. N. (1975) *Activity. Consciousness. Personality.* Moscow: Politizdat.

Lobok, A. M. (2001) *Probabilistic World.* Ekaterinburg: Evrika.

Lovitt, C. R. and Goswami, D. (Eds.) (1999) *Exploring the Rhetoric of International Professional Communication.* Amityville, NY: Baywood.

Mamardashvili, M. K. (2007) *The Necessity of Oneself.* Moscow: Labirint.

Maralov, V. G. (2003) *Pedagogy of Non-Violence.* Moscow: Nauka.

Nagata, A. L. (2006) "Transformative learning in intercultural education." *Rikkyo Intercultural Communication Review,* 4.

O'Brien, A. and Eriksson, A. (2010) "Cross-cultural connections: Intercultural learning for global citizenship." In M. Alagic and G. Rimmington (Eds), *Locating Intercultures: Educating for Global Collaboration* (pp. 29–50). New York: Macmillan.

Palmer, P. J. (1998) *The Courage to Teach.* San Francisco, CA: Jossey-Bass.

Ruben, B. D. (1989) "The study of crosscultural competences: Traditions and contemporary issues." *International Journal of Intercultural Relations* 13: 229–240.

Rubenstein, S. L. (2008) *Personality's Self-Consciousness and the Way of Life.* Moscow: Nauka.

Sercu, L. (2004) "Assessing intercultural competence: A framework for systemic test development in foreign language education and beyond." *Intercultural Education* 15: 73–89.

Spitzberg, B. H. (1991) "An examination of trait measures of interpersonal competence." *Communication Reports* 4: 22–30.

Spitzberg, B. H. and Cupach, W.R. (1984) *Interpersonal Communication Competence.* Beverly Hills, CA: Sage.

Vygotsky, L. S. (1999) *Pedagogical Psychology.* Moscow: Nauka.

Williams, M. (2011) "Assessment." Fulbright Teacher at KSAEL 2011–2012.

Zinchenko, V. P. (2004) *Man Self-Developing.* Moscow: Trivola.

6

MAKING THE SHIFT TOWARDS A MEANING-BASED PARADIGM IN EUROPEAN HIGHER EDUCATION

A Spanish Case Study

María Luisa Pérez Cañado

Introduction

The decade that is just beginning marks an important crossroads for European Higher Education (HE). We are living in what Mehisto (2008) terms a period of disjuncture, characterized by the tension between the previous order and a new approach which changes the status quo. In Europe, the creation of the European Higher Education Area (EHEA) through what has come to be known as the Bologna Process is serving as a powerful lever for change and is promoting the supercession of a teacher-controlled banking model of education in favor of a more critical, meaning-based, and student-centered paradigm, where teachers pull back from being donors of knowledge to become facilitators. The profound changes in competency development, methodology, groupings and learning modalities, teacher and learner roles, materials and resources, or evaluation become paramount in making this shift to a more social-constructivist, student-led scenario, as they entail overcoming the almost exclusive reliance on ex cathedra lecturing prevalent in many European universities by incorporating a more action-oriented, discovery-based, and dialogic pedagogy.

The present chapter reports on how the curricular innovations brought about by the adaptation to the European Credit Transfer System (ECTS) are being approached within language degrees at the University of Jaén in Spain, where the need to adapt methodologically to the EHEA has informed two government-financed research projects whose outcomes, in turn, have guided and reoriented teaching practice. It begins with a consideration of how all these curricular and organizational levels of language teaching are being affected by the shift to a meaning-based paradigm. It then goes on to furnish research evidence from these projects (ADELEEES[1] and FINEEES[2]) on how language degrees piloting the

ECTS across Europe are conforming to student-centered pedagogies, as compared to the traditional methodology. They also probe the attitudes these new options are generating in participating stakeholders. Multiple triangulation (data, methodological, and investigator) has been employed in the studies, which present a mixed quantitative–qualitative research design with both descriptive and inferential statistics and grounded theory analysis. After outlining their objectives, procedure, instruments, sample, and methodology, the main results regarding the adaptation to all curricular levels propounded by the EHEA will be presented jointly. The final part of the chapter will foreground the most important conclusions as to where we stand in this arena at the 2012 crossroads.

Making the Shift to a Meaning-Based Paradigm: From Policy to Practice

The practical implementation of the ECTS is affecting all curricular and organizational levels of language teaching in Higher Education. For many (e.g., Benito and Cruz, 2007; Blanco, 2009; Poblete Ruiz, 2006), the cornerstone of the transformation is to be found in the application of competency-based teaching. In our specific European university context, the introduction of the concept of *competencies* has been considered "one of the major changes in university education in Europe in the last five years" (Pennock-Speck, in press). Poblete Ruiz (2006) compares the paradigm shift involved in making the transition to a competency-based model with the Copernican one, given its transcendent and far-reaching effects. The notion of competency involves not only knowledge, but also skills, attitudes, and values, and entails the capacity to perform successfully in an academic, professional, or social environment. Thus, competencies represent an initial attempt to overcome the traditional European university model based on transmission of knowledge through ex cathedra lecturing (Tudor, 2006) in favor of a student-centered, meaning-based one where critical thinking skills are promoted (Pérez Gómez *et al.*, 2009a). They do not, however, preclude knowledge or content; quite on the contrary, they comprise and mobilize it, infusing it with new life by transferring and applying it to real-world contexts, complex situations, or problem resolution (Pérez Gómez *et al.*, 2009a; Perrenoud, 2008). They consequently involve what Barnett (2001, p. 32) terms a shift from "knowledge as contemplation" to "knowledge as operation," and provide a more nuanced and unambiguous formulation of what the university graduate should be able to know and perform upon completion of tertiary education (Blanco, 2009, p. 13). The ultimate aim of the competency-based model is thus to form flexible and adaptable professionals who can apply competencies to the varied, unforeseeable, and complex situations they will encounter throughout their personal, social, and professional lives (Cano García, 2008; Pérez Gómez *et al.*, 2009b), and who can thus become active and useful citizens in our democratic society.

However, if there is an aspect of language learning which is most immediately affected by the implementation of the ECTS, it is *methodology* (Giménez de la

Peña and López Gutiérrez, 2006, p. 10). The European Declarations and Communiqués from 2005 onwards have placed the onus on Higher Education Institutions (HEIs) to introduce innovative methods, student-centered pedagogy, and lifelong learning into the teaching process. In Jiménez Raya's words (in press), "European universities are introducing new pedagogies in response to changing social demands." In this sense, the application of the ECTS is radically transforming the conception and nature of teaching at the tertiary level across Europe. The emphasis is now on successful learning rather than on the teaching provided, and a stronger student focus guides curricular reorientations. Previous methodologies are called into question (Pozuelos *et al.*, 2006) and a greater diversity is adopted. The transition needs to be made from a "bulimic" education learning where the students merely reproduce what they have learned, to a more critical learning that sticks. Contrary to the traditionalist stance which sees teaching as transmission of knowledge and learning as reproduction of contents (Pérez Gómez *et al.*, 2009c), post-secondary teaching is now held to be concerned with equipping learners with the tools they need to find, select, use, and interpret the vast amount of data they have within their reach (Pérez Gómez *et al.*, 2009a). Competencies such as critical thinking skills or the ability to synthesize and analyze should be developed, and the move needs to be made towards a self-directed, autonomous learning where students' independence, involvement, and participation are fostered. Meaning-based methodologies should thus involve knowledge creation rather than transmission and learning by construction rather than instruction. It is what Wegerif (this volume) refers to as making the transition from education as transmission to education as dialogue. They also entail equipping learners with the strategies they need to deploy throughout the rest of their lives to continue learning.

Just as the almost exclusive reliance on the lock step lecture has been overcome by manifold student-centered methodological options, so has the traditional theory/practice dichotomy observed in most European universities been superseded by a range of different classroom organizations and learning modalities. On the one hand, the local EHEA literature (Bueno González *et al.*, 2008; CIDUA Report, 2005; Pérez Gómez *et al.*, 2009a, 2009d) discerns four different *types of groupings*: the whole group (comprising all the students in a particular subject), the basic group (with 20 to 50 students), the work group (from 4 to 6 students), and autonomous work. And, on the other, De Miguel Díaz (2005, 2006) distinguishes a set of varied *learning modalities*, which are grouped within in-site tuition (theoretical sessions, practical sessions, seminars and workshops, external training, and tutorials) and independent work (group and individual work and study). All these groupings and modalities acquire a particularly sharp relief against the backdrop of active, student-led learning. They become crucial elements in aiding students in the learning process, whilst catering to their individual learning styles.

These diverse learning arrangements have involved a noteworthy change in the *university lecturer's role*, as numerous authors document (e.g., Durán *et al.*, 2006; Ron Vaz *et al.*, 2006). It is widely agreed that a successful implementation of the

Bologna Process is ultimately reliant on the substantial transformation of the teacher's role, who is required to become a pathfinder as opposed to a path follower (Jiménez Raya, in press). In addition to maintaining the role of expert transmitter of knowledge in the more traditional lock step contact sessions, teachers must also be motivators, stimulators, and creators of a positive classroom atmosphere. It is important that they create a climate of confidence, affective security, empathy and emotional cooperation where the learner feels confident to explore, make mistakes, obtain feedback, and continue trying (Madrid and Hughes, in press). They thus need to embody the two sides of dialogic education which Wegerif (this volume) pinpoints: teachers should both provide the necessary scaffolding for learners and be ready to pull back when necessary in order to nudge students forward in constructing their own learning process. Students, in turn, have to learn to take responsibility for their own learning. They are no longer passive recipients or empty vessels who accumulate and repeat the information received (Domingo *et al.*, 2007), but, rather, the protagonists of the learning process. They are expected to be more autonomous and independent (Martínez Lirola, 2007; McLaren *et al.*, 2005; Ron Vaz *et al.*, 2006); more active and participative in classroom activities (Giménez de la Peña and López Gutiérrez, 2006); more creative (Domingo *et al.*, 2007; Martínez Lirola, 2007; Pérez Cañado, 2009b); and more involved in the decision-making process (Taibi, 2006). This increased engagement on the part of the student favors more significant learning, greater retention of knowledge, and transfer to real-world situations, as Potosky, Spaulding, and Juzbasich (this volume) underscore.

Didactic materials and resources, with ICT figuring prominently among them, are pivotal in bringing about this reconfiguration of teacher and student roles and in operating the shift to a learner-centered pedagogy of autonomy (Pérez Gómez *et al.*, 2009d). In addition to being one the core generic competencies which most European universities have worked into all their Bologna-adapted degrees, the potential of technological or digital competence for enhancing the student-centered learning process has been underscored in the official EHEA literature. According to Benito and Cruz (2007, p. 104), ICT is not a mere fad, but a crucial tool which, in combination with the EHEA, will foster pedagogical innovation and allow all the agents involved in the teaching–learning process to expedite knowledge-building and competency development.

Finally, the changes which need to be implemented in terms of *evaluation* in the EHEA are as profound as those which have been witnessed for methodology, teacher and learner roles, or materials. Indeed, significant readjustments need to be effected in competency-based evaluation for it to promote a student-centered learning environment in HE, alongside other curricular aspects (Löfgren, in press). This final curricular aspect must be completely attuned to and coherent with the competencies and methodology followed (Benito and Cruz, 2007; Cano García, 2008). In competency-based assessment, knowledge should be evaluated, but always alongside the other components of a competency—abilities, attitudes, and skills. It needs to be integral or holistic, criterion-referenced, process-oriented, feedback-focused, relevant and authentic, transparent, and more diversified. This new type of assessment thus involves a shift from an evaluation *of* learning to an evaluation *for* learning (Benito and Cruz, 2007, p. 87).

Using Pedagogy to Guide Research: A Spanish Case Study

How has this shift to a student-led scenario been carried out in actual on-the-ground classroom praxis? The practical application of the ECTS to all these curricular and organizational aspects is now examined in a more specific context via a Spanish case study: that of the degree of English Philology at the University of Jaén, which has been involved in the piloting of the new credit system for well over half a decade, ever since it was selected in 2004–2005, alongside 13 other degrees, to partake in the experimental program for the implementation of the ECTS in Andalusia.

At the end of this first year of piloting (in the late spring of 2005), a brief questionnaire was administered to the participating stakeholders (students and lecturers) to determine the way in which the pilot experience was playing itself out (García García, 2005). The outcomes showed that neither cohort perceived substantial change in the ECTS methodology, nor did they believe it implied improvement in the learning activity. Furthermore, the students did not see their professors as fully committed to the proper development of the pilot project, and the ECTS guides were not considered to clarify the syllabus or methodology. The only aspect for which the ECTS was viewed as potentially positive was to foster future international mobility. Given these disheartening outcomes, the pilot experience did not seem to be off to a very auspicious start, and the concern that such teacher and student perceptions could curtail the ECTS implementation process at our university led to the creation of a specific research group (ESECS—English Studies in the European Credit System—www.esecs.eu), whose remit was to promote student-centered pedagogies through didactic innovation and to conduct both qualitative and quantitative investigations into the effects of these initiatives. This research group carried out two large-scale, outcome-oriented, and largely complementary studies which allowed the ECTS implementation process to be honed and recalibrated where necessary and which provided valuable information for the design of the new Bologna-adapted degree of English Studies at our university.

ADELEEES

Objectives

The first of these studies, ADELEEES, was an essentially qualitative endeavor, aimed at designing, validating, and applying four sets of questionnaires to measure the degree of satisfaction of professors and students, to determine the main methodological aspects involved in the teaching–learning process, to estimate the real workload of both agents, and to analyze the competencies which are actually developed and evaluated in language degrees. Its ultimate aim was to carry out an in-depth analysis of the current application of the ECTS to language teaching in Europe in order to effect the necessary readjustments prior to designing the new degree structures. The questionnaires (designed in four different versions: English, Spanish, for teachers, and for students) were applied not only at the local (Jaén) and national level (Spain), but in all those degrees (over 15 different ones[3]) piloting the ECTS in language studies across Europe.

Procedure and Instruments

Once they had been designed, the questionnaires were validated via a twofold process. In order to guarantee their validity and reliability, they were initially submitted to the expert ratings approach (with six external experts) and, subsequently, to a pilot study. After introducing the modifications suggested by the experts, the surveys were administered to a representative sample made up of 10 teachers and 54 students in the degree of English Philology at the University of Jaén, in December 2008 and January 2009. The feedback received from both agents of the teaching–learning process led us to reformulate the phrasing of certain items, add information and new questions, specify data, break down questions, and reduce the length of certain questionnaires (particularly that pertaining to competencies, where the initial 82 closed items it subsumed were grouped into a final 52).

The data obtained in the pilot study were used to analyze the reliability or internal consistency of the questionnaires (February 2009). It was determined using *Cronbach* α, and the extremely high values obtained for this coefficient guaranteed the reliability of both surveys (see Table 6.1).

The administration of the questionnaires followed their design and validation. In order to increase return rates, a series of strategies were deployed, in line with Brown's recommendations (2001, pp. 85–89). In order to reach as wide an audience as possible across Europe, an online system of application, *Survey Monkey*, was chosen for the questionnaire.

TABLE 6.1 Reliability of the questionnaires

Questionnaire	Number of Subjects	Number of Items	Cronbach α
Competencies students	54	81	0.955
Competencies teachers	10	81	0.846
Methodology students	54	51	0.858
Methodology teachers	10	51	0.817
Satisfaction students	54	43	0.896
Satisfaction teachers	10	43	0.914

Sample

The total number of respondents amounted to nearly 500, a majority of them students (see Figure 6.1). The composition of both cohorts is similar (albeit with a greater variety in the teachers' case): they are predominantly female participants, of Spanish nationality, studying or working at Spanish universities, and within English studies degrees. Thus, this means the outcomes obtained are particularly representative of and useful for our immediate context.

Statistical Methodology

Employing the SPSS program in its 16.0 version, data analysis was carried out via the following statistical operations:

1. To determine the reliability of the questionnaires, *Cronbach* α was used.
2. To carry out the four-pronged diagnosis of the adaptation of language degrees to a meaning-based paradigm, the following descriptive statistics were employed:

    2.1. Central tendency measures:

        2.1.1. Mean
        2.1.2. Median
        2.1.3. Mode

    2.2. Dispersion measures:

        2.2.1. Range
        2.2.2. Standard deviation

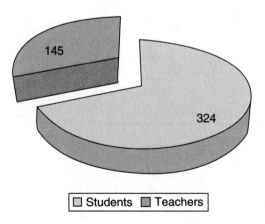

FIGURE 6.1 Total number of participants

3. To determine if there were statistically significant differences between students' and teachers' perceptions, Analysis of Variance (ANOVA) and the *t* test were used.

FINEEES

Objectives

In turn, the second research project, FINEEES, seizes the unique situation offered by the University of Jaén—where the same subjects are taught often by the same teachers employing two different methodologies: an ECTS stream within English Philology and a traditional methodology branch in English Philology and Tourism—in order to conduct a quasi-experimental study into the effects of both methodologies, factoring in a series of co-variates, such as gender, motivation, and performance on the university entrance exam.[4] It then completes the study with qualitative focus group interviews which employ methodological and investigator triangulation. Their objective was to carry out a diagnosis of the main strengths and weaknesses of the implementation of the ECTS in English Philology at the University of Jaén, comparing the functioning of the new credit system (in English Philology) with the traditional one (in English Philology and Tourism), again with a view to having our outcomes feed into the design of the new degree structures at our university.

Procedure and Instruments

Both an extended and more reduced protocol were employed for the data-gathering component of the study, where 11 key variables were considered:

1. Information received on the European Credit Transfer System in general and through the course catalogues in particular.
2. Development and evaluation of competencies.
3. Independent study: workload and effort.
4. Types of groupings and learning modalities (lectures, seminars, tutorials, self-directed learning).
5. Methods and materials used.
6. Coordination among subjects, professors, assignments, etc.
7. Overlaps and/or deficiencies in the curriculum.
8. Evaluation.
9. Student–teacher rapport.
10. Teacher commitment.
11. Global assessment of the curriculum.

The focus group interviews took place in March 2009, over the course of eight hours (roughly two hours per group). After each year of study had been divided into four subgroups and an investigator had been assigned to each one, a general introduction was given to the whole class on the objectives of the project. Each subgroup then devoted an average of five to ten minutes to the discussion of each variable. The students' perceptions were recorded using methodological triangulation, as three different data-gathering procedures were employed: a secretary within each subgroup of students was in charge of summarizing the main ideas set forth; the investigator responsible for that particular subgroup also took detailed note of the discussion in a more extended protocol; and digital recordings were made of each group intervention. Subsequently, a global debriefing was carried out again with the entire cohort, in order to foreground the main ideas and to value the experience. Investigator triangulation (Brown, 2001, p. 228) then allowed each supervisor to write up their own conclusions, which were collated in several meetings in order to arrive at the desired SWOT analysis.

Sample

Here, the total number of participants amounted to 208, distributed throughout the four years of both degrees (see Table 6.2 for the breakdown of the sample).

Methodology

For the qualitative analysis of the focus group interviews, grounded theory (Glaser and Strauss, 1967) was employed to code the data and draw meaning from it. In order to categorize, synthesize, and identify emerging patterns in the open-response data, three analytic strategies were employed within it.

TABLE 6.2 Sample of subjects (FINEEES)

Grade	Male students	Female students	Total
EP Freshmen	5	14	19
EP Sophomores	5	8	13
EP Juniors	2	6	8
EP Seniors	2	8	10
Total EP	14	36	50
EP + T Freshmen	15	38	53
EP + T Sophomores	14	31	45
EP + T Juniors	4	16	20
EP + T Seniors	6	34	40
Total EP + T	39	119	158
Total	53	155	208

Results and Discussion

The outcomes of both studies, presented jointly in this section, allowed a detailed portrayal of where our university stands in conforming to Bologna standards in our English degrees. The results are glossed in terms of all the curricular and organizational aspects being affected by the ECTS in language studies.

To begin with, vis-à-vis competencies, it transpires that, while the ECTS branch is aware of their existence, development, and evaluation, the traditional methodology strand is completely unfamiliar with the concept. However, within the new credit system, both teachers and students acknowledge that they are not only rarely being incorporated into the curriculum, but also very seldom being evaluated, with the learners even questioning whether their professors are prepared to implement and assess competencies. This circumstance is consistent with the results of other authors (Madrid and Hughes, 2009; Nieto García, 2007; Ron Vaz *et al.*, 2006), who stress that greater awareness of competencies needs to be raised.

Regarding *learning modalities* and *types of groupings*, our results show that the ECTS strand seems to be relying less on ex cathedra lecturing and the memorization of contents (something which is consistent with the findings of Ron Vaz and Casanova García, 2007) and that more independent work and practical activities are gradually being worked into the curriculum. However, according to the students, we are still not incorporating the full gamut of groupings and modalities which the ECTS places at our disposal. The type of grouping which is most used in the ECTS, according to this cohort, is individual work, followed by the whole group (entire class) and pair work. The work group (4 to 6 students) and the basic group (with 25 to 30) are rarely used, so that, apparently, these two novel options recommended by the CIDUA (2005) report are not, from the learners' point of view, being adequately incorporated. This lack of variety is also evident in the learning modalities employed. In a very homogenous way (the standard deviation is comparatively low in this heading), the interviewees consider that the most widely used option is the theoretical class, followed by the practical session, which is also considerably employed. However, seminars and workshops, group and individual tutorials, and conference attendance are scantily or not at all used. Seminars still have "fuzzy limits," as they are simply used to continue advancing with the theoretical contents of the program or are not taught at all, thereby being used as a sort of study hall period for autonomous student work. This is consistent with the study conducted by Madrid and Hughes (2009), which found that seminars were not adequately incorporated, and with Pascual Garrido's conclusions (2007), which suggest that the number of subjects which fully incorporate the variety of groupings and modalities advocated by the EHEA is reduced. The instructors' view of the use of groupings is considerably more optimistic than that of the learners, as they consider that the full range of options is being incorporated to a greater extent, with the theoretical class being relegated to a secondary position within their teaching.

In turn, in the traditional methodology group, our data reveal that the students have an excessive amount of traditional contact hours (as documented by Ron Vaz *et al.*, 2006), which leaves little time for independent work. There is a distinct imbalance between theoretical and practical hours (in line with Pascual Garrido's, 2007, findings), with teachers often foregoing the latter to continue advancing with the "content" of the program. Thus, whole class lecturing and some practical hours where the group is subdivided into two parts are the only learning modalities employed within this pre-ECTS methodology. It is therefore not surprising to find that the cohort urgently requests practically oriented subjects, with more than just "content," and which can be applied to the professional sphere.

The previous outcomes for both groups are consistent with those obtained for *methodology*. On the one hand, the ECTS cohort of students acknowledges that a more active and participative methodology is being incorporated within ECTS pilot schemes, in line with what Ron Vaz *et al.* (2006) and Ron Vaz and Casanova García (2007) highlight. Practical exercise resolution, oral presentations, and more autonomous learning are gradually finding their way into the curriculum, although, in line with the results obtained in previous headings, the most widely employed method is still lock step lecturing. This once more diverges from the teachers' point of view, who consider ex cathedra lecturing is at the bottom of the list (occupying a sixth place among other more student-centered options). There is, however, agreement between both stakeholders in reporting the infrequent use of virtual learning environments, computer-assisted language learning, and external training. This again starkly contrasts with the traditional methodology group. Self-directed learning which favors autonomy and the development of critical thinking skills are clearly absent from the current curriculum, and there is a marked predominance of theoretical hours where "bulimic" learning (transmission–memorization–reproduction) is embraced, in detriment of a more critical learning that sticks.

Reinforcing these findings are those pertaining to *materials and resources*. Here, there are more similarities than differences between the teachers' and students' perceptions. Those resources related to ICT (Second Life, videogames, digital storytelling, wikis, blogs, webquests, teaching software) are once again very sparsely used. These findings are surprising, particularly considering the extremely beneficial effects which ICT is exerting on language learning and competency development, as has been revealed by a notable number of recent studies (Alcantud Díaz, 2010; Brígido Corachán, 2008; Brígido Corachán and Zaragoza Ninet, in press; Ceballos Muñoz, 2010; Gregori-Signes, 2008; Jordano de la Torre, 2008; Pennock-Speck 2008, 2009; Ware and O'Dowd 2008; Zaragoza Ninet and Clavel Arroitia 2008, 2010), which vigorously support the incorporation of these resources into the language classroom. The textbook, educational web portals, *realia*, audio and video material, and online and print dictionaries are not very frequently employed, albeit more assiduously than those materials related to new technologies. On the opposite side of the cline are materials compiled or created by the teacher, PowerPoint presentations, and Internet downloads, which come across as the resources most frequently employed by teachers.

The outcomes obtained for *evaluation* are consistent with those of previous headings. The picture which can be gleaned from our data in terms of assessment in the ECTS similarly harks back to a traditionalist stance. There is a predominance of long-answer objective testing, which favors the memorization and reproduction of contents. The final exam with long essay-like questions still overshadows all other evaluation techniques within the ECTS, although a greater diversity in strategies can also be discerned, as, according to the participating students, other evaluation procedures are also frequently incorporated for competency-based assessment, such as papers and projects, task-based testing, oral presentations, and observation techniques. Less commonly employed are short-answer and multiple-choice objective tests, reports and/or diaries on practical sessions, and oral interviews. Portfolios, self-assessment systems, attitude scales, and global assessment sessions are hardly ever used.

According to this second cohort, the most commonly employed assessment technique is task-based testing, followed by papers and projects, observation techniques, oral presentations, and long-answer objective tests (which, according to the students, are the most regularly employed). Short-answer objective testing is also generally used. The lowest means and modes (1) are obtained for oral interviews, multiple-choice tests, self-assessment, global assessment sessions, diaries on practical sessions, portfolios, and attitude scales. The results for many of these aspects agree with those of the learners.

Finally, in the traditional methodology group, the evaluation systems employed reinforce the transmission of information model to an even greater extent: they are not diversified (as the final exam is the almost sole assessment procedure) or transparent (the students ask for greater information on the breakdown of their final marks). Furthermore, the predominant evaluation technique is long-answer objective testing, which, as has been said, favors memorization and reproduction of contents. Ongoing or formative assessment is practically non-existent.

If there is a notable divergence between the ECTS and traditional methodology groups in the prior curricular aspects, in the following *organizational ones*, a much greater harmony exists between the two cohorts. In terms of *workload*, our studies reveal that, for teachers, the preparation of a single ECTS subject in one semester takes up 24.1 percent of the total amount of work they should be devoting not only to teaching, but also to research and administrative duties. The students are also investing an average of 500 more hours a year than they should be, with an exponential increase in the independent work they need to carry out being documented from freshman to senior year. Contact hours are regarded as excessive, and projects and assignments tend to accumulate, especially at the end of each semester. These findings largely coincide with those of the traditional methodology group, albeit with less weight being attached to independent work within this other teaching system.

A further organizational aspect affects the *information received* on each type of system: our outcomes reveal that it is clearly insufficient (something which concurs with Pascual Garrido's, 2007, and Madrid and Hughes', 2009, results), although ECTS course catalogues are now regarded as clear and useful. In turn, the main *deficiencies* identified by the interviewees are the lack of use of English and oral work on the language, and of its practical application to the professional sphere. The most outstanding overlaps relate to literature and grammar subjects in current degree structures. The interviewees ask that these niches be urgently filled in the new plans of study. A conspicuous lack of *coordination* is discerned for both groups (although it is much more salient in the ECTS), among subjects, with respect to assignments (with a resulting accumulation at the end of each semester), and even between the theoretical and practical parts of specific subjects. This is consistent with the studies conducted by Madrid and Hughes (2009), Pascual Garrido (2007), and Ron Vaz *et al.* (2006), and points to one of the most glaring lacunae of the Spanish university: the often times worrying individualism which characterizes its teaching endeavors (Zabalza Beraza, 2004). This lack of coordination is particularly salient in the ECTS, which is not surprising if we consider its greater variety in groupings, methodology, and evaluation. On the positive side, however, it appears that the new credit system is fostering closer student–teacher *rapport* and increasing teacher *commitment*, with more personalized attention and enhanced communication being documented especially in the ECTS (something which accords with Pérez Cañado, 2009a, and Ron Vaz and Casanova García, 2007).

Finally, when asked to *globally assess* each teaching system, the outcomes are much more positive in the case of the ECTS strand. The traditional methodology branch voices its discontent as regards the excessively teacher-dominated methodology and exam-based evaluation system, and with respect to the lack of practical activities, of connection to the job market, and of oral communication in English. However, the ECTS stream, while acknowledging the increased workload which the new system entails, considers it to be heightening active, participative, self-directed, and critical learning and ultimately having positive repercussions on their preparation ("*We are going to be one of the best prepared cohorts,*" one student claims).

Conclusions

Thus, what are the broader implications which can be learned from these studies conducted at the University of Jaén? As benefits of our process of adaptation to the EHEA, we can highlight the considerably positive view which teachers harbor; the fact that there is awareness of competence development and evaluation; the greater methodological and evaluative diversification which is gradually making its way into the curriculum; or the considerable commitment which teachers are evincing to the new credit system.

However, our outcomes have also revealed a set of deficiencies or lacunae which need to be addressed in order to foster the effective functioning of the new system. To begin with, it would be highly advisable to promote global assessment or focus group sessions with both students and teachers in order to reconcile the two significantly different visions which our study has shown they hold regarding the adaptation to the EHEA. These sessions would foster dialogue, communication, and coordination among the protagonists of the process, something essential for the adequate implementation of the ECTS.

According to our data, it would also be necessary to provide additional information to both agents on competencies: what they consist in, how to work on them, and how to incorporate them into the evaluation process. Clearly, it would be advisable to design courses, seminars, or workshops to this end.

It also becomes paramount to take into account the increased workload which the new system involves for both students (including more realistic and feasible contents, fewer competencies, and a more reduced number of papers and projects in each subject) and teachers (ensuring their teaching load is compatible with other research and/or administrative duties). This would contribute to increasing the commitment and satisfaction of both cohorts within the ECTS.

In terms of methodology and evaluation, the suggestions for improvement are manifold. It would be desirable to reinforce external training in order to strengthen the link with the professional sphere; to increase the variety of groupings and modalities beyond the traditional theory/practice dichotomy; to deploy seminars adequately; to incorporate ICT to a greater extent; to diversify the types of tutorials and evaluation techniques; and, overall, to make the shift from a transmissive and memoristic model of education to a more critical, student-centered paradigm. Increasing information about the full implications of the ECTS and solving the overlaps and deficiencies in the curriculum would also be desirable, and learning from the best practices of others (particularly, from North American and northern and eastern European universities) would be especially valuable.

Notes

1   *Adaptación de la Enseñanza de Lenguas al EEES: Análisis del estado actual, establecimiento de redes europeas y aplicación a los nuevos títulos de grado*, Ministerio de Ciencia e Innovación, Programa Estudios y Análisis, Ref. EA2008-0173, 2008–2009.
2   *La Filología Inglesa en el Espacio Europeo de Educación Superior*, evaluated by the ANEP, 2008–1010, Universidad de Jaén, Plan de Apoyo a la Investigación, Acción 16, Ref. UJA_08_16_35.
3   Among them, English Studies, Translation and Interpretation, Teacher Training: English as a Foreign Language, Tourism, Spanish Philology, French Philology, German Philology, Languages and Cultures, and Pedagogy were the most representative.
4   These results are currently being analyzed.

References

Alcantud Díaz, A. (2010) "El relato digital educativo como herramienta de incorporación de las nuevas tecnologías a la educación superior: una experiencia práctica en Filología Inglesa." *Lenguaje y Textos* 31: 35–47.

Barnett, R. (2001) *Los límites de la competencia. El conocimiento, la educación superior y la sociedad.* Barcelona: Gedisa.

Benito, A. and Cruz, A. (2007) *Nuevas claves para la docencia universitaria en el Espacio Europeo de Educación Superior.* Madrid: Narcea.

Blanco, A. (Coord.) (2009) *Desarrollo y evaluación de competencias en educación superior.* Madrid: Narcea.

Brígido Corachán, A. M. (2008) "Collaborative e-learning in the European Higher Education Area (EHEA): Towards a peer-assisted construction of knowledge." *GRETA. Revista para Profesores de Inglés* 16: 14–18.

Brígido Corachán, A. M. and Zaragoza Ninet, M. G. (in press) "What's happening? Expanding the ESL classroom through educational social network sites." In M. L. Pérez Cañado and J. Ráez Padilla (Eds), *Solving the Competency Conundrum: An International Perspective* (in press). Frankfurt am Main: Peter Lang.

Brown, J. D. (2001) *Using Surveys in Language Programs.* Cambridge: Cambridge University Press.

Bueno González, A. *et al.* (2008) *Informe de la Red CIDUA de la Licenciatura de Filología Inglesa.* Universidades Andaluzas.

Cano García, M. E. (2008) "La evaluación por competencias en la educación superior." *Revista de Currículum y Formación del Profesorado 12.* Available online from: http://www.ugr.es/local/recfpro/rev123COL1.pdf (accessed June 29, 2010).

Ceballos Muñoz, A. (2010) "Tutorías electrónicas transversales: una manera innovadora de acompañar a los estudiantes de las titulaciones de idiomas." *Lenguaje y Textos* 31: 49–59.

CIDUA. (2005) *Informe sobre la innovación de la docencia en las universidades andaluzas.* Sevilla: Consejería de Ecuación, Junta de Andalucía. Available online from: http://www.uca.es/web/estudios/innovacion/ficheros/informeinnovacinjuntaabril2005.doc (accessed November 12, 2010).

De Miguel Díaz, M. (Ed.) (2005) *Modalidades de enseñanza centradas en el desarrollo de competencias. Orientaciones para promover el cambio en el marco del EEES.* Oviedo: Universidad de Oviedo.

De Miguel Díaz, M. (Ed.) (2006) *Metodologías de enseñanza y aprendizaje para el desarrollo de competencias. Orientaciones para el profesorado universitario ante el Espacio Europeo de Educación Superior.* Madrid: Alianza Editorial.

Domingo, A., Chiloeches, A. and García, V. (2007) "Un paradigma cliente-empresa como método docente." In *Actas de las jornadas nacionales de intercambio de experiencias piloto de implantación de metodologías ECTS* (actas en CD). Badajoz: Servicio de Publicaciones de la Universidad de Extremadura.

Durán, M. A., Peralta, J. L., Gallego, C. and Montalbán, F. M. (2006) "Análisis de una encuesta de evaluación de la experiencia piloto de implantación del crédito europeo en las titulaciones de Relaciones Laborales y Trabajo Social." In *Actas de las jornadas de trabajo sobre experiencias piloto de implantación del crédito europeo en las universidades andaluzas* (actas en CD). Cádiz: Universidad de Cádiz.

García García, L. (2005) European Higher Education Area at the University of Jaén. First

Steps towards a Common European Higher Education and Research Space. Invited talk at Leeds University. June 2005.

Giménez de la Peña, A. and López Gutiérrez, F. (2006) "La actividad docente en el modelo ECTS." In *Actas de las jornadas de trabajo sobre experiencias piloto de implantación del crédito europeo en las universidades andaluzas* (actas en CD). Cádiz: Universidad de Cádiz.

Glaser, B. and Strauss, A. (1967) *The Discovery of Grounded Theory: Strategies for Qualitative Research.* Chicago, IL: Aldine.

Gregori-Signes, C. (2008) "Integrating the old and the new: Digital storytelling in the EFL language classroom." *GRETA. Revista para Profesores de Inglés* 16: 43–49.

Jiménez Raya, M. (in press) "Exploring pedagogy for autonomy in language education at university: Possibilities and impossibilities." In M. L. Pérez Cañado and J. Ráez Padilla (Eds), *Solving the Competency Conundrum: An International Perspective* (in press). Frankfurt am Main: Peter Lang.

Jordano de la Torre, M. (2008) "Propuesta para la práctica y evaluación de la competencia oral en los estudios de Turismo a distancia de acuerdo con el EEES." *GRETA. Revista para Profesores de Inglés* 16: 50–57.

Löfgren, K. (in press) "Competency-based corrective feedback in higher education second language teaching: Perspectives from empirical research and the Common European Framework of Reference for Languages." In M. L. Pérez Cañado and J. Ráez Padilla (Eds), *Solving the Competency Conundrum: An International Perspective* (in press). Frankfurt am Main: Peter Lang.

McLaren, N., Madrid, D. and Bueno, A. (Eds) (2005) *TEFL in Secondary Education.* Granada: Editorial Universidad de Granada.

Madrid Fernández, D. and Hughes, S. (2009) "The implementation of the European credit in initial foreign language teacher training." In M. L. Pérez Cañado (Ed.), *English Language Teaching in the European Credit Transfer System: Facing the Challenge* (pp. 227–244). Frankfurt am Main: Peter Lang.

Madrid Fernández, D. and Hughes, S. (in press) "Competencies for foreign language teacher education." In M. L. Pérez Cañado and J. Ráez Padilla (Eds), *Solving the Competency Conundrum: An International Perspective* (in press). Frankfurt am Main: Peter Lang.

Martínez Lirola, M. (2007) "El nuevo papel del profesor universitario de lenguas extranjeras en el proceso de convergencia europea y su relación con la interacción, la tutoría y el aprendizaje autónomo." *Porta Linguarum* 7: 31–43.

Mehisto, P. (2008) "CLIL counterweights: Recognising and decreasing disjuncture in CLIL." *International CLIL Research Journal* 1(1): 93–119.

Nieto García, J. M. (2007) "Sobre convergencia y uniformidad: La licenciatura en Filología Inglesa desde la perspectiva de un coordinador de titulación." In *Actas de las II jornadas de trabajo sobre experiencias piloto de implantación del crédito europeo en las universidades andaluzas* (actas en CD). Granada: Universidad de Granada.

Pascual Garrido, M. L. (2007) "Problemas y soluciones de la implantación de créditos ECTS en la titulación de Filología Inglesa en la UCO." In *Actas de las II jornadas de trabajo sobre experiencias piloto de implantación del crédito europeo en las universidades andaluzas* (actas en CD). Granada: Universidad de Granada.

Pennock-Speck, B. (2008) "The implementation of ICT in the second-cycle History of the English Language module at the Universitat de València." *GRETA. Revista para Profesores de Inglés* 16: 65–70.

Pennock-Speck, B. (2009) "European convergence and the role of ICT in English Studies at the Universitat de València: Lessons learned and prospects for the future." In M. L.

Pérez Cañado (Ed.), *English Language Teaching in the European Credit Transfer System: Facing the Challenge* (pp. 169–185). Frankfurt am Main: Peter Lang.

Pennock-Speck, B. (in press) "Teaching competences through ICTs in an English degree programme in a Spanish setting." In M. L. Pérez Cañado (Ed.), *Competency-Based Language Teaching in Higher Education* (in press). Amsterdam: Springer.

Pérez Cañado, M. L. (2009a) "The European Credit Transfer System: Enhancing creativity in teachers and students." *Humanising Language Teaching* 11(1). Available online from: http://www.hltmag.co.uk/feb09/mart03.htm (accessed June 29, 2010).

Pérez Cañado, M. L. (2009b) "Debunking EHEA myths: Common ECTS misconceptions and why they are wrong." *International Education Studies* 2(4): 15–24.

Pérez Gómez, A., Soto Gómez, E., Sola Fernández, M. and Serván Núñez, M. J. (2009a) *La universidad del aprendizaje: Orientaciones para el estudiante.* Madrid: Ediciones Akal, S.A.

Pérez Gómez, A., Soto Gómez, E., Sola Fernández, M. and Serván Núñez, M. J. (2009b) *Aprender en la universidad. El sentido del cambio en el EEES.* Madrid: Ediciones Akal, S.A.

Pérez Gómez, A., Soto Gómez, E., Sola Fernández, M. and Serván Núñez, M. J. (2009c) *Los títulos universitarios y las competencias fundamentales: Los tres ciclos.* Madrid: Ediciones Akal, S.A.

Pérez Gómez, A., Soto Gómez, E., Sola Fernández, M. and Serván Núñez, M. J. (2009d) *Contextos y recursos para el aprendizaje relevante en la universidad.* Madrid: Ediciones Akal, S.A.

Perrenoud, P. (2008) "Construir las competencias, ¿es darle la espalda a los saberes?" *Red U. Revista de Docencia Universitaria* 1. Available online from: http://www.redu.m.es/Red_U/m2 (accessed June 29, 2010).

Poblete Ruiz, M. (2006) "Las competencias, instrumento para un cambio de paradigma." In M. P. Bolea Catalán, M. Moreno Moreno and M. J. González López (Eds), *Investigación en educación matemática: Actas del X Simposio de la Sociedad Española de Investigación en Educación Matemática* (pp. 83–106). Zaragoza: Instituto de Estudios Altoaragoneses y Universidad de Zaragoza.

Pozuelos, F. J., Conde, A., Alonso, P., Cruz, R. and Rodríguez, J. M. (2006) "La colaboración docente como marco para el desarrollo de la experiencia piloto ECTS de la Titulación de Psicología." In *Actas de las jornadas de trabajo sobre experiencias piloto de implantación del crédito europeo en las universidades andaluzas* (actas en CD). Cádiz: Universidad de Cádiz.

Ron Vaz, P. and Casanova García, J. (2007) "El crédito europeo y los resultados académicos en la titulación de Filología Inglesa en la Universidad de Huelva." In *Actas de las II jornadas nacionales de metodologías ECTS* (actas en CD). Badajoz: Servicio de Publicaciones de la Universidad de Extremadura.

Ron Vaz, P., Fernández Sánchez, E. and Nieto García, J. M. (2006) "Algunas reflexiones sobre la aplicación del crédito europeo en la Licenciatura de Filología Inglesa en las universidades de Andalucía (Córdoba, Huelva y Jaén)." In *Actas de las I jornadas de trabajo sobre experiencias piloto de implantación del crédito europeo en las universidades andaluzas* (actas en CD). Cádiz: Universidad de Cádiz.

Taibi, M. (2006) "Reconsidering tutorials and student-lecturer power relationships in language subjects." *Porta Linguarum* 6: 33–39.

Tudor, I. (2006) "Trends in higher education language policy in Europe: The case of English as a language of instruction." Paper presented at the ECORE Conference Challenges in Multilingual Societies. June 9–10, Brussels, Belgium.

Ware, P. D. and O'Dowd, R. (2008) "Peer feedback on language form in telecollaboration." *Language Learning & Technology* 12(1): 43–63.

Zabalza Beraza, M. A. (2004) *Guía para la planificación didáctica de la docencia universitaria en el marco del EEES*. Santiago de Compostela: Universidad de Santiago de Compostela.

Zaragoza Ninet, M. G. and Clavel Arroitia, B. (2008) "ICT implementation in English Language and English Dialectology." *GRETA. Revista para Profesores de Inglés* 16: 78–84.

Zaragoza Ninet, M. G. and Clavel Arroitia, B. (2010) "La enseñanza del inglés a través de una metodología *blended-learning*: Cómo mejorar el método tradicional." *Lenguaje y Textos* 31: 25–34.

7

MEANING-CENTERED INTEGRATIVE INSTRUCTION IN LEARNING COMMUNITIES

Harriet Shenkman

Learning communities have been extensively practiced in colleges and universities in the United States and they have been identified as a high-impact practice by the Association of American Colleges and Universities (Kuh, 2008). The key goals have been to encourage integration of learning across academic courses and to involve students in an intensely engaging experience that fosters effort and persistence. The learning community structure also provides the opportunity for meaning-centered learning. This chapter will summarize the history of learning communities and explore how one aspect, an integrative meaning-centered approach, intensifies this experience and helps make what students are learning relevant to their conception of themselves in the world and to their future lives. As Potosky, Spaulding, and Juzbasich (this volume) note, meaning making is a constructive process that organizes our experiences. Learners represent the subject, not the receiver of educational activities. Instructors accordingly do not transmit information. Instead, they co-create experiences with learners and for learners to process. In the learning community structure, where teams of faculty work together to create engaging learning environments for students, the opportunity for this type of learning experience is made possible in numerous ways. Specific examples of this approach to teaching will be drawn from a learning community program at one community college at the City University of New York. In addition, possible approaches to measuring learning outcomes of meaning-centered activities will be explored.

A Brief History of Learning Communities in the United States

Learning communities in both two-year, four-year and research universities have been practiced widely in the United States, especially for first-year students. In the Second National Survey of First-Year Academic Practices, as many as 60 percent of responding institutions had adopted some form of learning community model (Barefoot, 2002). This curricular model consists of two or more classes linked together to form a cohort of students with various social and supplemental supports. Tinto (1997), an early advocate, has written about learning communities and their ability to foster social integration and collaborative learning and to strengthen curricular coherence. The social integration and engagement has been achieved through a variety of methods and structures including block programs, planned social events, service learning projects and residential arrangements. Integration of the curriculum is achieved through shared syllabi, academic assignments and projects, and common themes across linked courses.

The underlying practice of establishing student learning communities is attributed to John Dewey (1938) and Meiklejohn's Experimental College at the University of Wisconsin (1932). Their work and ideas encompassed the democratic ideals of both social interaction and community building (Zhao and Kuh, 2004). After its initial start the learning community model was renewed in the 1960s. The Washington Center for Improving the Quality of Undergraduate Education was formed at Evergreen State College in 1998 (www.evergreen.edu/washcenter) to support institutions that responded to the National Institute of Education's recommendation that learning communities be established. The idea was that the learning community model would foster a sense of community and be a particular help to an increasingly diverse student population with needs for extra support.

In recent years the American Association of Colleges and Universities has identified learning communities as a high impact educational practice, one among several widely tested teaching and learning innovations which show substantial educational benefits, especially for college students from historically underserved backgrounds. According to Kuh (2008), the key goals are to encourage integration of learning across courses and to involve students with "big questions" that matter beyond the classroom. Many learning communities explore a common topic and/or common readings through the lenses of different disciplines. Big questions and overarching issues are made manifest through thematic integrative structures and in this chapter thematic structures are seen as enabling meaning-centered education. These structures require the faculty to move from specific experiences for student learning in individual classrooms toward negotiated collaboration of common goals.

We must ask at the onset what we mean by meaning? The implication for many years in education was that meaning resides in the one who expresses the meaning. In other words, we look to the author, the expert, or the professor. Today we have moved from an emphasis on the meaning intended by the author and translated by the instructor to a focus on the meaning understood by and derived by the student. In other words, we have moved toward a learner-centered view of teaching and learning and a more open meaning-making process. We want to foster and facilitate this process. We also want to know what students have learned, how they have transformed their own understanding of the world, and we want to give them the opportunity to express their newly formed meanings.

Community Colleges

Learning communities are particularly popular as an intervention to support first-year developmental students at the community college. Often times a developmental course is linked with a credit bearing course and other times several basic courses in English and Mathematics are linked together in formation of at least three courses termed a cluster. This model is intended to foster social integration and collaborative learning which, in turn, has been postulated to have an effect on increased effort, academic performance, and retention. However, the effect on retention and graduation is difficult to prove. National Center for Postsecondary Research (May 2008) reports that rigorous studies as to the effectiveness of learning communities in terms of increasing long-term persistence and graduation rates are limited. Instead of making claims that learning communities lead to greater retention and higher graduation rates, Washington Center now emphasizes intentional integration as the key goal.

> Students persist in their studies if the learning they experience is meaningful, deeply engaging, and relevant to their lives. We know from campus visits—especially sitting in on classes—that if institutional energy goes to designing models and organizational structures without a similar attentiveness to teaching and learning, opportunities are squandered. The camaraderie of co-enrollment may help students stay in school longer, but learning communities can offer more: curricular coherence; integrative, high-quality learning; collaborative knowledge-construction; and skills and knowledge relevant to living in a complex, messy, diverse world.
>
> *(Lardner and Malnarich, 2008, p. 30)*

Curricular Integration and Common Themes

An essential element to a meaning-centered pedagogical approach is the organization of an integrated curriculum around common themes developed by the clusters within the community. This instructional practice enables the faculty to construct shared teaching and learning experiences. Integration may include planned integrated syllabi, joint assignment, common readings, joint projects, and themes that are shared during the class and made visible in peer presentations at a culminating event.

Another key practice that characterizes the next phase of learning community work is the implementation of integrative assignments which have the intentional aim of cross-disciplinary integration. Malnarich and Lardner (2003) describe the heuristic they have developed for designing learning experiences for students in three steps: The first step asks the faculty: what do you want students to know and be able to do in the individual courses you are teaching? The second step makes a public issue or larger question the subject of substantive work. This includes integrating knowledge from the different disciplines in the cluster. The skills in the individual courses are used and contextualized in doing this work. Students learn to do research, theorize, read, write, reason quantitatively, and synthesize information. Two additional elements are provision for students to reflect on their work and provision for students' work to become public. The third step emphasizes the resources learning communities need to draw upon to enrich student learning.

Thematic Work and Meaning-Centered Learning

The heart of meaning-centered activities in the learning community is the thematic work made possible by cross-disciplinary structures. By emphasizing themes across the linked courses, meaning is made more apparent and central and students new to academic content are more easily able to bring their own personal experience into learning. At Anne Arundel Community College, for example, learning communities offered clusters in Fall 2011 with themes such as *Now Who's Wearing the Pants?*; *Evolution and Revolution of Gender Roles?*; and *Saving the Planet: One Bite at a Time* (http://www.annearundel.edu). The themes are predetermined and designed to attract students to the course. In other instances, faculty members decide with the students upon the common theme for the semester after the course has begun. In either case, the themes are the critical glue that brings various areas of information and ideas together into a coherent whole. This approach encourages students to think about a subject and relate it to themselves. It also allows students to apply concepts to society issues and larger concepts of significance to their community. It encourages students to seek out relationships between disciplines and bits of information and to formulate their own integrative understanding or meaning. The meaning ultimately resides with the student and his ability to express his new found understanding. In the second section of this chapter, we will describe how thematic integrative instruction was undertaken in the First-Year Learning Community at Bronx Community College of the City University of New York.

Thematic Integration in Learning Communities at Bronx Community College

At Bronx Community College of the City University of New York, the majority of students are first-generation college students from underserved communities.

English is often not their first language. A small first-year learning community has been functioning at the college for more than five years. The community consists of five or six clusters of three courses each offered to first-year students who are shown through a uniform entrance examination to require at least one remedial noncredit course. Our learning community is an intentional restructuring of student and faculty time to build community and foster an integration of curriculum. We seek to foster connections between students, between students and faculty, between faculty and counselors, and between developmental course work and academic disciplines. Clusters consist of a developmental course in mathematics, English or reading, an academic discipline such as sociology, psychology, or environment science, and a college orientation course taught by faculty who also function as counselors. Time is built in for faculty to meet weekly to focus upon student needs and to plan for integration of learning. There is a planned orientation session and a culminating showcase where students have an opportunity to share their work with peers and faculty across clusters.

Faculty and students in each cluster develop a theme and explore the theme in their unique way, integrating the skills and content of the individual course into the thematic project. During several sessions throughout the semester, faculty members have the opportunity to develop their thematic approaches and share their planning and issues. The themes are understood through the individual experience of students, and, at the same time, lend themselves to a larger understanding of the human experience and the world beyond their individual experience. It is essential that the projects engage the students and seem relevant to the life they know.

The task of the faculty is to establish the themes in conjunction with students, gather the resources, both readings and film, and shape the experience. They must also integrate the work into the learning outcomes of the individual courses and establish a timeframe in which all the learning activities can be accomplished. Finally, the learning community clusters participate in a culminating event at which the work is presented to all the student and faculty in the First-Year Learning Community. This presentation usually involves the use of digital media. Students are encouraged to use digital storytelling and multimedia tools to share their work and technology assistance is provided to students in creating their presentations.

Each semester the themes and events change based upon the decisions of the new faculty and student cohorts. Over the years, the learning community clusters have produced themes and related activities that have been engaging and meaningful to students. In the 2008 spring semester, the themes included *One World, One Love, The Monte Carlo Experiment, Tolerance, Where I'm From, Leadership and the Community*, and *Environmental Issues*. Described below, in the words of faculty, are four among many meaning-centered thematic projects.

In the first project, the students use their own social standpoint to explore social issues in American society. In the second, students write, narrate, and act out digital stories that showcase their own individual identities while they study psychology. The third project has a global perspective. Students from the Bronx and from South Africa create an anthology of their stories of personal empowerment. And in the fourth project, ESL students interview local community leaders and create a digital story of the interviews. The cluster projects are developed to be shared in a showcase at the end of the semester and serve as an impetus for integrative work.

"One World, One Love" Learning Community

Our PowerPoint projects of Fall 2007 Learning Community Showcase were centered around our belief that when we share our experiences from a sensitive and critical perspective, others listen, learn and change. Having researched important social issues in America, namely, drug abuse, domestic violence, crime in New York City and welfare dependency, our students in the "One World, One Love" learning community presented the real life experiences of people suffering from these afflictions, statistical data that supported the need to address these social problems, as well as made suggestions for their resolution. As a team of students and teachers, we made a commitment to inspire the audience through an honest and heartfelt presentation of the issues using an enthusiastic voice and video clips of interviewees who spoke about their plight. At the onset of the project, we avowed to choose topics that emanated from our own experiences in the hope that our experiences met those of the audience. Indeed, the instructors and counselor on the team believed that it is only from our own social standpoint that we can speak truthfully and effectively.

We also believed that learning occurs at the point where real life experience meets the academic content. Having students represent their findings in various forms that included technology, statistics, the written word, images and voices reinforced their learning of the material in a profound way.

(Reynoso et al.*, 2007)*

Identity

After sharing CUNY graduation statistics by racial/ethnic cultural classifications with students, we decided to collectively challenge simplistic analysis of students' talents and the multiplicity of challenges that impede their academic success. Students are writing, narrating, and acting out short digital stories that showcase the individual identities they bring to the learning community. At the same time students are critically reflecting on what they are currently learning and how forces like gender, biology, culture, and development shape their group identity as a cluster.

Identity formation is at the core of psychology. Changing behaviors so as to succeed in college is at the core of OCD. Learning to summarize, reflect on, and incorporate the ideas of others is at the core of English 02. All of these courses offer opportunities to both reflect on current identities and to build skills that challenge the idea of identity as something static. The core of the connection across the three courses is the idea of how the self affects the whole, and the whole affects the creation of the self.

(Coss Aquina et al., *2011)*

Empowerment

This anthology is a collection of personal stories of empowerment written by students at Bronx Community College, New York City, USA, and at the University of KwaZulu-Natal, Durban, South Africa. All the authors of these stories are taking a basic writing class and have had to overcome many challenges in order to become college students. This anthology is a way to celebrate their achievement and to inspire other students to be high achievers, despite the challenges they may face in college and in life.

These stories are very different from each other because they were written by students who had very different lives. All these stories, however, share the same theme: empowerment. To us, editors of this anthology, empowerment means to do better in life, to uplift oneself, and to strive through hardships by building confidence. Each of these stories shows a different aspect of empowerment by looking at how students can take control of where their life is going, despite all the challenges.

(Parmegiani et al., *2010)*

Community Interview Digital Story Project

Students enjoyed working on the community leader interview project for a number of reasons: The project encourages them to get to know at least one leader in their neighborhoods and interact with her or him. This is very inspiring and empowering for our students. Many of them talked to me about the person they interviewed with great admiration and a certain pride in knowing such an accomplished and caring person. I assisted students with the editing of their interviews even though this semester they were rushed to finish, and I didn't get to work with all of the students. A crucial part of the project is that the students hand in to Jordi the questions they would like to ask the community leader they chose, and the three of us will go over the questions at one of our weekly meetings. The students thus receive feedback on the specificity and appropriateness of their interview questions early on in the development of their project, assuring them if they are on the "right" track or alerting them if they are not asking relevant questions. This is also a great opportunity for students to look at the content of their interviews in a more analytical way, which ties back to previous class discussions on what are the outstanding qualities of people who make a difference in the lives of others.

(Treglia, 2009)

In each project, students are integrating content and developmental skills and examining discipline-related issues central to their lives. The topics are generative as defined by the assignment heuristic (May, 2010) of the Washington Center. They are relevant to the students and society, central to one or more disciplines, accessible through multiple means, and connected to other topics taught. Faculty members meet weekly and at least three times a semester as a whole to refine the projects and share feedback about student response and performance. A powerful aspect of these projects is that students are transforming what they have learned in all three classes into their own integrative understanding with the purpose of making it public by sharing it with their peers. PowerPoint presentations and digital stories produced by students become artifacts of student accomplishment that are shared with peers and with the next cohort of students.

Faculty members were asked to reflect on their experience as faculty. A representative response from one team follows (Osborne *et al.*, 2009):

Each faculty member in the learning cluster was able to use his or her skills and creativity in the design of the integrated activities. This made our teaching more enjoyable and stimulating, which has had positive repercussions on the way students responded to the learning objectives we had set.

Each instructor was able to rely on his/her skill set, but also on the skill set of the group. This made it possible to create projects that would have been beyond our reach, had we worked individually.

Measuring the Results of Meaning-Centered Student Outcomes

The success of the First-Year Learning Community has been measured by traditional means such as final grades and rates of withdrawal. The First-Year Learning Community has shown over the span of five years higher average grades across courses as compared with the same courses taken by the general freshman population and lower student withdrawal rates. Student surveys have indicated positive responses in terms of engagement. In one survey, for example, 93 percent of students wrote positive responses to the question: how did you feel about the learning community experience?

Although surveys and student writing have been used to show the effects of engagement and academic data from individual classes have been assessed, it has been difficult to systematically measure the integrative aspects of content and the meaning-centered nature of the experience. Miller (2005) sheds light on the complexity of trying to assess integrative learning. A vital first step is defining the goal. In the Learning Community effort described above, integrative learning involves blending knowledge and skills from a content, developmental, and orientation perspective to create meaning for the students. A methodology might involve rating student writing for signs of integrative thinking using checklists or rubrics. Miller describes a general checklist used at New Century College at George Mason University which includes a check box for "connections across course experiences" with ratings ranging from making insightful connections to unsatisfactory connections. The showcase end-term digital projects might also be rated for making insightful connections.

A more complex methodology was developed by Mino (2006) as part of a Carnegie Scholars project. In a three-stage study investigating integrative learning by students in a learning community, he used the general SOLO Taxonomy as a course-level assessment rubric in stage one, and in stage two he attempted to study the precise elements of integration and meaning making in student writing. He identified twelve different interdisciplinary linking mechanisms in student writing, including embedded quotes, use of metaphor, personal experience, integrative questioning, and theory application. The third stage in Mino's approach was called "Link Aloud." It provided a visual and auditory representation of integrative learning. Briefly, students were asked to select one of their assignments and discuss the interdisciplinary connections they made. The student interviews were transposed into visual concepts maps using a verbal protocol analysis methodology. The process resulted in a map of connections made between subject matters and a number of highlighted words and phrases that activated relevant audio links, which provided detailed explanations in the students' own voices. This third stage is an opportunity for students to reflect about their own learning and meaning making, the process itself leading to moments of additional discovery. Mino calls this last stage "a pedagogy of guided reflection."

Lardner and Malnarich (2008/9) explored the assessment of integrative learning and advocate a focused response to student work using a protocol that guides attention to specific evidence of integration. They experimented with a collaborative approach in which a team of faculty moves through a set of questions which allows them to notice, value, and raise questions about student work.

The assessment practices described have potential for measuring meaning-centered outcomes achieved in learning communities. Practitioners now recognize that an integrative meaning-centered approach is a deeper and more valid focus although measurement of outcomes is a challenge. In the future, more ways should be devised and perfected to measure this important outcome in learning communities and validate the critical benefits to student learning.

References

American Association of Community Colleges (2007) *AACC Research and Statistics: Community College Fast Facts.* Washington, DC: American Association of Community Colleges. Available online from: http://www2.aacc.nche.edu/research/index.htm (accessed August 2, 2011).

Barefoot, B.O. (2002) *National Survey Results.* Available online from: http://www.firstyear.org/survey/survey2002/index.html (accessed October 19, 2007).

Coss Aquina, M., Ingram, T. and Guishard, M. (2011) *Integrative Learning, CTE Day Brochure.* New York: Bronx Community College, CUNY.

Dewey, J. (1938) *Experience and Education.* New York: MacMillan.

Kuh, G. D. (2008) *High Impact Educational Practices: What They Are, Who Has Access to Them, and Why They Matter.* Washington, DC: American Association of Community Colleges.

Lardner, E. and Malnarich, G. (2008) "A new era in learning-community work: Why the pedagogy of intentional integration matters." *Change* 40(4): 30–37.

Lardner, E. and Malnarich, G. (2008/9) "Assessing integrative learning: Insights from Washington Center's national project on assessing learning in learning communities." *Journal of Learning Communities Research* 3(3): 1–20.

Malnarich, G. and Lardner, E. (2003) "Designing integrated learning for students: A heuristic for teaching, assessment and curriculum design." *Washington Center Occasional Paper*, Winter, 1. Evergreen State College.

Meiklejohn, A. (1932) *The Experimental College.* New York: Harper.

Miller, R. (2005) "Integrative learning and assessment." *Peer Review* (Summer/Fall): 11–14.

Mino, J. J. (2006) *The Link Aloud: Making Interdisciplinary Learning Visible & Audible.* Available online from: http://www.cfkeep.org/html/snapshot (accessed February 16, 2012).

Osborne, G., Gonzales, M. and Parmegiani, A. (2009) *First-Year Learning Community Summary Report.* New York: Bronx Community College, CUNY.

Parmegiani, A., Osborne, G. and Fortune, M. (2010) *Transforming Lives Through Education: An Anthology Edited by Students at Bronx Community College.* New York: Bronx Community College, CUNY.

Reynoso, N., Thomas, V., Wilson, J. and Cukras, G. (2007) *First-Year Learning Community Summary Report.* New York: Bronx Community College, CUNY.

Tinto, V. (1997) "Classrooms as communities: Exploring the educational character of student persistence." *Journal of Higher Education* 68(6): 599–623.

Treglia, M. (2009) *First-Year Learning Community Summary Report.* New York: Bronx Community College, CUNY.

Washington Center for Improving the Quality of Undergraduate Education Learning Communities National Resource Directory (2011) Available online from: http://www.evergreen.edu/washcenter/directory (accessed February 1, 2012).

Zhao, C. and Kuh, G.D. (2004) "Adding value: Learning communities and student engagement." *Research in Higher Education* 45(2): 115–138.

8

TRUE COLLABORATION

Building Meaning in Learning Through Sharing Power With Students

Anton O. Tolman and Christopher S. Lee

We cannot create genuine communities of practice for students until we allow faculty to participate too . . . Only if the teachers are learners too, and if they are seen to be learners, can they genuinely model deep learning for the apprentice learners in the community.

(John Tagg, 2003, p. 263)

Introduction

The goal of facilitating an environment where students construct meaning is largely impeded by the current "Instruction Paradigm" (Tagg, 2003) that continues to saturate higher education. In this model, instructors—experts in their respective disciplines—disseminate content to students, primarily through lecture, and the metaphor of "coverage" is invoked as if transmission of content equates to student development (Tagg, 2003). Transmitting knowledge into the minds of students is the implicit instructional goal, a process Freire (1993) has described as the banking concept of education, "in which the scope of action allowed to the students extends only as far as receiving, filing, and storing the deposits" (p. 53). In contrast, a constructivist explanation suggests that learning is the outcome or result of meaning-making processes in the learner, a combination of new information and experiences that must be blended with one's prior understanding and personal history (Potosky, Spaulding, and Juzbasich, this volume).

In the Instruction Paradigm, the primacy of content is imposed upon students externally, assumed by all parties to be the obvious purpose of education; faculty, perhaps unintentionally,[1] disregard students' internal construction of knowledge and meaning, what Potosky, Spaulding, and Juzbasich (this volume) refer to as an *intrapersonal* dialogue. Instructors often fail to provide any rationale for the significance of class content or structure; they are the authority, the one who deems the "truth" that should be transmitted to students, a process that Wegerif (this volume) names *monologic*. It is a one-way, top-down system where the role of students is primarily submission to the authoritative voice and decisions of the professor. Student progress is commonly assessed based on recognition or recitation of factual knowledge, with minimal focus on metacognitive awareness, making it difficult for students to build meaning and develop as learners. Measurements of learning target what the instructor deems correct, not the students' own understanding, rendering students voiceless in their own education. Students also have little or no input regarding instructional practices, assignments, and aspects of course governance. This opaque educational existence only serves to provide students with a view of course assignments as "busy work" rather than opportunities to learn. Such practices actually foster student resistance to collaborative learning and meaning creation; they see no point in building knowledge with others because doing so may not match the instructor's expectations.

Potosky and her colleagues (this volume) argue that meaning arises primarily through multiple channels of dialogic communication, including collaborative and interpersonal dialogues between student peers as well as students and instructor and a personalized, internal, and reflective dialogue within the mind of the student. The monologic classroom (Wegerif, this volume) almost never generates the type of environment that is conductive to encouraging, sustaining, or expanding the potential of these forms of meaning-related communication. Indeed, as Tagg (2003) so deftly points out, higher education has been designed primarily as a credit-granting system, focused on delivery of instruction rather than on promoting student learning or creation of meaning.

In such an educational environment, instructors may approach the classroom with a fixed perception of the power dynamics between student and teacher. This is clearly evidenced by edict-driven syllabi that seem to treat students like criminals[2] (Singham, 2007) and generate an environmental subtext of instructor versus student. Teachers assume almost total control over the educational process in their classroom. As passive recipients of information with minimal control over their education, students find little motivation to create meaning. As Wegerif (this volume) notes, "If meaning is a kind of thing, then you can transmit it. If meaning is a dialogue, then you have to participate in it." In order to more effectively facilitate the process of truly developing meaning in students' education, faculty must move towards true collaboration by sharing *real* power with students. Only then will students be empowered in a classroom no longer focused solely on content but will be building skills and habits of mind that are rooted in foundational knowledge (see AAC&U, 2007), where the instructor no longer dictates to students every detail of what to learn but where students and instructors decide together what is most important and how to learn it most effectively. Such an environment is dynamic, dialogic, respectful, and encourages student motivation to learn and to find personal and professional meaning in the learning process. Potosky and colleagues note (this volume) that meaning-making can only begin when learners are exposed to the opportunity to experience something; a classroom built around principles of authentic sharing of power between instructor and students provides a setting where those opportunities can be constructed.

This chapter will discuss common reasons why faculty resist sharing power, examine the empirical literature related to collaborative power sharing, and provide practical suggestions regarding needed changes and practices that faculty can implement to effectively share power and help students create meaning in their own education.

Legitimate and Problematic Reasons That Faculty Resist Sharing Power

For many faculty, making the leap from an instructor-based view of the classroom to one based on collaborative partnerships with students can be the most difficult of a set of needed changes (see Weimer, 2002). Faculty have a list of objections—some legitimate, some problematic—that seem to justify maintaining the educational status quo. For instance, how much power is too much? How can faculty measure student maturity when it comes to allowing increased decision-making? At what point do instructors begin to abandon their ethical responsibilities to teach? Although these concerns have some validity, they should not pose decisive barriers against power sharing; many of these worries rely on questionable assumptions about student learning, the role of instructors, and the nature of power sharing. The potential long-term negative outcomes to students when power is exclusively retained by the instructor may overshadow most of these concerns. As Singham (2007) has noted, "controlling environments have been shown consistently to *reduce* people's interest in whatever they're doing, even [those] that would be highly motivated in other contexts" (p. 55).

Perhaps the most frequently cited concern is that sharing power with students will inevitably lead to chaos in the classroom; this worry may also be closely connected to faculty anxiety that students lack the intellectual maturity to make important decisions about their own learning. Doyle (2008) describes this claim, pointing out that faculty possess "a fear of losing control of the class, having to pick up the pieces when students make poor decisions" (p. 96).

Fear of losing control particularly manifests in introductory level courses; however, Weimer (2002) argues, "the fact that students need to be prepared for learner-centered approaches is not an endemic reason that justifies . . . making *all* [emphasis added] the decisions about their learning for them" (p. 25). Concerns about the learning environment can be reduced by exposing the assumption that Weimer alludes to: that sharing power is a dichotomy: either instructors assume the traditional autocratic role or submit to potentially unrealistic decisions of students. Doyle (2008) suggests that context should inform the degree of power distribution in the classroom (p. 105). Rather than a dualistic view of power sharing, this more realistic alternative is to see decision-making as a continuum, taking into account situational constraints (class size, type of class, course level, administrative assessment standards, etc.) and allowing instructors to incrementally experiment with methods of sharing power.

Another, perhaps more legitimate, criticism regarding power sharing is the concern that doing so abdicates ethical and professional obligations to teach. As previously discussed, this dichotomous metaphor is misleading, and reflects a distorted view of power sharing. Giving students total control over their grades is, obviously, irresponsible and unethical. Involving students to an appropriate degree in a variety of course decisions (see below) based on an assessment of situational constraints is clearly not the same thing. As Weimer (2002) has noted, "Most faculty control decision making about learning so completely that the possibility that they will transfer too much power too quickly seems remote" (p. 44). Thus, it seems highly unlikely that unethical extremes of power sharing are frequent.

A more subtle form of faculty resistance to sharing power may arise as a reaction to student resistance to active learning methods. For many reasons, some of them legitimate, students may resist an instructor's efforts to enhance their learning; these behaviors are easily interpreted by faculty as laziness, lack of vision, or indifference to the value of education. Many instructors may be unaware of the complex interactions of student cognitive development, cultural forces, negative previous experiences that shape expectations, and their perceptions of the value and costs of making changes (Tolman and Kremling, 2011). By interpreting student behaviors in this way, faculty may naturally reach a conclusion that sharing power with students would be counterproductive. In this way, faculty reject the potential of *dialogic* communication with students (Wegerif, this volume) in preference to the monologic approach with which they are familiar and comfortable.

Unfortunately, relatively few faculty have received intensive training in how to teach. The oft heard refrain is that professors teach "as they were taught," and there is much truth to this aphorism. Instructors are accustomed to the instructional paradigm, to lecture-based classes where the professor makes all decisions. Although they may chafe at some of the constraints imposed by a monologic environment, it is what they are used to, the mental image that arises when they think of "teaching." Moving into an environment where students have real power to influence decisions, class policies, content, or assignments can generate reactions ranging from discomfort to anxiety. This may be true even for those professors who may believe such a change can be managed without disruption or losing control of the classroom. This source of resistance is *internal*, resulting from the disruption of existing mental models of a professor's role; ironically, this is often exactly what instructors ask students to face when they learn, but it is easier to impose such a discomfort on others than to face it oneself. Fortunately, as with all sources of resistance described here, this challenge can be managed and overcome.

Last, faculty may fear violating departmental or institutional policy by power sharing with students or worry about tenure or promotion. Some professors may claim they cannot act because departmental policies require explicit authoritarian statements to be included in the syllabus. They overlook the fact that departmental policies are created by faculty, and they are in a position to change them. The Instruction Paradigm's factory model of education (Tagg, 2003) has no room for power sharing and those who adopt innovative means to assist students in creating personal meaning from their education may face criticism from those who tacitly or explicitly endorse its provisions. Senior faculty or tenure committees may be willing to label innovative teaching methods as ineffective or inept because such practices violate their own expectations of authoritarian power in the classroom. Department chairs, administrators, and faculty colleagues supportive of student empowerment share an obligation to put in place safeguards and protections to assist faculty seeking to make these changes.

These commonly cited concerns among faculty with sharing power deserve thoughtful consideration and even effective action such as policy changes, but they should not be permitted to impede the advantages that can come from providing students with a voice in their own education. Many faculty defend current practices by claiming they already share power to an appropriate degree and that change is unnecessary. Empirical data is helpful in evaluating this claim.

Empirical Patterns in Faculty Power Sharing

Most faculty sincerely want students to succeed, to connect *what* they are learning in a meaningful way to *why* that content is important in students' lives. When asked directly, many faculty indicate that they listen to students, giving them a chance to express their thoughts and voices to influence the direction and nature of their own learning. If this claim were true, it should be visible in the course syllabus, the document that reflects the overall philosophy and approach of the course and that defines the learning environment for students.

Unfortunately, many university syllabi do not reflect the ideals and aspirations of the faculty who create them. Wasley (2008) notes that syllabi have increasingly come to be seen by faculty and administrators as legal contracts full of "exhortations and enunciations" of class and university policies. She proposes several reasons for this pattern including institutional mandates and attempts to avoid conflicts with students. Wasley notes that some faculty even require students to sign the syllabus, an action that cements the impression of an authoritarian and adversarial classroom environment. In contrast, Singham (2007) describes the "rule infested, punitive, controlling syllabus" as an artifact that has contributed to the degradation of higher education and advocates for a collaborative discussion of how the course will proceed between instructor and students, but it is unclear how often such a practice actually occurs.

Empirical data to evaluate faculty power sharing practices are very rare in the literature. Baecker (1998) conducted a preliminary study examining pronoun use in a small sample of college syllabi. Her goal was to understand the way faculty use pronouns to negotiate power issues. Out of 15 syllabi examined, she found relatively few that were "balanced" between the instructor's use of "I" and the more dominant use of "you" for students. She reported that "you" was used in these syllabi 55–82 percent of the time with the use of "I" ranging from 9 to 38 percent of the time. Baecker noted that regarding the use of "we," faculty were sometimes signaling collaboration, although they usually used the pronoun "falsely," to diffuse or hide the instructor's power or to coerce students into believing a statement instead of a true indicator of community or collaboration.

From a broader perspective, Cullen and Harris (2009) devised a rubric for evaluating the degree to which course syllabi demonstrated the instructor's intent to create a learner-centered classroom environment, including building a community of learners, sharing power and control, and clear links between assessment and learning outcomes. They evaluated syllabi from two academic units at a public comprehensive university, involving a total of 25 faculty. Overall, the results suggested that both units scored low with little evidence of power sharing with students.

Tolman *et al.* (2009) carried out a more comprehensive investigation at a public western teaching university using data from a random sample of 94 faculty syllabi from five different colleges or schools. The sample was stratified by instructor gender, course level (upper or lower division), and college/school with a sampling frame of 40 percent of the full-time faculty teaching in the unit.[3] The authors developed a new instrument, the Faculty Immediacy and Power Sharing Inventory (FIPSI), to evaluate the syllabi on the two major dimensions of power sharing and interpersonal warmth or "immediacy." Three trained students rated the syllabi and a point-by-point analysis demonstrated a high degree of inter-rater reliability (90.2 percent overall).

The Power Sharing scale on the FIPSI consists of 14 items that measure several power sharing concerns including authoritarian ("you will," "required") or demeaning (assuming students will cheat) language, student choices and involvement in content, course policies, and assignment decisions. A professor's score may range from a low of −2 (highly punitive or demeaning language) to a maximum of 12 on this scale. No significant differences or interactions were found for gender or course level. Table 8.1 demonstrates the results from this sample of professors.

These results suggest real cause for concern. Across almost one hundred professors from five different colleges or schools, evidence of power sharing with students was rare and a significant percentage of these syllabi used language that was authoritarian, demanding or that stated or implied that students were untrustworthy and could be punished.

Although empirical research in this area is scant, it is entirely consistent with

TABLE 8.1 Descriptive statistics from the FIPSI Power Sharing scale

Statistic	Value
Highest score	5
Lowest score	−2
Mean (s.d.)	0.46 (1.3)
Median	0
25th Percentile	0
50th Percentile	0
75th Percentile	1
94th Percentile	2
Syllabi scoring below 0	20%

Note: N = 94; Scale score has a minimum of −2 to a maximum possible score of 12; FIPSI = Faculty Immediacy and Power Sharing Inventory

the theoretical argument that there is a need for change. Faculty may genuinely desire for their students to learn, and they may believe that they are adopting approaches to helping students become independent thinkers who may contribute to society. However, their behavior, at least as manifest in the document that describes and lays out their approach to teaching and their course design, does not show evidence of it. It is possible that on some campuses, especially those with an intensive research focus, the situation may be even worse. As Barr and Tagg (1995) noted in their seminal article, "For many of us, the Learning Paradigm has always lived in our hearts. As teachers, we want above all else for our students to succeed. But the heart's feeling has not lived clearly and powerfully in our heads" (p. 13).

Moving Towards Collaboration and Power Sharing: A Dialogic Conversation

Faculty will not move away from rigid and authoritarian course designs to meaning-centered learning until they see a reason to do so. While it is possible that instructors may increase awareness of the need for this change on their own, most would benefit from external support. Discussing collaborative classroom environments with experienced mentors and colleagues who have been experimenting with power sharing in the same discipline may help faculty think through ways to apply these concepts effectively. Teaching circles where colleagues gather regularly to read a scholarly work, discuss, and devise changes in teaching methods provides a vital link to the literature that could provide some "cover" during tenure reviews. Requesting a classroom observation from colleagues experienced at collaborative work with students may also be helpful. Faculty Learning Communities can generate scholarly analysis of the issues and propose solutions adapted to the specific campus environment via white papers or recommendations. Additionally, the role of faculty developers may be critical in achieving forward momentum.

By incorporating collaborative principles into new faculty orientation, campus-wide programs and workshops, and providing consultation, faculty developers can provide the needed vision and technical support to enable faculty to begin to see the advantages of sharing power and feel more confident in doing so. Developers can also work with faculty over time, to assist them as they move through the learning curve involved in changing one's paradigm and behaviors. This learning curve involves making significant changes to one's underlying assumptions as well as to one's teaching practices.

The first major obstacle for faculty may be the most difficult to overcome because it is at the core of professional identity: eliminating a mindless adherence to content. In contrast to their typically limited training in teaching and student learning, faculty are disciplinary experts, very familiar with course content that they believe is important for all students to learn. This imbalance promotes a tendency to focus on content to the exclusion of other vital course objectives (e.g., development of critical thinking, oral and written communication, etc.). For example, survey courses purport to prepare students for later learning in the discipline or to provide a wide general overview of a field. In such courses, faculty may sincerely believe it is necessary to review 15 chapters of material in a semester to achieve these goals. This creates a time pressure to lecture, to transmit information in a monologic manner, and to avoid any approach or method that may "use up" precious class time. Many faculty do not consider design elements that would encourage students to learn basic, foundational concepts on their own outside of the classroom. Similarly, concerns for student input are meager because the professor believes there is not enough time for them. Yet, the reality is that most factual content is likely to be forgotten, vital skills development is sidelined, and students become passive recipients in an authoritarian regime that leaves little time for creating personal meaning.

However, if faculty can recognize the value of collaboration and sharing power, they can take a broader view of content. For example, Abnormal Psychology is a widely offered survey course in most Psychology/Social Science departments. Tolman (2011) describes a set of five course objectives, only two of which are focused on content. Others are devoted to skill development and a personal understanding of social stigma. These other objectives drive class time towards collaborative activities including student involvement in deciding course assignments, content to be reviewed, and course policies. Students are actively involved in meaning creation because they customize the course material to their own learning interests and needs; they connect content to their personal lives and the world. Whether or not students go on to graduate study, they leave class with an understanding of professional and ethical thinking, development of key skills, and recognition of the social costs of stigma. If they do move forward to graduate work, they will later take a plethora of advanced courses focusing on assessment, diagnosis, treatment, and so forth, that duplicate and extend what they learned at the undergraduate level. This use of overarching core themes that are broader than just content coverage, as well as the *utilization* of course content to achieve meaningful aims, becomes possible when faculty leave behind their exclusive focus on the purpose of class as reviewing or transmitting content.

Second, faculty should give up the idea of the course design and syllabus as a contract and resist any administrative efforts to that end. Such a focus only promotes a legalistic mentality that is necessarily adversarial. It can also promote the idea that students are entitled to exactly what is written down and are not required to do anything beyond those boundaries. Reed (2009) argues that, in fact, syllabi do not function as contracts and there is no substance to this perspective. By viewing the syllabus and related course design as a dialogue or ongoing negotiation between an instructor and students, collaboration becomes not just a possibility but a necessary element of education. Another starting point to avoid the problems described in existing syllabi above is for faculty to make genuine changes to the language and content of their syllabi, emphasizing the classroom as a community of learners and reducing language that automatically blames or assumes certain behaviors on the part of students (e.g., plagiarism, non-attendance, etc.). For example, faculty could replace phrases in the syllabus that note that students "will" do X, or "are required" with phrasing that describes how "we" may achieve course objectives or that emphasizes student selection of options that will best help them to learn. Instructors could also emphasize the "we" of the classroom community rather than single out students as separate from the instructor. Such linguistic changes, if genuine, promote a sense of dialogue and interaction rather than a monologic transmittal of requirements from authority.

Regarding practices, faculty should think of students as partners in the learning process. Keeping in mind the course organizing themes, faculty should begin by preparing students for a collaborative classroom starting with the first day of class. Students usually expect a passive learning environment and many, especially successful students, have learned how to survive and operate well in such an environment. Regardless of the value of a dialogic conversation with students about the meaning of their learning, the content, and course structure, students may need time to acclimate to this idea. Faculty need to explain the reasoning behind the class (Doyle, 2008), describe the students' role, validate their voice, and demonstrate throughout the semester that this is not a "trick" or false front. One way to do this is to utilize a set of questions on the first day of class as a fulcrum for a discussion about the relative importance and purpose of gaining factual information, learning how to apply information, and development of lifelong learning skills (Smith, 2008). These questions can then become the foundation to help students see the value in taking an active role in their own education, and it shares with them a vision of their role: they are not there to memorize and repeat back factual information on course assessments; they are there to personally develop the knowledge and skills essential to their own lives and careers. Beginning the class with this dialogue with students, and reframing education as a dialogic, rather than monologic process, emphasizes the importance of "continuous re-creation of meaning" (Wegerif, this volume) instead of a static process. Approaching students this way helps to develop the "long time horizon" described by Tagg (2003).

Once students share a vision of the value of a collaborative classroom, faculty can consider various options for student empowerment ranging from the approach recommended by Singham (2007) where students essentially co-author the syllabus and shape the learning experiences, to other spaces on the continuum where students may co-author (via a Wiki or in-class groups) course policies, weight course grading, and help to select content (especially in survey courses). Instructors may offer a set of mandatory assignments that establish a foundation for learning expected of all students while simultaneously offering a significant portion of the grade based on student-selected assignments drawn from a menu of options or that they propose. Mastery learning is another example. In mastery learning (e.g., Gentile, 2005; Lally and Gentile, 2009), students utilize formative assessment to learn and relearn until they achieve specific standards of competence on fundamental course objectives without comparison to how other students are performing (criterion vs. norm-referenced performance). Instructors may then negotiate with students the levels of achievement expected for enrichment objectives and how that achievement relates to final grades. These approaches and others can be combined or blended in a medley that suits the course content and promotes not only student empowerment and participation but that enhances their learning.

Last, those who understand the vital nature of this effort must work to create an environment supportive of collaborative meaning-making. Faculty development efforts could focus on workshops, reading circles, mentoring by experienced faculty, and other opportunities to help faculty understand the importance of these shifts and to catch a vision of what could be done. For faculty, making the transition to a power sharing classroom is not a simple process, and they would benefit from guided adaptation and experimentation. Administrators and department chairs can work with tenure policies and guidelines to ensure they are friendly to innovative and important changes such as these; indeed, administrators and faculty should be encouraged to consider changes to existing documents in order to reward or incentivize collaborative methods. Power sharing in the classroom should be seen as evidence of sound pedagogy and approaches to helping students learn, factors that should *increase* the probability of tenure in institutions that value teaching. This shifts faculty perceptions toward adopting collaborative methods from a list of negatives to a series of strong positives and might encourage faculty to begin purposeful implementation. Department chairs and faculty developers can work together to put into place mentoring systems where faculty with experience in designing and implementing learning partnerships with students coach and assist their colleagues.

Conclusion

Facilitating a collaborative classroom environment and providing students with choices that impact their education is vital in order to divorce teaching practices from the current instructional, monologic paradigm and more fully enable genuine construction of meaning. When faculty recognize and alter their underlying assumptions and come to see students as partners, collaborators in learning, change is possible. Only then will students become active agents, participants in an ongoing creation of meaning through dialogue both communal and intrapersonal, rather than passive recipients in their education. Such an environment creates opportunities for learners to "cognitively reconstruct experiences in ways that are meaningful to them" (Potosky, Spaulding, and Juzbisch, this volume). Faculty can be freed from an autocratic role that damages themselves and students and likewise become a vibrant participant in a meaningful dialogue. The problems that may arise from the idea of sharing power with students merit further discussion but do not justify a complete resistance to change. Change may be difficult but it need not paralyze; faculty can incrementally make the shift by incorporating the proposed suggestions discussed above. Meaning-centered learning will not become widespread until faculty begin to make significant commitments to fostering a learning environment that empowers and motivates students to be part of their own education.

Acknowledgments

We would like to acknowledge the vital contributions of three students to the empirical study reported in this chapter: Melissa Ercanbrack, Erik Hunt, and Laura Gorman.

Notes

1   Tagg (2003) provides an in-depth analysis of how the structure of higher education reinforces the Instruction Paradigm, including how faculty can unintentionally impede student learning and the construction of meaning, which he refers to as "Theories-in-Use" (p. 13).
2   One recent study published in *Police Practice and Research* ranks universities as inferior to police agencies regarding management practices. Bayley (2011) notes, "Universities deliver classes and hope for education in just the way police deliver patrol or criminal investigation and hope for the prevention of crime" (p. 313).
3   The school of education was oversampled because of relatively small numbers of faculty in that school.

References

Association of American Colleges and Universities (AAC&U) (2007) College learning for the new global century: A report from the National Leadership Council for Liberal

Education and America's Promise. Washington, DC: Association of American Colleges and Universities. (Also available at www.aacu.org).

Baecker, D. (1998) "Uncovering the rhetoric of the syllabus." *College Teaching* 46(2): 58.

Barr, R. B. and Tagg, J. (1995) "From teaching to learning—a new paradigm for under-graduate education." *Change* 27(6): 12–26.

Bayley, D. H. (2011) "Et tu brute: Are police agencies managed better or worse than uni-versities?" *Police Practice & Research* 12(4): 313–316.

Cullen, R. and Harris, M. (2009) "Assessing learner-centeredness through course syllabi." *Assessment & Evaluation in Higher Education* 34(1): 115–125.

Doyle, T. (2008) *Helping Students Learn in a Learner-Centered Environment.* Sterling, VA: Stylus.

Freire, P. (1993) *Pedagogy of the Oppressed.* London and New York: Penguin.

Gentile, J. R. (2005) "Improving college teaching productivity via mastery learning." In J. E. Groccia and J. E. Miller (Eds), *On Becoming a Productive University* (pp. 291–301). Thousand Oaks, CA: Corwin Press.

Lally, J. P. and Gentile, J. R. (2009) "Classroom assessment and grading to assure mastery." *Theory into Practice* 48: 28–35.

Reed, D. (2009) "Is a syllabus a contract?" Available online from: http://www.unitedstatesjurisprudence.com/page5.html (accessed December 7, 2012).

Singham, M. (2007) "Death to the syllabus!" *Liberal Education* (Fall): 52–56.

Smith, G. A. (2008) "First day questions for the learner-centered classroom." *National Teaching and Learning Forum* 17(5): 1–4.

Tagg, J. (2003) *The Learning Paradigm College.* San Francisco, CA: Anker (Jossey-Bass).

Tolman, A. O. (2011) "Creating transformative experiences for students in Abnormal Psychology." In R. L. Miller, E. Balcetis, S. R. Burns, D. B. Daniel, B. K. Saville and W. D. Woody (Eds), *Promoting Student Engagement* (Vol. 2, pp. 136–145). Avail-able online from: http://teachpsych.org/resources/e-books/pse2011/vol2/index.php (accessed December 7, 2012).

Tolman, A. O., Ercanbrack, M. and Hunt, E. (2009) "How are we doing in sharing power with students?" Paper presented at the Teaching Professor Conference, Washington, DC, June.

Tolman, A. O. and Kremling, J. (2011) "Using Metacognitive Instruments to Reduce Student Resistance to Active Learning." Workshop presented at the 23rd Annual Con-ference of the International Alliance of Teacher-Scholars (Lilly West), Pomona, CA, March 12.

Wasley, P. (2008) "The syllabus becomes a repository of legalese." *The Chronicle of Higher Education* 54(27): A1.

Weimer, M. (2002) *Learner-Centered Teaching: Five Key Changes to Practice.* San Francisco, CA: Jossey-Bass.

PART III

Enhancing Meaning-Centered Teaching and Learning

9

MEANING'S SECRET IDENTITY

Russell A. Hunt

Introduction

The word "meaning," most of the time, is a noun. But like many English words, it has a secret identity, and appears once in a while in its guise as a verb ("to mean"). The first time I realized what a powerful difference this might make was when I picked up M. A. K. Halliday's book about the language development of his infant son, and considered its title: *Learning How to Mean* (1975). As a long-time teacher of literature, I had been conditioned to think of "meaning" as something in a text or piece of discourse, as something you found, or disputed about, not something you did. At best, it was something you "made." The implications of this change in thinking have been playing out for a number of years, both in my practice as a teacher and in my writing and thinking about how language works and how, throughout our lives, we develop our abilities to use its power as a tool for thinking and for engaging with others. Placing "meaning" as a verb, rather than a noun, at the center of my practice and thinking, has amounted to putting action at the focus of my curricula rather than material, and has pulled into focus much of the reading about language and learning that has guided my thinking and research.

I will attempt here to outline the theoretical and practical basis of this way of thinking about language, and then to demonstrate some of the ways in which putting meaning at the center of classroom practice opens up new approaches to learning. One of the most powerful implications of this change in focus has to do with how text is used. A text as a repository of a "meaning" (or even more than one) is fundamentally inert and unchanging; our perception of it may vary according to our situation, but the text itself is assumed to be passive. Thinking of the ways in which a text is an act of meaning, however, brings creator and reader into an active relationship, and means that texts must always be seen, understood, and used as social actions, with specific writers and readers, in the same way as oral language is. This entails, I argue, rethinking the way writing is used in educational contexts: it promotes a move from using writing as a method of assessment to using it as a method of conducting discussions; it affords making classroom written language more like the authentic written language by which we conduct science, scholarship, and, indeed, most complex human activities. Most important, it affords learning how to use written language as a tool for further learning.

The Social Action of Meaning

In the late twentieth century we began to hear a lot about language as a social phenomenon, from people working in a wide variety of disciplines. I was particularly influenced by the work of Kenneth Kaye (1982; Kaye and Charney, 1980) and Jerome Bruner (1983), who were concerned with the very earliest beginnings of mental life in infants, and who helped me see that Vygotsky (1978; see also Wertsch, 1983, 1986) was right when he said, a half century or more ago, that intelligence itself was a social phenomenon, intimately connected with that most social of phenomena, oral language. These ideas were also shaped by work on the development of literacy in young children—especially, in my case, Frank Smith (1988), Jerome Harste (Harste *et al.*, 1984) and Judith Newman (1991). From them I learned that written language must be "meaningful"—that is, as I now understand it, it must be taken, understood, responded to, as a social action—in order for it to be something children want, and need, and are thus enabled, to learn.

I had been aware for some time that second language theorists like Stephen Krashen (1981) and teachers like Anne Freadman (1988) had shown that the best way to learn a language is to use it in real social contexts, for genuine social purposes. And of course in composition studies, "social process" was the dominant catchphrase of the early nineties. Scholars like Karen Burke LeFevre (1987) and James A. Reither (1985; Reither and Vipond, 1989) made it clear that not only composition and revision, but invention itself is profoundly social. Even in literary theory, a dialogic view based on Bakhtin (1986) became increasingly important.

It was the Bakhtinian view of language that helped me to understand that it is the utterance, not the phoneme, the word, the sentence or the text, that is what we need to attend to. The utterance is any instance of language in use, bounded by a change of speakers—one utterance ends, another is a response to it, and still another is a response in turn. The utterance is always created and formed and shaped as a response to a previous utterance or utterances, and it is always created and formed and shaped in anticipation of a responding utterance. Language, Bakhtin told me, is an unending dialogic web of cross-connected utterances and responses, each piece of writing or speaking, each utterance, depending on its occasion and context for its very existence, for its comprehensibility (for an illuminating take on this view of the primacy of context, see Wegerif, this volume).

"As an utterance," Bakhtin says, "(or part of an utterance) no one sentence, even if it has only one word, can ever be repeated: it is always a new utterance (even if it is a quotation)" (*Speech Genres* 108). It is, in other words, an act of meaning. The speaker or writer—and, of course, the hearer or reader—are meaning.

Perhaps equally important has been my introduction to speech-act theory, the set of ideas pioneered by J. L. Austin (*How to Do Things with Words*, 1962) and developed since by many others, for me perhaps most productively by Mary Louise Pratt (1977). The idea that language was not primarily a bundle of facts but a series of intentional acts remains central to my conviction that we should more consistently think of "mean" as a verb.

More recently, my understanding of this process has deepened as I discovered, mostly through the work of Robin Dunbar (1998; see also Leslie, 1987), the extensive literature on what is called in psychology "Theory of Mind." This concept, first introduced in the late seventies by Premack and Woodruff (1978), posits that central to our humanity is our ability to understand the mental states of others around us, to infer their intentions from their actions, and to grasp when they do, and when they don't, share our perceptions of the world. The classic studies which helped us all understand this had to do with discovering that children only developed this ability somewhere around the age of four. They showed that younger children didn't, and older ones did, have the ability to know, for example, that the box they knew to contain not Smarties but pencils, might be thought by someone else to contain Smarties, or to realize that the person who didn't see the object hidden will not know where it is (see, e.g., Gopnik and Astington, 1988). The implications of this for the human ability to mean—to engage in transactions mediated by meaning—seem clear; what is also clear is that it is learned, and can develop and deepen over time (and, as has been frequently noted, can fail to develop, as in various autism-spectrum disorders).

What This Means for Meaning

Once we've accepted that language is at this deep and fundamental level a social process, our notion of what meaning is must change radically. It has been clear for decades that traditional definitions are less than adequate, of course. Michael Reddy (1979), for example, pointed out how, when we use what he termed a "conduit" metaphor for describing language, we are led to think (wrongly) about language as a sluice down which chunks of meaning, like pulp logs, are channeled from sender to receiver, arriving essentially unchanged. Frank Smith (1985) called this the "information-shunting" model. According to that model, meaning isn't particularly problematic: it is just information that is somehow contained in text. Our recurrent use of phrases such as "meaning making" (cf. Wells, 1986, or Potosky, Spaulding and Juzbasich, this volume) runs the risk of falling into a tacit assumption that meaning is a constructed object. Our job as speakers and writers is to get the information into the conduit; as listeners and readers, to get it out.

It's perfectly clear, however, that in at least some cases (were I pushed to the wall, in fact, I would argue that this is virtually always true) the social situation in which a particular syntactic structure is uttered effectively shapes what it means, and does it without much help or interference from the kinds of internal structures that a computer program could apprehend. Information can be shunted from one computer to another, but a computer cannot mean.

If you listen to any naturally occurring oral conversation for more than two or three minutes, you discover that the meanings of the overwhelming majority of oral utterances are in fact determined not so much by their lexical or semantic properties and syntactic structures, but much more powerfully by a sort of unspoken, continuously renegotiated social contract between the participants in the conversation. Rupert Wegerif (this volume) makes this point very thoroughly.

Casual conversational irony, for example, is enabled entirely by theory of mind: if I don't deploy the social resources necessary to presume that you would know that I know, and know I know it, that there's a blizzard in progress, I would simply think you were wrong to say, "Lovely day out there," as you stagger in, covered in ice, or that you were crazy enough to think that it actually was lovely.

"Tell me about it," I might reply.

We both know that you certainly don't mean that it's lovely, and that I'm not asking you to tell me anything at all. How is it that we mean these things to each other? Although we might not all talk the same way about how we have used those sentences to mean, it's clear that we would all share the theory of mind that allows us to make the right sense out of them (most of the time).

Against the background of this rather elaborate argument, let me see if I can now say what I've come to mean by "mean." I think it has a good deal to do with what sociolinguistics has taught us to think of as "point." Most relevant here is the work of Labov (1972) and Polanyi (1979, 1985) on the way conversational stories allow tellers and listeners to share "points." To state the insight I draw from their work as simply as possible: when I recount an incident in a conversation, if you were to attend to what I say as though it were a series of factual assertions to be remembered, you would almost certainly lose the "point" utterly. I mean, but you don't get it.

A Conversational Model of Literate Meaning

There is an extrapolation to be made here, from oral meaning to literate meaning. It is not a truth universally accepted that the kinds of observations of how language works in oral communication (and oral language learning) actually also apply to the more theoretical and distant kind of meaning we make with a pen or keyboard. However, the continuity between oral and written language development is regularly asserted, especially by people working with the development of literacy in young children, and occasionally by others like Bakhtin, who regularly refers to utterances as including everything from a one-word response to a novel, and even occasionally by scholars writing about literature, ranging, for instance, from Pratt (*Toward a Speech-Act Theory of Literary Discourse*, 1977) to Zunshine (*Why We Read Fiction: Theory of Mind and the Novel*, 2006). My own conviction is that to analogize the development and practice of literacy to the development and practice of what Roger Brown (1973) famously called "a first language" is a powerful tool for thinking about literacy learning and practice at a level beyond childhood.

No one would dispute, of course, that there are fundamental differences between language as it exists in oral exchanges and as it exists in writing. The central issue is the extent to which written language functions pragmatically to serve the sorts of intentional social functions that Dunbar and Halliday (and Austin) identify as central to oral discourse, and, equally important, the extent to which the way individual humans develop and extend their linguistic competence is parallel in the two different situations.

One argument for their fundamental difference arises out of the apparent inertness of written language. Unlike talk, it just sits there. And indeed, there are many occasions when it is virtually impossible to see a particular piece of text as bearing, or having the potential to bear, the kind of social intention that is central to this view of meaning as an act.

A helpful way to think about this is to use the distinction Bakhtin draws between "text" and "utterance." He contrasts the set of words and syntactic structures used by someone in a given situation (the text) with what the people in the situation actually use the text for (the utterance). In the case of the example I used earlier, the four words, "Tell me about it," constitute the text: the utterance is a quite different act of meaning in the situation I presented from what it is when I offer the same string of signifiers as an example in this paragraph—and, of course, would be quite different again when the four words occur in a new situation. Combining my term and Bakhtin's distinction, it's possible to say that texts which resist being made into utterances—whether because of the situation, the users, or the string of signifiers themselves—are what I have called "textoids" (Hunt, 1989, 1993).

Examples of language which occur in such circumstances can indeed, I would agree, lack entirely the kind of social meaning I've been describing. One thing that is clearly important about such lack of meaning is that, as I have argued elsewhere (1987, 1989), it makes it much more difficult for us to use to their full potential our powerful language learning abilities and propensities. Just as a child achieves the miraculous learning of language in infancy by using language to participate in the society around her, so older learners can use the same engagement with meaning in the same way. But, ironically, if we are looking for examples of language transactions which are of that peculiar, sterile, meaningless kind, the best possible place to find them is in school and university. I would contend, in fact, that the written language events which occur in educational contexts are virtually all like that.

I should make clear here, by the way, that when I say that such authentically meaning-centered language is hard to find in educational contexts, I am not asserting that education is dominated by empty language exercises, rote learning and memorization, etc. Such educational practices are still extant, of course, but I would argue that even more "enlightened" practices are trapped in this inauthenticity. Particularly distressing examples of this are my own (presumably enlightened) practices as a teacher of English over the first 25 years of my career, and what seem to me to represent some of the best and most imaginative and thoughtful strategies among my professional colleagues. When we examine those assignments and those strategies in the light of this notion of meaning as social event, I think that we discover some challenging truths, and further, that some facts about student reading and writing that we've all known and accepted with a good deal of equanimity for years take on a new urgency.

Teaching Without Meaning

Let me consider an example from my own teaching, one I have recounted elsewhere (Hunt, 1993). Once upon a time I asked an introductory literature class to read the Ernest Hemingway short story "Hills Like White Elephants" and write their own responses to it. This was late in the course, so they'd had time to learn, if they were ever going to, that this was not a test, and that individual and peculiar responses would be valued—or at least would not be "marked down." Covertly, I was hoping to find out how many students knew, before we discussed the story in class, that the "operation" that's the implicit subject of the whole elliptical conversation between the two Americans waiting at a railway station in Spain is an abortion. More overtly, I was trying to help the students use their writing to explore and extend their own understanding of the story before we discussed it in class.

The writing they handed in to me was appalling, of course (not more appalling than usual, naturally, but still of a kind that you'd only ever expect to see in an introductory literature class). What I saw at the time were the incomplete and ungrammatical sentences, the complete lack of transitions, the absence of any sense of direction (or, indeed, of the existence of a reader out there beyond the page), and the highly skilled evasion of the story's central issue. Based on those papers—virtually every one of which amounted to a highly general summary of the discussion between the two characters, and elaborately phrased and entirely abstract value judgments about the artistic merit of the text—I absolutely could not tell whether any of them had constructed a "meaning" for the story that was even remotely related to mine. My own had to do with the impact of the sudden discovery of pregnancy on this carefree, adolescent, Hemingway-style relationship.

I can no longer find that set of papers among my souvenirs, but virtually any English teacher will be able to supply comparable sets from her own experience (the classic description of this experience, of course, is Mina Shaughnessy's (1977) account of the influx of basic writers into her teaching). My conclusion then, and the conclusion most of my colleagues have drawn from similar stacks of papers, was that most of the students couldn't write, and in fact that when you came right down to it they couldn't read either.

It will not come as a surprise that I now think rather differently about that situation. I now think that the problem wasn't a matter of the students' capabilities at all, but something quite different. The situation in which the students were acting was one which virtually guaranteed that both their reading and their writing would be of the kind that I have been describing as meaningless—that is, completely disconnected from any real social occasion or motive, any reason to mean.

First, consider the reading. The students were reading as part of a class assignment. Whatever I might say to them about the assignment (and at the time I didn't say much), they knew that their job with school assignments was to read, decode, store and remember. Most of the texts they had encountered in school, of course, from basal readers to history and science textbooks, were really textoids, that is to say, were treated as such because they were disconnected from any immediate social context. They were not manufactured and created, or distributed, because someone wanted to mean something to a real audience. They were created because certain pieces of information had to be encoded in a language whose rhetorical choices and limitations were determined not by readers and writers, but by readability formulas and the intense scrutiny of banks of editors, consultants, censors and curriculum committees.

But it's also true that even when "real" texts, actively meaning, are encountered in school—stories written by Hemingways, poems written by Frosts or Collinses, even (very rarely) expositions written by John McPhees or Stephen Jay Goulds—they are normally encountered in situations where it's extremely difficult to treat them as anything other than textoids. The possibility that the author, like the person across the table telling a story, might be meaning—might be engaged in sharing values and inviting the reader to construct points—is obliterated by the fact that the story is, in reality, the possession of, and is being offered to the student by, the textbook and the teacher—by the educational institution. It is not being offered by its speaker or author. And it's being offered not as an utterance, but, as Anne Freadman (1988, p. 7) said about any instance of French in French class, "an example" of something, a pretext for a test.

Even more powerfully, the students knew (however cleverly I thought I'd concealed it) that they were being tested. Everyone was, after all, reading the same story—obviously some would understand its "meaning" better than others. Whatever I might say about differences in interpretation being okay had been said to them by many teachers before me—just as sincerely, and just as deceptively. They knew there was a "right answer," a correct "hidden meaning," and, furthermore, they knew that, as always, the teacher was the person who had it. My illusion that I could change a dozen years' worth of hard-learned lessons with a few weeks' exhortations was not only ill-founded, it was also in an important way dishonest: there was a right answer, and I did have it. It involved abortion.

In the terms of the model of reading I described earlier, what we have is a situation in which the text, for the right reader and in the right situation, clearly would have afforded an engaged, pragmatic, dialogic, "real" reading for meaning. But the situation and the reader powerfully pulled for an empty, asocial search for isolated chunks of information. If I were to try to characterize the process of reading as it occurs in such a situation, I might contrast it with what happens in an oral conversation. If the speaker says something incomprehensible, you hold on to it and look (wait actively) for understanding, on the assumption that the speaker is intending something—you impute coherent pragmatic intentions to the speaker. In a situation involving what you are treating as a textoid, however, you make no such assumption and so when something incomprehensible or incongruent is encountered you simply pass it over—or, at best, you try to memorize it for the test.

My first point about that assignment, then, is that—primarily because of the situation—the reading that the students did was virtually guaranteed not to have meaning at its center. It is a rare student who in such a situation can read the story as though it might have some purchase on her, as though it were being told to her by someone who had a reason for telling it and to whom it was possible to impute normal human intentions, someone who was meaning. Such a student would be one with a highly developed ability to ignore the real situation in favor of a fictional one, a student with what I've come to call a powerful pragmatic imagination. Another way to describe such a student is to say that she's already a reader. Still another thing one might say about her is that she doesn't need much help from a teacher.

Now, let's think about writing in that situation. My second concern has to do with the potential role meaning might play in the writing the students did on the basis of this reading. What was it possible for them to mean in what they wrote in that situation? With whom could they have been trying to make contact, and what values, structures of knowledge, judgments of importance and patterns of expectation could they have been trying to share? From their point of view, they could hardly expect to have anything to mean—something that would serve their immediate social purposes—about the story. Having something to say is not easily distinguishable from having someone to say it to, and in the view of those students—even after a few months' evidence of ignorance and incompetence on my part—I already knew everything there was to know about stories. I was, after all, the teacher.

I could tell them—I probably did tell them—to write not as though to me but as though to a general reader; I might even have specified a general reader who had already read the story (to avoid long, pointless summaries). But the ability to engage such a mythical rhetorical reader in the active process of composition is a rare one. It requires the writer to use that imaginary figure to decide, for instance, in specific instances—moments where, to use James Britton's phrase (Britton *et al.*, 1975), the language is being shaped at the point of utterance—precisely how much reference to the events of the story is necessary for that reader, and what inferences that reader can be called upon to make. It calls on her to decide which ideas can be backgrounded, or treated as "given," and which need to be fore-grounded and treated as "new" (as Clark and Haviland, 1977, described the nec-essary components of an authentic social exchange).

To synthesize such an audience requires the kind of powerful pragmatic imag-ination that a very few students—the readers and the writers—have managed miraculously to attain. Very few of my students—then or now—have it. It's hard to imagine where they might have acquired it, other than in the sort of uncom-mon home where—as Gordon Wells (1986) demonstrated so clearly—attitudes toward books and language create writers and readers.

A resource which a skilled writer often turns to in such a situation is her knowledge of how writing of the kind she's trying to produce sounds, or looks. Rather than using the real situation to generate purposes and readers, she uses as a model the strategies by which this kind of audience have, to use Ede and Lunsford's (1984) useful term, been "invoked" by other, similar texts. But my students had never in their lives read anything like what I was asking them to write—like, that is, the sort of thing teachers had increasingly been asking them to write throughout their school careers. No wonder they didn't produce such great texts—and no wonder they didn't learn very much that was of use to them from the exercise. Everything about the situation virtually forced them to treat the text they were reading as a textoid, and to produce textoids in response to my assignment. For them, an occasion to mean, in the sense of to engage socially, or to share structures of evaluation and understanding, or "point," was just about entirely absent from the situation. They didn't read to see what someone meant, or write to mean. Nor, not at all incidentally, did I read what they wrote as though I thought they were meaning: I read it to assess what they knew and their ability to write—a completely different matter.

It is not, of course, true that written language is usually divorced from this kind of immediate pragmatic meaning. It is, I contend, the peculiar situation of lan-guage in the school situation that divorces it from meaning and renders it a simu-lation of meaning, an example of English. In the last few years, in fact, students encounter many examples of written language which are not radically divorced from immediate pragmatic situations. Forms like text messages, email, Facebook postings and tweets, have given students experience with written language that has the possibility to mean, immediately, to another human being.

If it is true that there are profound and fundamental differences between the processes of reading and writing when conducted as empty simulation exercises and when conducted for meaning (as I am defining it), then it seems to me that much of the adventurous and exciting theoretical and practical work in composi-tion and in the teaching of literature, and the use of writing in other disciplines, may be pretty much beside the point. Separated from the act of meaning, language itself tends to become an empty, pointless exercise.

Why is this a problem? After all, surviving university does demand that one develop the skill of processing and retaining information from text, and there have been scores of studies aimed at finding ways of helping students get even better at this. What's wrong with it?

I've spent much of my career looking at this problem, watching students failing, for example, to understand the ironic stances in many of the writers I ask them to read in my literature classes and wondering why it was that when Jonathan Swift's earnest accountant proposes using roast baby to address Ireland's famine and overpopulation problems, or when Robert Browning's Duke explains how, well, unsatisfactory his last Duchess was, students rarely find the irony delightful. More commonly, they're shocked at the idea of roast yearling child served up at a christening, or want to know where Ferrara is, whether Klaus of Innsbruck actually existed, and whether this is going to be on the exam.

In the absence of pragmatic context and intention, reading tends to become a passive act of decoding and storage, and interpretation and response tend to wander into an endless maze of free association and unfettered fantasy. "Analysis of literature" in English classes is often this sort of exercise. More pervasively, the creation of term and research papers becomes, especially since students are awash in online text, at best what Rebecca Moore Howard (1999) has called "patchwriting," in which students assemble (with or without attribution) pre-existing chunks of text.

When students read, and write, in the unmeaning ways afforded by the situation they're in, the ideas and arguments are not attached to each other in strings of socially embedded acts of meaning: they are isolated gobbets of data, infochunks to be warehoused as carefully as possible—and which rarely survive the date of the examination, because they're attached to nothing else in the warehouse.

Unless meaning is at the center, none of the conventional language-based activities is likely to provide much opportunity for learning how to handle language when meaning is at the center. Even more seriously, I think, the predominance of these kinds of activities in educational institutions tends to inculcate one lesson very powerfully: written language, especially in academic settings (which should, I think, be seen as the peculiar case, rather than Odell's writing "in non-academic settings"), does not mean.

Indeed, it seems obvious that in other circumstances, involving engaged social actors with active intentions, and who have active, flexible, theories about the minds of others, written language affords being used as a tool with which to mean. We can, and regularly do, mean in writing as we mean in speaking.

Alternatives

The obvious question to be raised at this point is whether there are any genuine, practical alternatives to the present situation. Are there ways, within the limits set by the institutional contexts teachers work in, to create situations in which student reading and writing is, in these terms, meaningful? If there is no alternative, what I'm arguing might be a theoretically interesting viewpoint, but would in practice amount to little more than a depressing and self-indulgent orgy of woe-crying and nay-saying.

Having said all that, I don't imagine it will be a surprise to discover that I believe there are alternatives. The ones I know most about are the ones occurring among some of my colleagues at St. Thomas, and it may be helpful here to describe a couple of specific examples of alternative ways of structuring learning, ways that hold, I think, real promise for addressing some of the problems I've been describing, for putting meaning, as a verb, at the center of the learning process.

The basic strategy entails creating situations in which student writing is read not by an approving or disapproving authority, but by someone who needs to know what the writer has to say, is open to being persuaded, enlightened, informed or amused by the writer's meaning, and whom the writer knows to be open to these effects.

One context which affords such writing and reading we call "Collaborative Investigation." In general, it entails creating a situation in which the class organize themselves into teams to cooperatively investigate some specific topic, using writing as the fundamental tool for that organizing, that investigating, and that cooperation. Here is one example of how that works in practice. I'm going to describe it as concretely as I can in the hope that specifying some of the ways in which the reading and writing is done in a situation which makes them rather different from more conventional models will suggest other alternatives in different disciplinary contexts.

I regularly require my introductory literature class to attend plays on campus or at the local professional theater during the year. One year not long after I'd started trying to develop ways to center my courses on meaning, I suggested (after we'd conducted for our own information a couple of collaborative investigations of productions we were going to see) that we prepare what we wound up calling a "Playgoer's Guide" to an upcoming professional production of Lillian Hellman's *The Little Foxes*. We began by getting hold of copies of the play and reading it. We didn't order 29 copies of a text; we shared library copies. We even shared the reading—by having groups read (and describe to each other) different parts of the play. We then generated questions about the play, Hellman, and the production. In this case, we did this by asking everyone to write down as many questions as they could in fifteen or twenty minutes; the class then formed into groups to read each other's questions and select a few to write on the blackboard. Then we edited and selected among those, and set up ad hoc groups to go to the library and find out what they could about particular questions—regarding, for instance, Hellman's life, the composition of the play, its historical background, its previous productions, and so forth. (Today, of course, much of this activity is conducted online.)

Each group prepared a short, concrete report (sometimes these took the form of a set of separate, individual reports; in other cases they were researched and written in collaboration). Each of these reports was photocopied and in class the next week each of a new set of groups received a sheaf of documents which included a copy of each of those first reports. They read and discussed them, and generated a new set of questions. Again these were written on the board, edited and discussed, and assigned to groups, which took the relevant reports, with their lists of references, and went back to the library to prepare further additional or elaborative reports.

The second round of reports were also distributed and read. We spent part of a class session arriving at a consensus as to what should go in the final handbook, and set up groups to combine various reports into sections of the handbook. These sections were finally edited by other groups, and then given to a secretary (me, as it happened) to be keyed into a computer file, laid out, and printed. The final handbooks were distributed in multiple copies to the class and left around the university a day or so before the play opened—they were, I might add, snatched up more rapidly than I could photocopy them, and a number of my students reported instances of being thanked for their work by people they hardly knew, who'd picked up copies somewhere. Since that time I often negotiate with companies to have the documents distributed with their own programs.

It may be important to point out that I was not the first or only or final reader of any piece of writing produced in this process; I did not mark, comment on or edit any piece of writing (except that because I was secretary I copy-edited and ran a spell checker on the final copy). There were no papers which were essays on, or interpretations or analyses of, the play. And it is certainly important to make clear that the document that was finally produced was far from wonderful—it's scrappy, sometimes superficial and in at least one case erroneous. But—like the texts produced on the way to it—it served an actual social function. It meant. And it was obvious to everyone involved that without the social interaction structured by all those intermediate texts, it would have been impossible to accomplish the final task or learn what we learned about Hellman and her play. Perhaps more important, in every case rhetorical decisions were made, at the point of utterance, in the light of obvious, real demands: the writers knew, or learned as they went, who would be reading this, and how much they knew—and even, to some extent, how they felt about it.

There are a variety of other ways in which the reading and writing that students do in connection with their learning can be made more obviously and practically functional, more clearly something written and read in order to mean rather than in order to demonstrate competence or exercise rhetorical skills. I have described a range of them elsewhere (e.g., Hunt, 1996, 2001).

One of the unmixed advantages of the advent of the age of the internet is that sharing student writing, and affording authentic responses to it, is far more convenient than in the days of photocopying and printing, though obviously there remain situations in which publication of hard copy works in a way that electronic media cannot.

What is most important is that such strategies are not difficult to come up with, once one has embraced the basic notion—that the way to create a context in which students are writing and reading for meaning is to put the writing and reading into situations where they serve purposes which the students can see as real and which they can adopt as their own. Where they can mean. The danger, of course, is that once you've embraced that notion, there isn't any going back: the changes and the discoveries acquire their own momentum. You get hooked.

In the age of the internet, of course, there are no more phone booths in which superheroes can change from their secret identity. Perhaps it's time for meaning to come out of the closet altogether.

References

Austin, J. L. (1962) *How to Do Things with Words: The William James Lectures Delivered at Harvard University in 1955*. (Ed. by J. O. Urmson). Oxford: Clarendon Press.

Bakhtin, M. M. (1986) *Speech Genres and Other Late Essays*. (Trans. by Vern W. McGee. Ed. by Caryl Emerson and Michael Holquist). Austin, TX: University of Texas Press.

Britton, J., Burgess, T., Martin, N., McLeod, A. and Rosen, H. (1975) *The Development of Writing Abilities (11–18)*. London: Macmillan.

Brown, R. (1973) *A First Language: The Early Stages*. Cambridge, MA: Harvard University Press.

Bruner, J. C. (1983) *Child's Talk*. New York: Norton.

Clark, H. H. and Haviland, S. E. (1977) "Comprehension and the given-new contract." *Discourse Production and Comprehension. Discourse Processes: Advances in Research and Theory in Discourse Production and Comprehension. Discourse Processes: Advances in Research and Theory* 1: 1–40.

Dunbar, R. I. M. (1996) *Grooming, Gossip, and the Evolution of Language*. Cambridge, MA: Harvard University Press.

Dunbar, R. I. M. (1998) "Theory of mind and the evolution of language." In J. R. Hurford, M. Studdert-Kennedy and C. Knight (Eds), *Approaches to the Evolution of Language: Social and Cognitive Bases*. Cambridge, MA: Cambridge University Press.

Ede, L. and Lunsford, A. (1984) "Audience addressed/audience invoked: The role of audience in composition theory and pedagogy." *College Composition and Communication* 35: 155–171.

Freadman, A. (1988) "'Genre' and the reading class." *Typereader: The Journal of the Centre for Studies in Literary Education* 1: 1–7.

Gopnik, A. and Astington, J. W. (1988) "Children's understanding of representational change and its relation to the understanding of false belief and the appearance-reality distinction." *Child Development* 59: 26–37.

Halliday, M. A. K. (1975) *Learning How to Mean: Explorations in the Development of Language*. London: Elsevier North-Holland.

Harste, J. C., Woodward, V. A. and Burke, C. L. (1984) *Language Stories and Literacy Lessons*. Portsmouth, NH: Heinemann.

Howard, R. M. (1999) *Standing in the Shadow of Giants: Plagiarists, Authors, Collaborators.* Stamford, CT: Ablex.

Hunt, R. A. (1987) "'Could you put in lots of holes?' Modes of response to writing." *Language Arts* 64(2): 229–232.

Hunt, R. A. (1989) "A horse named Hans, a boy named Shawn: the Herr von Osten theory of response to writing." In C. M. Anson (Ed.), *Writing and Response: Theory, Practice, and Research* (pp. 80–100). Champaign-Urbana: National Council of Teachers of English.

Hunt, R. A. (1993) "Texts, textoids and utterances: Writing and reading for meaning, in and out of classrooms." In S. B. Straw and D. Bogdan (Eds), *Constructive Reading: Teaching Beyond Communication* (pp. 113–129). Portsmouth, NH: Heinemann-Boynton/Cook.

Hunt, R. A. (1996) "Some strategies for embedding writing in dialogic situations." *The Point: The Newsletter of SCENT–UPEI's Senate Committee on the Enhancement of Teaching* 5(1): 3–4.

Hunt, R. A. (2001) "Making student writing count: The experience of 'from the page to the stage.'" In G. Tucker and D. Nevo (Eds), *Atlantic Universities' Teaching Showcase 2001: Proceedings.* Halifax, Canada: Mount St. Vincent University.

Kaye, K. (1982) *The Mental and Social Life of Babies: How Parents Create Persons.* Chicago, IL: University of Chicago Press.

Kaye, K. and Charney, R. (1980) "How mothers maintain 'dialogue' with two-year-olds." In D. R. Olson (Ed.), *The Social Foundations of Language and Thought: Essays in Honor of Jerome S. Bruner* (pp. 211–230). New York: Norton.

Krashen, S. D. (1981) *Second Language Acquisition and Second Language Learning.* Oxford: Pergamon.

Labov, W. (1972) *Language in the Inner City: Studies in the Black English Vernacular.* Philadelphia, PA: University of Pennsylvania Press.

LeFevre, K. B. (1987) *Invention as a Social Act.* Carbondale, IL: Southern Illinois University Press.

Leslie, A. M. (1987) "Pretense and representation: The origins of 'theory of mind.'" *Psychological Review* 94(4): 412–426.

Newman, J. M. (1991) *Interwoven Conversations: Teaching and Learning Through Critical Reflection.* Toronto: OISE Press; Portsmouth, NH: Heinemann.

Odell, L. (1985) "Beyond the text: Relations between writing and the social context." In L. Odell and D. Goswami (Eds), *Writing in Nonacademic Settings.* New York: Guilford.

Odell, L. and Goswami, D. (1982) "Writing in a non-academic setting." *Research in the Teaching of English* 16(3): 201–224.

Polanyi, L. (1979) "So what's the point?" *Semiotica* 25(3/4): 207–241.

Polanyi, L. (1985) *Telling the American Story: A Structural and Cultural Analysis of Conversational Storytelling.* Norwood, NJ: Ablex.

Pratt, Mary Louise (1977) *Toward a Speech-Act Theory of Literary Discourse.* Bloomington, IN: Indiana University Press.

Premack, D. G. and Woodruff, G. (1978) "Does the chimpanzee have a theory of mind?" *Behavioral and Brain Sciences* 1: 515–526.

Reddy, M. J. (1979) "The conduit metaphor—A case of frame conflict in our language about language." In A. Ortony (Ed.), *Metaphor and Thought* (pp. [284]–324). Cambridge: Cambridge University Press.

Reither, J. A. (1985) "Writing and knowing: Toward redefining the writing process." *College English* 47(6): 620–628.

Reither, J. A. and Vipond., D. (1989) "Writing as Collaboration." *College English* 51(8): 855–867.

Shaughnessy, M. P. (1977) *Errors and Expectations: A Guide for the Teacher of Basic Writing.* New York: Oxford University Press.

Smith, F. (1985) "A metaphor for literacy: Creating worlds or shunting information?" In D. R. Olson, N. Torrance and A. Hildyard (Eds), *Literacy, Language, and Learning: The Nature and Consequences of Reading and Writing* (pp. 195–213). Cambridge: Cambridge University Press.

Smith, F. (1988) *Joining the Literacy Club: Further Essays into Education.* Portsmouth, NH: Heinemann.

Vygotsky, L. S. (1978) *Mind in Society: The Development of Higher Psychological Processes.* (Ed. by M. Cole, V. John-Steiner, S. Scribner and E. Souberman). Cambridge, MA: Harvard University Press.

Wells, G. (1986) *The Meaning Makers: Children Learning Language and Using Language to Learn.* Portsmouth, NH: Heinemann.

Wertsch, J. V. (1983) "The role of semiosis in L. S. Vygotsky's theory of human cognition." In B. Bain (Ed.), *Sociogenesis of Language and Human Conduct* (pp. 17–31). New York: Plenum.

Wertsch, J. V. (1986) *Vygotsky and the Social Formation of Mind.* Cambridge, MA: Harvard University Press.

Zunshine, L. (2006) *Why We Read Fiction: Theory of Mind and the Novel.* Columbus, OH: The Ohio State University Press.

10

HOW TO ENHANCE MEANING-CENTERED WRITING AND READING

Anne Ellen Geller

> I only wrote three major papers for [one course], none of them come to mind as "valuable" considering I only did them to get it out of the way.

> I only had to write simple journal responses (no revision necessary) and lab reports. I can't really imagine any writing assignments that were particularly valuable.

> In Personal Values we took our newly found philosophical understanding and debate skills to establish arguments about issues we are passionate about and thoroughly defend their validity. We learned by researching our topic, thinking analytically, and using new found skills.

> The final paper in Are We Modern Yet? asked us to present the arguments of the modernists and postmodernists and take a position. It really helped me to finally understand what the postmodernist argument was and had a great impact upon my worldview.

As the first two of the opening four quotes reveal, students sometimes complete courses feeling as if they "only" did what was required of them in writing and describe finding little value or meaning in their course-based writing and reading. But meaning-centered writing and reading tasks can affect students' growing sense of who they have been, who they are, or who they will be (Carroll, 2002; Herrington and Curtis, 2000; Hilgers *et al.*, 1999; Kells, 2007; Thaiss and Zawacki, 2006). And by interrogating more deeply when and why and how some students, like the authors of the second two quotes above, have found value and meaning in the required work they do for classes, there is much we can learn about how to provide more meaningful reading and writing opportunities for all students.

We tend to measure the value of reading and writing assignments by the degree to which these assignments help students meet course goals and outcomes.

In classes focused on transmitting disciplinary content, we assign reading and writing to help students learn, understand, and retain information, concepts and theories. In courses more focused on skills—writing courses or discipline-based methods courses, for example—our goals and outcomes may also have to do with what students can show us in writing about how they make use of the approaches and methods we have asked them to practice. Perhaps less transparent is that these reading and writing tasks are also *disciplinary*, examples of knowledge production and communication "owned" by particular disciplines and often described as "disciplinary genres" (Swales, 1990). Faculty may also prioritize writing for active learning and inquiry, utilizing an array of informal writing assignments to engage students in inquiry and reflection (see Bean, 2011).

If we need confirmation we should value writing in meaning-centered teaching and learning, we need only turn to the research that has shown students are invested in classes where they write on a regular basis. Take, for example, Richard Light's (2001, p. 55) oft-quoted finding from *Making the Most of College*:

> The relationship between the amount of writing for a course and students' level of engagement—whether engagement is measured by time spent on the course, or the intellectual challenge it presents, or students' level of interest in it—is stronger than the relationship between students' engagement and any other course characteristic.

Or consider Lee Ann Carroll (2002), who finds in a longitudinal study reported in *Rehearsing New Roles: How College Students Develop as Writers*: "Writing that brings together academic learning and 'hands-on' experience seemed to rate especially highly with students" (p. 58). Carroll also notes that in terms of "literacy development, these experiences expand students' knowledge base, offer new environments and roles to play, and bring together academic and personal learning" (p. 60). Also, although Arum and Roska (2011) have been critiqued for focusing on the number of pages students read and write, and for using the CLA test as a measure of student learning, their recent and much discussed *Academically Adrift: Limited Learning on College Campuses* claims: "When students are asked to read and write in their courses, when academic coursework is challenging, and when higher-order thinking is included in the coursework, students perform better on tests measuring skills such as critical thinking and writing" (p. 93).

The data for this chapter come from a pilot study[1] conducted in the spring of 2004 at a small private liberal arts university in the northeast United States. The institution calls itself "increasingly selective" in its 2011 common data set, but according to the National Center for Education Statistics (www.nces.ed.gov) accepted 68 percent of its applicants for fall 2011. In this study, first-year students (78 percent of whom went on to graduate in six years) were invited to complete a web-based survey at the end of their second semester. The survey's 13 short-answer questions prompted students to reflect on their experiences reading and writing during their first year (see appendix for the questions). The 64 responses received represent approximately 12 percent of the first-year class (about 2,200–2,300 enrolled undergraduates).[2] I have taken a grounded theory approach (Strauss and Corbin, 1998, p. 12) to analyzing and making sense of the survey responses, using open coding to develop categories that lead to theory building (Strauss and Corbin, 1998, pp. 101–121). I read and re-read the survey data searching for reoccurring patterns in student responses. I collected these patterns, grouped them with codes, and then cross-checked my sense of these patterns and codes with re-readings of the survey data. I completed one round of analysis in 2004 and 2005 and captured that analysis by writing research memos and drafting profiles of selected individual students in the study. I returned to the data in 2011, again re-reading the survey responses and writing memos about patterns and codes I saw in the responses. Both rounds of analysis pointed to the existence of some shared experiences among the 64 students.

While I refer to students' answers to many of the survey's questions throughout this chapter, I focus primarily on the themes that emerged from patterns in the responses to question four on the survey, which read: "Describe a writing assignment from this year that seemed valuable to you. Why do you feel this writing assignment was valuable? (Be specific.)" In this study, the short survey responses seldom provide extended explanation of the courses students took, their professors' teaching methods, the students' writing processes or the particulars of assignments. But even though students' descriptions of their writing and reading experiences are brief, these descriptions provide information about when and why students had derived some meaning from their writing and reading.

In this study, one assignment—Causes and Consequences of the Iraq War—stands out because eight different students cited it as the most valuable assignment they did in their first year of college, and all eight students describe the meaning they found in the project. There may be quite mundane reasons so many students chose Causes and Consequences of the Iraq War as their most valuable assignment. For example, the course in which students wrote the assignment had a large enrollment and serves as a required gateway course for the interdisciplinary undergraduate program in international studies. These first-year students had graduated high school in the spring of 2003 when Iraq was invaded. They had watched through the 2003–2004 academic year as the war evolved, so the topic was also particularly relevant. But analysis of the comments the eight students offered about this assignment reveals students understood how this writing assignment required them to make meaning of their lives and the times they were living in using scholarly lenses and stances, and thus the writing project also led them to both interrogate and strengthen the beliefs they brought into the course with them.[3]

In what follows, I discuss students' experience of Causes and Consequences of the Iraq War as the primary data source. I also include student reflections on a variety of other assignments cited as valuable. These additional reflections reveal students found meaning in assignments that allowed them to experience something new through writing and assignments that allowed them to combine their own experiences, interests, and/or passions with academic ideas—something they often term "the personal."

Finding Value and Meaning in Required Coursework in the First Year of College

Because this study was designed to account only for students' descriptions of—and reflections on—their reading and writing in their first year of college, I didn't ask students to contribute the actual assignments their professors provided. But I do believe that it is possible to piece together the requirements and expectations of the Causes and Consequences of the Iraq War assignment through students' descriptions of their experiences of researching and writing the project. And these requirements and expectations are shaped by notions of what writing and reading need to do in this task—be a means of researching and exploring the topic, of writing a final draft, and of connecting students' personal beliefs to larger public beliefs.

All of the students who offered Causes and Consequences of the Iraq War as their most valuable assignment acknowledged in some way that they had to, as one student wrote, "gather and analyze a lot of information about current politics" and all said the assignment had informed or affected their thinking about the conflict because, as one student wrote, it "demanded that we pay attention not only to history and what we learned in class but also to current events" to end up with "a very clear and supported opinion about the war." One student's explanation of the assignment was "we could claim any cause we wanted to as long as it was researched and we had evidence supporting our claim." And another of the eight students wrote: "I had not been very politically conscious, but that class allowed me to learn about what was going on in our world." In this way, required work for a class gave her an opportunity—and the encouragement and support she needed—to reflect on the world outside the classroom. From the descriptions students offered of the assignment it is also clear that students had chances to hear one another's opinions ("It was also interesting seeing other students' opinions on the matter"), were stretched as communicators ("It gave me a chance to express my opinion and also evaluate myself on the ability to persuade a large group of people") and learned to integrate challenging texts they had never before read into their own thinking and writing ("Writing it exposed me to a whole bunch of new ideas, which made me stoked. In particular Immanuel Wallerstein's take on it about US hegemony"). In other words, as one student summed up the experience: "Not only did it improve my research and writing skills but also furthered my knowledge of a very important current event."

What students experienced researching, developing and writing Causes and Consequences of the Iraq War was just the type of learning researchers like Marcia Baxter-Magolda propose leads to students' self-authorship, "a shift from uncritical acceptance of external authority to critical analysis of authority to establish one's own internal authority . . . the capacity to define one's beliefs, identity and social relations (Baxter Magolda 2001; Kegan 1994)" (Hodge *et al.*, 2009, p. 16; see also Lee's discussion of Baxter Magolda in this volume). Throughout the students' descriptions of writing Causes and Consequences of the Iraq War is language that hints at how this process worked on two levels—what was non-negotiable and negotiable about the project within the stated goals of the course and how those goals led to students' ownership of their own view of the war. The students use verbs like "forced," "demanded," and "required" to explain the expectations for collection of research ("forced me to gather and analyze a lot of information about current politics" and "required me to do research which showed me aspects I had never considered before"). But in their responses, they also often link what they were required or forced to do with what they were "allowed" and encouraged to do—"the assignment required me to go through the many different causes and decide which were the most influential in the start of the war" or "the encourage-ment to form your own thoughts backed by well researched information." These first-year students thus completed the assignment aware of the degree to which they were developing an informed and personal view on something of importance, in a sense a personal view that becomes a public view because of their engagement with the task: "This was valuable because it forced me to gather and analyze a lot of information about current politics which I would have been too lazy to do on my own. Now I have a very clear and supported opinion about the war."

Causes and Consequences of the Iraq War required students to practice new and exciting ways of weighing and presenting information to explain their beliefs about world events to themselves and to others. As Virginia Lee points out in this volume, a reading, researching and writing project like this one prioritizes independent inquiry that can "help students see the connections between the abilities they are developing in their communities of inquiry at the university and the broader societies they will inhabit following graduation" (p. 163). And Causes and Consequences of the Iraq War was not the only assignment that combined independent inquiry with course learning. For example, one student offered a description of a research paper for an AIDS in Africa class "on any topic pertain-ing to the pandemic that we had not covered extensively in class" and said "I appreciated this assignment because it gave opportunity to do outside research and apply the knowledge we had picked up in class to our own findings."

Learning to Do Something New In or Through Writing

The Causes and Consequences of the Iraq War writer who said that the project gave her "practice writing concisely and a way to really learn and process infor-mation that is applicable to my life" and the student who was "stoked" about Immanuel Wallerstein and felt the project "exposed" him to "a whole bunch of new ideas" are examples of the way students described learning to do something new in/through writing. Even students who did not identify an assignment as valuable because of the act of writing it added, as a part of the response, that the assignment was also valuable because of what it taught them about writing or because of what they experienced as they wrote it. In those responses students used phrases like these: the writing "took me out of my comfort zone," the writing "forced us to look outside the box," the writing "made me analyze our perception of the world, challenging me to think about things that we normally just accept and take for granted."

When students found they were novices at the writing they were asked to do, they felt discomfort but still noted the experience as valuable. One student said even though the valuable assignment—a 25-page paper—was "very stressful it helped me build a lot of confidence in my ability," and one noted that in the project she named valuable she "had accomplished more than in most other papers." Another student offered this experience: "I wrote what I thought was a decent paper. Through the revision process and my meetings with the professor I was forced to think about the organizing of my writing in a way that was much more critical, gave attention to developing the idea, and the overall flow." A third student offered "It was the hardest paper I have ever had to write . . . Because of the difficult content, the in-depth analysis required, and the length, the paper was worth writing." Sometimes the learning (and satisfaction) came from writing a new genre. A student named a book review as her most valuable writing assignment and said, "since I had never written one before, completing this paper was a great learning experience." Writing in new genres, with a new size or scope of writing project, and with new processes were all cited as meaningful experiences.

Some students described their valuable experiences more cumulatively. One said "I had to put all my previous knowledge of paper writing into this specific paper," but it was "the most thoughtful piece of work I have done." And a student who had to write two to three pages in Spanish analyzing a book read in Spanish said the assignment was "absolutely the most valuable writing I had to do because not only did it challenge me to think in Spanish, but it forced me to use all the grammar skills I had learned over the years" and with excitement present even in her survey answer, she added "Now I have the ability to not only speak the language with confidence, but to read it, understand it and write it." Sometimes time spent within a discipline and a disciplinary assignment led to students feeling they had more expertise: "My final essay for Mexican cinema was extremely valuable as a cumulative assessment of my understanding of cinematography and Mexican culture; it also allowed me to be much more independent in my interpretations and overall understanding of a film."

If many students saw what they could do in writing, others were disillusioned by a lack of challenge. As one disappointed student wrote of his experiences in his first year of college: "I had hoped that I would be expected to write something a little more difficult. I have had papers assigned that I was able to write in about an hour before the class and still get a good grade." In contrast, he did note an assignment he found valuable because it was "the only paper that I actually had to research and write over and over again."

Connections to the "Personal"

As I noted earlier, in writing Causes and Consequences of the Iraq War some students found themselves more personally invested or interested in the topic than they might have realized they would become, and that is obviously because the "topic" was not restrictive even as it was limiting. Students had to work toward an individual opinion about the causes and consequences of the war, but it was clear to them that there were many documentable stances that could be developed from examining evidence. As one student writer noted of the assignment: "This was helpful to me personally because I was becoming more informed." And this was not the only assignment reported in the study that positioned students' thinking in relation to well-established arguments. The directive to carefully take on someone else's thinking was replicated in a challenging philosophy assignment another student noted as valuable. He was "required to create an argument . . . against modern philosophers" and said the assignment was "difficult since [he] had to search for holes in the philosophers' arguments" and the philosophers "made sure that most counter arguments could not be made against them."

Over and over again, students described valuable assignments using the word "personal." "Personal" was often clarified as having the opportunity to "write about a topic I felt passionately about," or writing about "real life topics or things I was interested in," or finding that along with research there was "room to put my own input in." When students felt this way about assignments they were "into writing it more." As one student offered: "I like to talk about things that I have an interest in instead of an assigned topic. I think it makes me work harder on it and put more effort into the paper." Students also connected "personal" to writing assignments that offered both choice and support and led to a feeling of accomplishment. As one student described a poetry portfolio she submitted in response to a philosophy assignment: "The choice and freedom allowed me in that assignment promoted a really thought out project . . . I was completely able to do what I wanted, while I still had direction in my assignment. I never felt lost or reckless."

As I've described elsewhere when students say they find an academic task "personal," it may be that they "feel more engaged in the work at hand and with one another" (Geller and Cantelmo, 2011, p. 218), and this was certainly true for some students in this study who felt individual investment in a writing project and individual learning as well as the power of the classroom community as support and/or audience. For example, a student in an acting class was asked "to write a monologue about a situation where you wished you had said something, but you did not, in fact, say it." The assignment was valuable, she said, because "it gave me a way to express my anger over something I thought I was through being bitter about, yet came to realize that it was still affecting me negatively. It forced me to do some self-reflection and to think about anger and forgiveness." Added to that, however, she said: "The best part was when each student shared his/her piece with the class . . . everyone has deeper layers under the surface."[4] Another student described being asked to "write about an example of activism . . . to choose an active group exercising activism and to discuss hardships they encounter as a result of global social pressures." She was asked to include her "own opinion on activism in general" as well, and she reported that the value in the assignment came from "the opportunity to explore a topic that is interesting to me (environmentalism) and to share my interest with the class and my professor. It also gave me the opportunity to find out more about the struggles environmental activists encounter."

Assignments that helped students find ways to use the material of a course to interrogate personal experiences, and, in the process, learn more about both course content and themselves were also powerful. In a striking example, a student cited an assignment for a course on the African Environment in which she wrote "about the war in Liberia and the chain of events that led to it." She said "I enjoyed this because I got the opportunity to learn more about my parents' native country." Though a longitudinal study of four students Herrington and Curtis (2000) found that "without explicit or implicit invitation from teachers to let their voices be heard from within their written forms, [students] disengaged from tasks as well as texts, writing less or less coherently and learning less in the process" (p. 361). Meaning-centered writing experiences should value students' voices and experiences, inquiry, dialogue, research and reflection. (See Lee in this volume for more on creating the teaching and learning contexts for such writing experiences.)

So Little Reading and Writing, So Little Value and Meaning

As the opening quotes to this chapter reveal, this survey also reminds us that some college students, even at this institution where classes tend to be small and are taught by full-time faculty, do little writing during their first year of college. So, although it seems almost too obvious to note, when students have few opportunities to write for courses they end up feeling as if they have done little valuable or meaningful writing.

In this survey, and from my own experience of talking with undergraduates about their writing across the curriculum, I hear the sarcasm and disappointment students express when their expectations of writing in college are not fulfilled. As one student, who reported keeping a journal outside of school, wrote in his survey response: "I wrote so little that I am having trouble even filling out this survey." Another student offered: "I had to write more in high school, so I expected more writing in college." And a third described three papers for an English class as her only writing in her first year of college and commented that "none of them come to mind as 'valuable' considering I only did them to get it out of the way." These writing experiences—or lack thereof—are especially troubling in comparison to the experiences described by students who found value and meaning in the writing they did in their first year of college. And these comments have a very different tone than those students who wrote to tell of writing they valued and were proud to have completed.

Students describe their reading experiences in similar ways. Most students in this study were challenged by the reading they did for their courses. Ten of the 64 students who responded to the survey cited their surprise at the volume of reading required for college courses and six noted the newness and difficulty of the texts they had to read in college ("getting used to the academic language has been my greatest trial"), but students found meaning in learning to manage the volume of reading and learning how to work to make sense of the required reading ("I have to engage my mind to understand a lot of it" and "one has to analyze and draw conclusions from the material. That was a skill that needed practice"). However, a few students reported they had learned they didn't "have to do a whole lot of" reading and said that for some classes the reading "is not as necessary as it is made out to be." When reading, like writing, was something students did to "get it out of the way," they didn't find value or meaning in the work. Many chapters in this volume describe the conditions that encourage and support meaning-centered education, and in such contexts learners must also be invited to write (and read) in meaning-centered ways. In other words, an inquiry-based, dialogic course striving to educate meaningfully should do more than ask students to read texts that are then summarized by a teacher and fed back to them on lecture slides and should do more than require students to write reflections that receive only a check in the teacher's log and are returned with no comments or questions from an interlocutor.

Teaching Practices Leading to Meaning-Centered Writing and Reading Assignments

If we listen to the 64 students of this small study, we can learn quite a bit about how to build meaningful reading and writing experiences for our students. With attentiveness to assignment design (see John Bean's *Engaging Ideas: The Professor's Guide to Integrating Writing, Critical Thinking, and Active Learning in the Classroom* and Christopher Thaiss and Terry Myers Zawacki's *Engaged Writers/Dynamic Disciplines*), faculty across the disciplines can be more explicit not just about what they are asking writers to do in assignments but also why they are asking writers to read, research and write as they are. To utilize these more explicit expectations and instructions (for example, be sure to note both causes and consequences of the Iraq War, write in the genre of a book review, search for holes in the philosophers' arguments), faculty may feel they are learning a whole new approach and vocabulary, but as Bean and Thaiss and Zawacki show, faculty value more than they express in a simple assignment like "write a paper" or "write an essay." And assignments with more explicit guidelines turn out to be simultaneously more connected to course content and disciplinary values and more open for students to imbue with their own experiences, interests and passions.

Working through stages of writing for and with students (as opposed to just assigning a paper and having one due date) is also a practice that leads to meaningful writing experiences for students in part because it allows for dialogue between teachers and learners, and a significant number of students described the valuable feedback they received from faculty and explained how that feedback affected their writing and revision process and their thinking. For example: "Professor X would always have a meeting with each student after each paper assignment and go over what could be improved as well as what was good about the paper" and "faculty helped with my brainstorming" and "yes, by being tough . . . pushing me to revise and be specific and articulate." And, after naming three faculty and the specific types of feedback provided by each, one student wrote with great metacognitive awareness: "In the year I attended X University, my writing grew with such incredible rapidity and I owe those three professors a debt of gratitude."

But similar to the frustration students expressed about being asked to do little writing, students also expressed frustration about how often they received no faculty comments on the writing they did. As one student said: "Professor _____ was very helpful in telling me where I needed to improve my arguments and theories. Some professors, on the other hand, didn't even return writing assignments, which allowed me no way to see where I was making my errors." And as another offered: "My journal responses were never handed back and my lab reports were always graded by TAs. I don't mind the latter as much as the former." And students who are already strong writers are sometimes those most likely to find little meaning— or challenge—in the feedback they receive—"I wrote papers for four different professors and received As on every paper I wrote with much positive feedback, but very little constructive feedback." A text like John Bean's (2011) *Engaging Ideas*, or scholarship of teaching and learning literature considering the relationship of disciplinary expertise (especially literature built on and from transformative practitioner research, see Taylor in this volume), learning and writing, can help faculty who believe they are content specialists and not teachers of writing learn how to meaningfully intervene in students' writing and thinking processes through informal writing, peer review and feedback through commenting.

Asking faculty to reflect on their own processes and experiences of learning, researching and writing (Haviland and Mullin, 2008; Thaiss and Zawacki, 2006) will also reveal to faculty that they are more prepared than they realize to talk about how they have experienced meaning-centered education through reading and writing and to recognize what prompted and supported their own meaning-centered writing and reading experiences when they were students. Throughout the responses first-year students describe the thrill and meaning that came from assignments through which faculty allowed them to imagine themselves as participants within a discipline or a profession. As one example, a student said "my Introduction to American Government research paper was very valuable to me because I would like to become a lawyer and this paper required me to learn many different legal terms and congressional definitions." Sometimes the writing in the disciplines assignments that led to meaning for students were those assignments focused less on the content knowledge of disciplines and professions and more on "procedural knowledge, writing as a way of knowing in a discipline" (Carter, 2007, p. 387). For example, one student described a literature assignment that asked him to "analyze characters from a Freudian or Jungian perspective," which he said was valuable to him because "I will likely be a psychology major, and this paper helped show me how psychology is valuable and applicable in other academic fields." In the third quote at the opening of this chapter the student described the satisfaction of applying the procedural knowledge of philosophy and combining that knowledge with a personal passion.

When faculty are involved with students as they read and write they are also able to get to know students well enough to encourage and support the inquiries students refer to as "personal." Many of the students who described valuable assignments as "personal" experienced assignments that provided opportunities for them to utilize what Juan Guerra (2008) terms their learning "incomes," "what students bring with them when they come to school" (p. 296). Whether those incomes were international experiences (or what Guerra terms "transcultural" experiences), familial or community experiences, languages other than English or other than standardized school English, interests in popular culture seemingly unrelated to course content, assignments students cited as meaningful to them allowed and encouraged students to see their in-class lives need not be kept separate from the rest of their lives. These personal connections may overwhelm some faculty and feel antithetical to the most superficial expectations of the education. As Peter Taylor notes in this volume: "Although educating for a higher level of consciousness might seem to be an insurmountable challenge given the historical inertia of formal education systems, there is cause for optimism that it is achievable" (p. 172) with the application of approaches to teaching and learning that include social constructivism, critical social theory and critical constructivism. And, if we are able to show teachers that it is so often both cognitive and affective connections that have brought them to their fields of expertise and that keep them imagining meaning-centered, meaningful writing informed by their passions (Thaiss and Zawacki, 2006) and their disciplines, they will be all that much more willing to invite students to bring their questions, opinions and lives into the classroom, to their reading and into their writing.

Appendix (Survey Questions)

This past year, for the first time, _____ University placed incoming students by a writing placement process—a questionnaire and a writing placement essay. In that questionnaire, you reflected on your own reading and writing experiences. As a follow-up, we hope you'll reflect on your first-year reading and writing experiences at _____. Please take the time to consider the questions carefully, answer them honestly, and help us reflect on reading and writing at _____ University.

We estimate that you will need 15–20 minutes to complete these questions. Please make sure that you have answered every question before submitting. Thank you.

Question 1: On average, approximately how many writing assignments **per week** have you had to write during your first year at _____ University?

On average, approximately how many writing assignments **per semester** have you had to write during your first year at _____ University?

Question 2: Which of your courses have been particularly writing intensive?

Question 3: This year, have you been required to write:

- more often than you expected?
- about as often as you expected?
- less often than you expected?

Question 4: Describe a writing assignment from this year that seemed valuable to you. Why do you feel this writing assignment was valuable? (Be specific.)

Question 5: Have faculty supported your writing this year? In what ways?

Question 6: What has surprised you most about writing at the collegiate level?

Question 7: What has surprised you most about reading at the collegiate level?

Question 8: What do you consider to be your greatest writing strength now, at the end of your first year of college? Did you gain this skill this year? (Be specific.)

Question 9: What is the most difficult aspect of writing for you now, at the end of your first year of college? (Be specific.)

Question 10: What sort of writing do you do outside of course assignments?

Question 11: Did you take Expository Writing this year?

Question 12: If so, do you think this was the right course for you? Why? Why not? (Be specific.)

Question 13: How would you best describe yourself?

- English is my native language
- English is not my native language; however, I speak and write English as fluently as I speak and write my native language
- English is not my native language. I do not speak and write English as fluently as I speak and write my native language

Notes

1 This study was reproduced on a larger scale in 2012 (with Michele Eodice and Neal Lerner) at St. John's University, Northeastern University and University of Oklahoma as "Seniors Reflect on Their Meaningful Writing Assignments: A

Cross-Institutional Study" supported by a 2010–2011 Conference on College Composition and Communication Research Initiative Grant.

2 Further specifics of the demographics of this survey sample: Four students in this sample self-identified as English as a Second Language (ESL). Of the 64 students, 24 took expository writing in their first year and 40 were exempted from the course by the placement essay they wrote and submitted in the summer before they began at this institution as first-year students. These percentages (ESL, students exempted from expository writing) are consistent with the institution's overall student profile. In any given year approximately 10–14 percent of the student population at this institution identify as ALANA (Asian-, Latino-, African-, and Native-American) and 8–11 percent identify as international students. This institution enrolls undergraduates of traditional college-going age, has four- and six-year graduation rates of approximately 70–78 percent, and approximately 90 percent of enrolled students have some form of financial aid.

3 I witnessed a similar current events-related phenomenon in the fall of 2008 when a professor at St. John's University facilitated an extracurricular science learning community event and invited undergraduates to an informal debate and discussion of the Science, Technology, Education and Mathematics (STEM) issues facing the US on the eve of the presidential election. Students were asked to choose an issue and write about Senator McCain's position, Senator Obama's position and their own position. This informal writing was students' "meal ticket" to the free learning community dinner and that could be the reason 130 students arrived with writing in hand. It may be just as likely, however, that many of these science-oriented students valued the opportunity to reflect on issues they cared about that would also inform their first ever presidential election votes. On their event exit slips they noted they felt informed and empowered as they prepared to vote.

4 See Wegerif, in this volume, for a discussion of how "a space of reflection that is both individual and collective" can also be created through internet-mediated dialogue.

References

Arum, R. and Roska, J. (2011) *Academically Adrift: Limited Learning on College Campuses.* Chicago, IL: University of Chicago Press.

Bean, J. (2011) *Engaging Ideas: The Professor's Guide to Integrating Writing, Critical Thinking, and Active Learning in the Classroom.* San Francisco, CA: Jossey Bass.

Carroll, L. A. (2002) *Rehearsing New Roles: How College Students Develop as Writers.* Carbondale, IL: SWR/Southern Illinois University Press.

Carter, M. (2007) "Ways of knowing, doing, and writing in the disciplines." *College Composition and Communication* 58(3): 385–418.

Geller, A. E. and Cantelmo, F. (2011) "Workshopping to practice scientific terms." In C. Paine, J. Harris and J. Miles (Eds), *Teaching with Student Texts: Essays Toward an Informed Practice* (pp. 210–219). Logan, UT: Utah State University Press.

Guerra, J. C. (2008) "Cultivating transcultural citizenship: A writing across communities model." *Language Arts* 85(4): 296–304.

Haviland, C. P. and Mullin, J. (2008) *Who Owns This Text? Plagiarism, Authorship, and Disciplinary Cultures.* Logan, UT: Utah State University Press.

Herrington, A. and Curtis, M. (2000) *Persons in Process.* Urbana, IL: NCTE.

Hilgers, T. L., Hussey, E. L. and Stitt-Bergh, M. (1999) "'As you're writing, you have these epiphanies': What college students say about writing and learning in their majors." *Written Communication* 16: 317–353.

Hodge, D. C., Magolda, M. B. and Haynes, C. A. (2009) "Engaged learning: enabling self-authorship and effective practice." *Liberal Education* 95(4): 16–23.

Kells, M. H. (2007) "Writing across communities: Diversity, deliberation, and the discursive possibilities of WAC." *Reflections* 11(1): 87–108.

Light, R. J. (2001) *Making the Most of College: Students Speak Their Minds*. Cambridge, MA: Harvard University Press.

Strauss, A. and Corbin, J. (1998) *Basics of Qualitative Research: Techniques and Procedures for Developing Grounded Theory*. Thousand Oaks, CA: Sage.

Swales, J. (1990) *Genre Analysis: English in Academic and Research Settings*. Cambridge: Cambridge University Press.

Thaiss, C. and Zawacki, T. M. (2006) *Engaged Writers/Dynamic Disciplines: Research on the Academic Writing Life*. Portsmouth, NH: Boynton/Cook.

11

SUPPORTING STUDENTS' SEARCH FOR A MEANINGFUL LIFE THROUGH INQUIRY-GUIDED LEARNING

Virginia S. Lee

Introduction

In the past fifteen years, many colleges and universities have adopted inquiry-guided learning (IGL) as a way to reform undergraduate education (for a sampling of eight institutions, see Lee, 2012). In the United States the report of the Boyer Commission on Educating Undergraduate Students in the Research University (1998) argued that using inquiry as a mode of learning capitalizes on the strength of the faculty in research. Inquiry is a part of the distinctive ecology of the research university in which faculty and students, both graduate and undergraduate, should participate. Universities in the United Kingdom, Australia, New Zealand and Canada have embraced the idea of the "teaching and research nexus" as a way to strengthen the links between teaching and research in institutions with a strong research component. In addition, other types of institutions of higher education including baccalaureate colleges and comprehensive universities have also adopted IGL, in many instances as part of an effort to become more like research universities.

The real promise of inquiry-guided learning, however, lies in the infusion of a spirit of inquiry that permeates every aspect of campus life. Inquiry is an essential human activity that makes meaning from experience. According to William Perry, the purpose of an organism is to organize, and what human beings organize is meaning: a sense of pattern, order, form, significance, and connection (in Daloz Parks, 2000, p. 19). In this context, the academic disciplines have developed as increasingly sophisticated sets of knowledge constructions, methodologies, and values for making meaning out of the specific realms of experience they explore and seek to understand (Doherty *et al.*, 2002). The challenge of inquiry-guided learning for institutions and instructors is reimagining the disciplines as sites of learning for students (see also Riordan and Roth, 2005) in addition to sites of scholarship for faculty members.

Further, to prepare students for "moral and meaningful lives in an increasingly interdependent world" (Walsh, 2006, p. 10), colleges and universities should create "a container in which our students can safely and genuinely experience confusion and conflict in all its complexity and can grow through and with it to greater wisdom and maturity" (p. 10). A key aspect of Walsh's challenge involves helping students see the connections between inquiry in the academic disciplines and in their own lives and learn the distinction between answering and living vital questions.

In the current higher education environment, the reimagining of the academic disciplines as sites of learning through inquiry-guided learning is a radical act if we fully understand its implications. Each student is an evolving self-in-society, deeply engaged in trying to make sense of her life as she seeks to answer fundamental questions such as "Who am I?", "What and whom do I care about?", and "How shall I live?" (Daloz Parks, 2000). One of the many challenges educators face is helping students link the living of these pressing questions with the traditional ways of making meaning in the academic disciplines. However, the task is both controversial and difficult due to the ascendancy of the research agenda, its attending epistemology and ethics of objectivism (Palmer and Zajonc, 2010; Kronman, 2007), and the growing expectation that higher education prepare students for lucrative careers following graduation. Recent research (Astin *et al.*, 2011; Astin and Astin, 1999) shows that faculty members are themselves caught in the horns of the dilemma: While faculty members report that questions of meaning and purpose are central to their own lives, they do not see it as their responsibility (nor do they feel able) to engage these questions with students.

This chapter explores the potential of the academic disciplines as sites of learning through inquiry-guided learning. It extends the traditional understanding of inquiry-guided learning as an initiation into the academic disciplines as forms of scholarship—sophisticated ways of making meaning of experience for a specialized community of inquirers—to include as well a companioning of students as they face and grow into life's pressing questions of identity and purpose. It offers a number of recommendations at both the course and institutional level, focusing primarily on the academic agenda.

Inquiry-Guided Learning: Inquiry as a Developmental Process

Inquiry is a developmental process. We see its mature expression in the scientist's search for the "God particle," the poet's struggle to find her unique voice, and the spiritual seeker's quest for a deepening relationship with the "Other." In contrast, perhaps the earliest expression of inquiry is the acquisition of language in the unfolding relationship between caregiver and infant, according to Bateson (2004) the archetype of the ideal learning environment. Naturally alert, curious, and capable of relationship, the healthy infant begins to develop the conceptual filters to make sense of the "blooming, buzzing confusion" (James, 1981/1890) that surrounds her. The caregiver supports this process using "motherese," the instinctual, simplified, repetitive, and exaggerated language adults use with infants. In all these examples, inquiry, whether independent or supported by a more mature human being, is a process of making meaning of experience as an expression of a developing self.

As traditionally understood, inquiry-guided learning promotes the acquisition of new knowledge, abilities, and attitudes through a learner's increasingly independent investigation of questions, problems, and issues using the ways and standards of inquiry in the disciplines. As Figure 11.1 illustrates, inquiry-guided learning is a subset of so-called active learning strategies that also belongs to a group of strategies Prince and Felder (2006) refer to as inductive teaching and learning methods. Instead of moving from general principles to applications, a more common instructional approach, instruction begins with specifics—a set of observations or experimental data to interpret, a case history to analyze, a complex real-world problem to solve or a question students really want to answer. As students try to analyze the data or scenario or solve the problem, they recognize a need for facts, rules, procedures, and guiding principles, which the instructor either presents to them or students discover themselves. Problem-based learning is a specific type of inquiry-guided learning that arose in fields such as medicine and engineering in which problem solving is a dominant mode of inquiry. Undergraduate research, properly structured, is also a type of inquiry-guided learning (Lee, 2011).

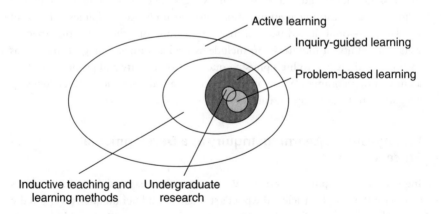

FIGURE 11.1 Inquiry-guided learning as a subset of active learning

Source: Lee (2012).

As we noted above, inquiry-guided learning requires instructors to imagine the forms of inquiry they conduct in their disciplines as contexts for learning rather than scholarship. An important aspect of using disciplines as contexts for learning is designing a set of inquiry experiences that is suitable to the developmental level of students. Using good pedagogical judgment, instructors need to balance manageable *challenge* with appropriate *support* (or "scaffolding"). Challenge is the degree of complexity in the inquiry, while support is the degree of structure provided (see Knefelkamp, 1974). Challenge and support can take a variety of forms in inquiry-guided learning. For example, the possibility of a variety of perspectives, open-endedness, scope, the number of distractors, and gaps in essential information all contribute to the challenge of an inquiry. In contrast, modeling, heuristics, guiding questions, rubrics, mini-lectures on aspects of the knowledge base relevant to an inquiry, assigned readings, direct instruction on important skills of inquiry (e.g., developing a research question and hypothesis, analyzing data, generating possible solutions), and feeder assignments leading up to a final report of an inquiry are all examples of support that can be used alone or in combination with one another (Lee, 2011).

Achieving the proper balance of challenge and support is a combination of science and art honed through experience. Knowing something about the cognitive development of college students, however, can hasten the process. The work of Belenky *et al.* (1986/1997), King and Kitchener (1994), and Perry (1970) alerts us to the kinds of difficulties most students will face as they learn through inquiry and, consequently, the kind of support they are likely to need. For most first-year students, learning through inquiry will be unsettling, because it violates their assumptions about the origins of knowledge and the role of instructors and students in the learning process (and even older students). Briefly, many entering students believe that knowledge is a repository of right answers known by instructors or found in textbooks. The role of the instructor is to tell students what they need to know and for students to give it back, preferably on an exam with clear right and wrong answers. Gradually students come to see the function of inquiry in knowledge construction (including the use of evidence to support an argument, warranted knowledge claim, judgment or decision) and the active role they share with the instructor and other students in the process of inquiry.

Inquiry-Guided Learning and the Development of Self

Interestingly the assumptions underlying environments that support inquiry-guided learning also promote the development of self-in-society or "self authorship" as described by Baxter Magolda (2001): knowledge as complex and socially constructed; the self as central to knowledge construction; and authority and expertise shared in the mutual construction of knowledge among peers. As a matter of fact, the ultimate recognition of these assumptions as central to meaning-making in the disciplines and the wider world is a critical developmental milestone as students move from dualistic through subjectivist and relativistic to committed ways of knowing (see Perry, 1970). Because knowing and valuing become contingent on context as students move into relativistic and committed ways of knowing, and because contexts constantly change, what one knows and values can change as well. These realizations prompt the restructuring of identity as the one who chooses to what to devote his energy and care as commitments (in Baxter Magolda, 2001, p. 20).

While all three of the assumptions above are controversial in the context of traditional educational practice in the academy, the centrality of the self in knowledge construction is particularly so. On the one hand, positivism—once the purview of the sciences only, but now embraced by most academic disciplines—assumes and values the self that stands at arm's length from experience (Palmer and Zajonc, 2010). The disinterested self coolly observes and analyzes experience in order to understand it as an objective truth or to manipulate experience for some purpose. On the other hand, the most sophisticated forms of inquiry acknowledge that the self is always interested, affecting and affected by the very experience it seeks to understand. Building on Heisenberg's uncertainty principle, modern physics openly recognizes that the act of observation itself alters experience; Margaret Mead, recognizing that her self was very much a part of her anthropological inquiries, worked continuously to hone herself as an observational instrument (Bateson, 2004); Barbara McClintock, the famed geneticist, cultivated empathy as a way of deeply knowing the behavior of genes in corn. Others, including variously Carl Jung, the Buddha, and Marion Milner (2011/1934) have used methods of empirical inquiry (e.g., observation, recording, reflection, critical thinking) towards greater self-knowledge and identity development. In other words, the evolving self, its ways of knowing, and the experience in which it resides interpenetrate and affect one another in many ways that many developmental theories systematically describe (e.g., Perry, 1970; Belenky et al., 1986/1997; Kegan, 1994).

With the above as background, let us consider the society of inquirers represented in Figure 11.2. The field of the largest circle represents raw experience. Each smaller circle represents a person embedded in experience with the arrow signaling a sense of purpose. Note that there are a number of persons with different purposes, each a self-in-society. The inset describes in greater detail the process of meaning-making through inquiry used by each person: at the center is the person herself, alert, attentive, and curious; around her is the accretion of her experience represented by knowledge (K), methods (M), and values (V), which she orchestrates to make new meaning in the form of new knowledge claims and decisions, the widest ring. Knowledge exists in the form of facts, concepts, theories, principles, and so on; methods in the form of the cognitive processes of observation, analysis, evaluation, and synthesis and their orchestration in critical thinking, problem solving, and the specialized methods of inquiry of the disciplines; and values or preferences in terms of what sustains our attention and sense of purpose and supports our judgments concerning the worth of knowledge

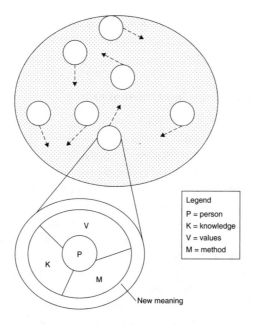

FIGURE 11.2 A schema of meaning-making in a community of inquirers

claims and decisions. (Note that the Vee diagram in Novak and Gowin, 1984, provided inspiration for some of the ideas regarding meaning-making through inquiry here.) Whether the society in question is a specialized community of inquirers such as the scientific community or civil society, meaning is negotiated with other participants, in the former through the formalized processes of peer review and publication and in the latter through consensus making. In comparison to the infant and the caregiver, note how much more extensive is experience, more developed knowledge structures, more sophisticated the methods of inquiry, more robust underlying preferences and values, and more complex the society in which meaning is tested and negotiated.

Returning to colleges and universities, what kinds of environments and practices prepare students to participate skillfully, responsibly, and even happily in advanced societies of inquiry? How can colleges and universities support students as they learn to integrate the knowledge, methods, and values of inquiry in the academic disciplines as ways of making meaning of experience with their own personal search for meaning and purpose?

Infusing a Spirit of Inquiry on College and University Campuses

The recommendations below, focused primarily on the academic agenda, work together to infuse a spirit of inquiry on college and university campuses and to create a container or "holding environment" (Walsh, 2006) in which students can grow into a vital and productive relationship with important and pressing questions of identity and purpose.

Create Supportive Learning Environments

Taking risks is essential for learning and development: venturing into unfamiliar territory, confronting and breaking down misconceptions, revealing incompetence, making mistakes, and using developing competencies under increasingly more difficult and complex circumstances. Research in neuroscience and the physiology of learning demonstrates the strong link between emotion and cognition; in the absence of the strong, positive emotions engendered by caring, deep engagement, motivation, and interest, little real learning occurs. Similarly negative emotions such as fear and shame, all too common in the traditional college classroom, retard learning due to "choking," the shutting down of higher-order thinking, and the activation of more primitive areas of the brain associated with the fight-or-flight syndrome. Further, classroom-based studies and extensive interviews with students affirm the findings of these theoretical studies. Research on large classes demonstrates the positive effects of personalizing the large class on student attendance and motivation to learn, particularly younger students. And undergraduate students repeatedly mention the importance of one-on-one interaction with instructors in supervised projects and the closer interactions with other students and instructors in small classes as important factors in their learning (see Lee, 2004). Strategies as simple as learning students' names, establishing ground rules, arriving early to class, keeping office hours and encouraging students to use them, providing prompt feedback, engaging in appropriate personal disclosure, and interacting with students in class together create a supportive environment for learning.

Establish Linkages Between Meaning-Making in the Academic Disciplines and in Students' Own Lives Early in the Undergraduate Curriculum

Over the past fifteen to twenty years, many colleges and universities in the United States have established first-year seminar programs: classes in which a faculty member engages a small group of students in an exploration of the questions, problems, and issues of his or her discipline and the methods used to examine them. Rather than being lost as a mere number in the large lecture classes typical of first-year study, students immediately become part of a small community of other first-year students with a faculty member who comes to know them personally. Small classes enable a sense of belonging, a predictor of retention and continuation to the sophomore year. They also establish expectations for university-level learning and provide a more sophisticated introduction to the academic disciplines and their methods of inquiry than the typical survey course.

At the same time that they are introducing students to the role of the academic disciplines in making meaning from experience, a smaller number of institutions also provide a set of seminars in which students actively explore questions regarding self and identity. At some institutions these seminars comprise the core curriculum, a common set of courses that all students take regardless of academic major. Often these institutions are religiously affiliated, although questions regarding self and value (see below) are frequently framed in secular terms. For example, at Dominican University (Chicago, Illinois) the first-year seminar "Dimensions of Self" is the first of four required seminars, one taken each year, in which students explore the search for meaning in ever widening contexts. Although each "Self" seminar has a different focus depending on the faculty member who teaches it, in all seminars students engage actively with these questions: What is the self? Is the self made, inherited, given, discovered? What are some of the key influences on a person's physical, emotional, spiritual, and intellectual development? How does the self interact with community (Dominican University, n.d.)? Seminars taken in later years continue the exploration of the implications of self, identity, and engagement in society: "Community, Culture and Diversity" (Sophomore), "Technology, Work and Leisure" (Junior), and "Virtues and Values" (Senior).

Consequently, early in their university study, at a time when it is especially important to embed learning in personal experience, students are exploring questions of their own identity through the methods of inquiry of the academic disciplines. Meaning-making in the disciplines and for the self forging a sense of identity and direction in the wider societies in which it lives are related.

Make Explicit the Role of Values and Valuing in Meaning-Making

Current trends in higher education such as the ascendance of positivism and relativism discussed more fully above have tended to discourage faculty members from incorporating discussion of personal values into the curriculum. However, students are actively exploring and seeking answers to what deeply matters to them and the grounds on which they make important life decisions such as their choice of career, life partner, and how they spend their time and money. For this reason, some have argued (e.g., Chickering *et al.*, 2006; Baxter Magolda, 2001; Daloz Parks, 2000) that colleges and universities should provide more explicit support as students struggle with these important life questions. The Association of American Colleges and Universities (AAC&U), a champion of liberal education in an increasingly interdependent world, has contributed to the creation of developmental rubrics for key competencies in a liberal education curriculum (see The Association of American Colleges and Universities, n.d.). These competencies include a set of four abilities related to Personal and Social Responsibility, three of which attempt to foster awareness of the values and assumptions that affect the quality of our engagement in civic society. Building on Krathwohl *et al.*'s earlier work (1964) on the development of habits and attitudes that embody our values, the approach to course design advocated by Fink (2003) incorporates two of six types of learning outcomes called "caring" (or "valuing") and "human dimension." As they design courses, instructors should help students understand themselves and others better through an exploration of academic material and why they should care about the disciplinary perspective offered in the course. Both the AAC&U rubrics and the Fink approach to course design offer helpful tools that instructors and institutions can use to support the identification of personal values and their consistent expression in the context of course work.

Despite these (and other) tools, the number of institutions that incorporate values and development explicitly into the curriculum is relatively small. For example, the curriculum at Alverno College (Milwaukee, Wisconsin) comprises eight liberal education outcomes or abilities, one of them being "Valuing in Decision Making." This ability represents "a process whereby a student examines her values, interprets the source of her values and her actions, practices taking multiple perspectives, and ultimately contributes to the development of values in the broader community" (see Character Clearinghouse, n.d.). At each level of the curriculum and in a variety of course contexts, students consider different dimensions of their own valuing process and how the process relates to their personal and work lives and to the societal structures related to their life and work. Consequently, students who graduate from Alverno have practiced "valuing in decision making" explicitly many, many times in numerous contexts. The experience of Alverno College shows that colleges and universities can support students' inquiry into their own values as a foundation for the personal decisions they make in their own lives as part of inquiry and meaning-making in the academic disciplines.

Design Learning Experiences That Support Independent Inquiry

In inquiry-guided learning, the task of instructors, departments, and the institution as a whole is the design of a coherent set of experiences in which students together wrestle with challenging questions, problems, issues, and situations; seek out necessary information from a variety of sources; design experiments, observe, record results, analyze and formulate conclusions; consider alternative solutions and select the best one given certain constraints; and then communicate their findings or solutions to an appropriate audience (Lee *et al.*, 2004). The degree of independence (i.e., the balance of challenge and support) that students exercise is a matter of instructors' discretion. A variety of frameworks have been developed to describe the proper balance of challenge and support for students at various developmental levels (see Lee, 2012).

The requirements of inquiry-guided learning also satisfy the educational conditions for students' development of self-authorship, that is, the ability to identify a personal sense of meaning and purpose along with the competencies to carry it out. In order to participate in a community of inquirers, students must confront ambiguity, develop and defend their own beliefs, negotiate the mutual exchange of knowledge, and practice respect, shared authority, and trust (Baxter Magolda, 2001). These aspects of participation hold equally for meaning-making in the academic disciplines as well as in the ever broadening societies of which students will be a part (see Figure 11.2).

Develop a Range of Opportunities for Students to Demonstrate and Reflect Upon Their Developing Competence

Often students do not understand what they are actually experiencing even as they undergo it. Consequently it is important that students name, in order that they can recognize, the competencies they are developing and to what degree at various points in time. In this vein, assessments are structured opportunities for students to demonstrate their growing ability to make meaning of experience through the process of inquiry and then reflect upon the strengths and weaknesses of their performance individually, with other students and with the instructor. Since the competencies of inquiry such as critical thinking, problem solving, decision making, communication, and social interaction develop slowly over an extended period of time, developmental rubrics for these abilities are a helpful adjunct to inquiry and a support for reflection and self assessment. Assessment should also address students' emotions including fear, anxiety, anger, and boredom as well as pride and joy in their participation in the process of inquiry.

The role of grading in the assessment of complex competencies as part of the evolving self is problematic. Ideally its function as a motivator for student engagement is less critical in inquiry-guided learning than traditional instruction: questions and problems are inherently motivating, and as part of a community of inquirers, students are swept up in the momentum of inquiry and accountable to others for their performance. If grading is an administrative necessity, the use of good developmental rubrics such as the VALUE rubrics developed by the Association of American Colleges and Universities (n.d.) establish expectations of performance at various developmental levels. Other strategies include counting assignments early in the term less and assessing more frequently, effectively minimizing the impact of any single performance on a student's grade.

Create Opportunities for Students to Use Their Competencies in Real World Contexts

Instructors and institutions should help students see the connections between the abilities they are developing in their communities of inquiry at the university and the broader societies they will inhabit following graduation. For example, the ability to identify a concern, ask robust questions about it, and seek answers (or frame problems and find solutions) in the academic disciplines applies equally to the spheres of home, community, work, and world. In other words, students can bring the same powers of attention, analysis, and synthesis to bear upon their deepest personal concerns as they can to the seemingly artificial or "academic" questions they encounter in the university.

There is a range of strategies to help students see the connections between the experiences they undergo in the university, the abilities they develop through these experiences, and their lives following graduation. Active learning strategies such as discussion, group work, role-plays, case studies, and simulations ground knowledge and concepts and their use in progressively more realistic contexts. Experiential learning in the form of consulting experiences as part of regular course work, service learning, internships, and study abroad engage students even more fully in the kinds of experiences they will encounter following graduation; structured opportunities for reflection are important to help students see the connection between academic work and these experiences. For example, Alverno College holds separate assessment days in which students enact named abilities developed across a range of courses in simulated experiences such as a committee meeting or an interview; members of the Alverno faculty and wider Milwaukee-community observe these experiences and assess students' performance at the same time that students assess their own performance. And at Stanford University students use design principles to create a life design for themselves (see Stanford Design Program, n.d.) based on their evolving sense of who they are and what they care about.

Strengthen Advising by Conceiving It as an Inquiry-Driven Process

Good advising is a far cry from the form that advising takes typically: a cursory check that students are meeting certain administrative requirements for graduation and a sign-off on a choice of courses for the upcoming semester. In fact, Richard Light (2001) notes that "[g]ood advising may be the single most underestimated characteristic of a successful college experience" (p. 81). He finds that the strength of good advising rests on two conditions:

1. a one-on-one relationship with a faculty member who knows and cares about the student, and
2. asking of unexpected questions that require students to make sense of the diverse experiences across their academic program and, in turn, see connections between their academic program and their personal values and goals.

Thought of in this way, advising is a form of teaching and learning driven by inquiry; occurs across the undergraduate experience, not only in the first year of study; and has its own curriculum (Campbell and Nutt, 2008). Laff (2006) likens advising to problem-based learning and a collaborative process of teaching and research that challenges students to question what they value in their own learning and why.

Conclusion

Historically colleges and universities in the United States have served a valuable function in preparing young adults for the demands of contemporary society. In recent times, however, the public perceives that higher education has abdicated this larger societal function, serving instead its own smaller, specialized societies in ways inscrutable and irrelevant to the general public. This situation, coupled with the rapidly rising costs of colleges and universities, has created a crisis in higher education.

As part of an effort to again prepare young adults for meaningful lives in contemporary society, colleges and universities need to re-imagine the academic disciplines as sites of learning through inquiry. In the process colleges and universities can become holding environments in which young adults can experience the confusion and conflict they will inevitably experience in their own lives and learn to grow into wisdom and maturity through that confusion and conflict. As a result colleges and universities will not only initiate young adults into the disciplines' sophisticated ways of making meaning of experience, but also companion them as they face and grow into life's pressing questions of identity and purpose.

There are a variety of strategies colleges and universities can use to infuse a spirit of inquiry throughout campus life and prepare students for enlightened and meaningful engagement in contemporary society: create supportive learning environments, establish linkages between meaning-making in the academic disciplines and in students' own lives early in the undergraduate curriculum, make explicit the roles of values and valuing in meaning-making, design learning experiences that support independent inquiry, develop a range of opportunities for students to demonstrate and reflect upon their developing competence, create opportunities for students to use their competencies in real world contexts, and strengthen advising by conceiving it as an inquiry-driven process throughout the undergraduate experience.

As the world becomes increasingly complex, the need for sustained preparation for enlightened participation in society is particularly acute. Without sustained attention to matters of identity and purpose and the competencies to fulfill that purpose, young adults are in danger of being tossed about on the surface of modern life and swept up in tides of popular opinion and the vagaries of the marketplace.

References

Association of American Colleges and Universities (n.d.) VALUE: Valid assessment of learning in undergraduate education. Retrieved December 15, 2011 from: http://www.aacu.org/value/rubrics/index_p.cfm?CFID=20879626&CFTOKEN=59566827

Astin, A. W. and Astin, H. S. (1999) *Meaning and Spirituality in the Lives of College Faculty: A Study of Values, Authenticity, and Stress.* University of California, LA: Higher Education Research Institute.

Astin, A. W., Astin, H. S. and Lindholm, J.A. (2011) *Cultivating the Spirit: How College Can Enhance Students' Inner Lives.* San Francisco, CA: Jossey-Bass.

Bateson, M. C. (2004) *Willing to Learn: Passages of Personal Discovery.* Hanover, NH: Steerforth Books.

Baxter Magolda, M. B. (2001) *Making Their Own Way: Narratives for Transforming Higher Education to Promote Self-Development.* Sterling, VA: Stylus.

Belenky, M. F., Clinchy, B. M., Goldberger, N. R. and Tarule, J. M. (1986/1997) *Women's Ways of Knowing: The Development of Self, Voice and Mind.* New York, NY: Basic Books.

Boyer Commission on Educating Undergraduate Students in a Research University (1998) *Reinventing Undergraduate Education: A Blue Print for American's Research Universities.* Stony Brook, NY: Stony Brook University.

Campbell, S. M. and Nutt, C. L. (Winter 2008) "Academic advising in the new global century: Supporting student engagement and learning outcomes achievement." *Peer Review* 92(2): 4–7. Downloaded December 21, 2011 from: http://www.aacu.org/peerreview/pr-wi08/documents/PR-WI08_AcademicAdvising.pdf

Character Clearinghouse (n.d.) 2011 Dalton Institute Award Recipient: Valuing in Decision-Making Department, Alverno College. Downloaded December 20, 2011 from: http://characterclearinghouse.fsu.edu/index.php/jon-c-dalton-institute-on-college-student-values/awards/691-valuing-alverno

Chickering, A., Dalton, J. and Stamm, L. (Eds) (2006), *Encouraging Authenticity and Spirituality in Higher Education* (Vol. 1). San Francisco, CA: Jossey-Bass.

Daloz Parks, S. (2000) *Big Questions, Worthy Dreams: Mentoring Young Adults in Their Search for Meaning, Purpose and Faith.* San Francisco, CA: Jossey-Bass.

Doherty, A., Riordan, T. and Roth, J. (Eds) (2002) *Student Learning: A Central Focus for Institutions of Higher Education.* Milwaukee, WI: Alverno College Institute.

Dominican University (n.d.) Core curriculum: Freshmen seminars. Downloaded December 15, 2011 from: http://www.dom.edu/departments/corecurriculum/seminars/freshmen.html

Fink, L. D. (2003) *Creating Significant Learning Experiences: An Integrated Approach to Designing College Courses.* San Francisco, CA: Jossey-Bass.

James, W. (1981) *The Principles of Psychology.* Cambridge, MA: Harvard University Press. Originally published in 1890.

Kegan, R. (1994) *In Over Our Heads: The Mental Demands of Modern Life.* Cambridge, MA: Harvard University Press.

King, P. M. and Kitchener, K. S. (1994) *Developing Reflective Judgment: Understanding and Promoting Intellectual Growth and Critical Thinking in Adolescents and Adults.* San Francisco, CA: Jossey Bass.

Knefelkamp, L. L. (1974) "Developmental instruction: Fostering intellectual and personal growth of college students." Doctoral dissertation, University of Minnesota, Minneapolis. (Dissertation Abstracts 36, 3: 1271A. 1975.)

Krathwohl, D. R., Bloom, B. S. and Masia, B. B. (1964) *Taxonomy of Educational Objectives: Handbook II: Affective Domain.* New York: David McKay Co.

Kronman, A. T. (2007) *Education's End: Why Our Colleges and Universities Have Given Up on the Meaning of Life.* New Haven, CT: Yale University Press.

Laff, N. S. (Spring 2006) "Teachable moments: Advising as liberal learning." *Liberal Education*, 36–41. Downloaded December 21, 2011 from: http://www.aacu.org/liberaleducation/le-sp06/documents/le-sp06__LEAP.pdf

Lee, V. S. (2004). IDEA item #1: "Displayed a personal interest in students and their learning." In M. Theall (Ed.), *POD-IDEA Notes: Instruction*. The IDEA Center. Downloaded December 27, 2011 from: http://www.theideacenter.org/sites/default/files/Item1Formatted.pdf

Lee, V. S. (2011) "The power of inquiry as a way of learning." *Innovative Higher Education* 36(3): 149–160.

Lee, V. S. (2012) "What is inquiry-guided learning?" In V. S. Lee (Ed.), *Inquiry-Guided Learning*. New Directions for Teaching and Learning, number 129. San Francisco, CA: Jossey-Bass.

Lee, V. S., Greene, D. B., Odom, J., Schechter, E. and Slatta, R. (2004) "What is inquiry-guided learning?" In V. S. Lee (Ed.), *Teaching and Learning Through Inquiry: A Guidebook for Institutions and Instructors*, pp. 3–16. Sterling, VA: Stylus.

Light, R. J. (2001) *Making the Most of College: Students Speak Their Minds*. Cambridge, MA: Harvard University Press.

Milner, M. (2011) *A Life of One's Own*. New York: Routledge. Originally published in 1934 under the name Joanna Field.

Novak, J. D. and Gowin, D. B. (1984) *Learning How to Learn*. New York: Cambridge University Press.

Palmer, P. and Zajonc, A. (2010) *The Heart of Higher Education: A Call to Renewal: Transforming the Academy through Collegial Conversations*. San Francisco, CA: Jossey-Bass.

Perry, W. G., Jr. (1970) *Forms of Intellectual and Ethical Development in the College Years: A Scheme*. New York: Holt, Rinehart, and Winston.

Prince, M. J. and Felder, R. M. (2006) "Inductive teaching and learning methods: Definitions, comparisons, and research bases." *Journal of Engineering Education* 95(2): 123–138.

Riordan, T. and Roth, J. (Eds) (2005) *Disciplines as Frameworks for Student Learning: Teaching the Practice of the Disciplines*. Sterling, VA: Stylus.

Stanford Design Program (n.d.) Designing your life. Retrieved December 15, 2011 from: http://www.stanford.edu/class/me104b/cgi-bin/

Walsh, D. C. (2006) *Trustworthy Leadership: Can We Be the Leaders We Need Our Students to Become?* Kalamazoo, MI: The Fetzer Institute.

12

RESEARCH AS TRANSFORMATIVE LEARNING FOR MEANING-CENTERED PROFESSIONAL DEVELOPMENT

Peter Charles Taylor

Introduction

How can higher education prepare prospective leaders of emerging nations to develop counter narratives that resist the non-too-subtle cultural and economic imperatives of globalization in which higher education is deeply implicated? This chapter considers how research professors can counter the hegemony of the encroaching Western modern worldview by harnessing new research paradigms to engage their postgraduate students—mature-aged professional educators—in meaning-centered professional development aimed at personal and cultural emancipation. Metaphorically speaking, I call this *research as transformative learning*, and it has characteristics that resonate with theories of experiential learning, dialogical learning and inquiry learning presented in other chapters in this book.

Research as transformative learning opens new epistemological spaces (without necessarily closing down old ones) for educators to examine the cultural situatedness of their professional practices. Researchers as transformative learners draw on constructivist, critical-social and arts-based epistemologies to examine reflectively, critically and imaginatively their lived experiences (as advocated by Potosky, Spaulding and Juzbasich, this volume), revealing the historical and sociocultural framing of their personal lives and professional practices. Researchers as transformative learners, especially those belonging to post-independent nations where indigenous cultures—knowledge systems, languages, worldviews, values, identities—were repressed for centuries by colonial powers, reinvest personally and professionally in their cultural heritage and are motivated to find ways of giving their culture an official curriculum presence alongside the Western modern worldview.

However, strengthening personal agency while working to achieve cultural emancipation is not easily won; it entails modes of higher-order thinking such as critical (self-)reflection, metaphoric imagining, dialectical reasoning, spiritual awakening and re-envisioning, to name a few. The honing of these higher-order thinking abilities involves dialogue with the self (intrapersonal) and with the other (interpersonal) in order that the emerging authority of the transformative learner's lived experience can resist the siren call of the "academic expert" whose largely ungrounded (psychological, philosophical, sociological) theorizing is writ large in the canon of (Western) research literature. Thus transformative learning engages the self in rich reconstructive dialogue (much as advocated by Wegerif, this volume). When it comes to writing the thesis, arts-based literary genres that facilitate dialogic, narrative and poetic voice, amongst others, are important to the empowerment of the researcher as transformative learner.

To illustrate the practicability and efficacy of research as transformative learning, I draw on the work of my recent doctoral graduates whose transformative research generated pragmatic philosophies of culturally situated education for respecting, celebrating and growing local cultural capital in the universities and schools of Mozambique and Nepal. But first a word about my own epistemology as an author of this chapter. What you are about to read is a culmination of more than 25 years of theorizing about my own practice as a research professor, endeavoring to practice what I preach to my graduate students: research as transformative learning. I have engaged long and hard in reflective inquiry into my own practice as graduate research teacher and graduate student mentor, drawing on contemporary qualitative methods such as critical reflection, narrative inquiry, grounded theorizing and arts-based research writing. A full account of this epistemology is available in other publications (e.g., Taylor, in press/2013, 2008; Taylor and Wallace, 2007; Taylor et al., 2012).

Education for a Transformed World

My role as a research professor in a university graduate center is to engage teachers of science and mathematics (and other disciplines) in postgraduate professional development. Most of my on-campus students come from African, Asian and Arabic-speaking countries, bringing rich diversity in cultural beliefs and values, social practices and languages. Some have grown up in traditional village lifestyles, most are from non-Western (but rapidly Westernizing) societies, and some from recently independent (postcolonial) nations. What each of these postgraduate students has in common is success in negotiating "cultural border crossings" (Giroux, 1993) into a Western modern worldview that has governed both their formal education, from primary school through university, and their professional practice as school teachers or university teacher educators.

During the first weeks of semester it becomes clear that few have reflected critically on their role as agents of enculturation of their own students into a Western modern worldview. Most students have not identified, let alone thought to challenge, the assumptions framing the curricula that govern their professional practices and, not surprisingly, they envisage educational research as a means of finding "the" answer to the question of "*How can student participation and achievement in science/mathematics education in my country be improved by modern teaching approaches?*" Such a well-intentioned question, however, does not necessarily afford a critical examination of the relevance of established curricula to the conflicting needs of their rapidly globalizing societies. Most are predisposed to reforming established teaching and learning practices in their schools and universities from within existing curricular structures, rather than seeking to reconceptualize their society's educational goals. Why is this? The answer lies in the invisible part of the political spectrum where hidden assumptions govern beliefs about the purpose of schooling, giving rise to an uncritical belief in a "one-size-fits-all" curriculum for modernizing societies worldwide. The following aphorism puts this succinctly: *The fish is unaware of the water in which it swims.*

I have sympathy with culture studies researchers whose work helps me to understand that my international students' uncritical sense of belonging to "developing" countries is potentially demeaning and disempowering (Schech and Haggis, 2000). For centuries the so-called developed world, particularly Western European nations, colonized, subjugated and oppressed peoples worldwide for political and economic gain (Desai and Nair, 2005). The European Enlightenment (Scientific Revolution/Age of Reason) gave rise to the concept of modernity, in which the unfolding present is regarded as superior to the seemingly fixed past, and to the Eurocentric discourse of "orientalism" which diminished the intellectual and social status of the culturally different other (Said, 1978). As The West's power spread with the discovery of the New World this "translated into a sense of superiority over those pre-modern societies and cultures that were 'locked' in the past—primitive and uncivilised peoples whose subjugation and 'introduction' into modernity became the right and obligation of European powers" (Ashcroft *et al.*, 2006, p. 145). Emilia Afonso (2002) recollects her experiences as a young child attending school in Portuguese occupied Mozambique.

> At that time, Mozambique was still considered to be a province of Portugal. At school we were taught about the courage and bravery of Vasco da Gama and Luis de Camoes. We learnt about the princes and princesses of Portugal. We learnt about important rivers in Portugal and many marvelous things about Portugal: the food, the drink, the people . . . We learnt the word "oliveiras", for the trees that produce olive oil, "famous in the entire world", my teacher said. We learnt the word "videiras" for the vines that produce grapes used to produce wine. We learnt about God, whom I understood to be a white man, and the devil, whom I understood to be a black man. We learnt how big Portugal was, how it extended from Europe to Africa. We learnt about the weather in Portugal and how it was

important that the Portuguese came to my country to save our souls "that before were lost".

(Gomez de Azurara, in Ferris, 1989)

Throughout the colonized world, education systems were set up as mirror images of those in the motherland with curricula designed to "civilize the natives" by assimilating them into the dominant cultural beliefs, values, practices and languages (or worldview) of The West. In this process local knowledge and language systems were suppressed and the cultural integrity, identities and livelihoods of colonized peoples were severely undermined (Veerma, 2004).

In the twenty-first century we live in a world largely dominated by the view that, in the so-called natural order of things, Western nations are exemplary models of material and social progress, a belief reinforced by our unarguable expertise in modern science and technology; and made glamorous by the resulting availability of lifestyle enhancing goods. Because science and mathematics education are seen to be the keys to modernization, a global export industry is flourishing served by Western universities specializing in postgraduate courses. Postcolonial scholars argue, however, that globalization of curricula and its "policing" by international benchmarking systems (e.g., Trends in International Mathematics and Science Study: http://nces.ed.gov/timss/) constitutes a form of neocolonialism (Semali and Kincheloe, 1999) that replaces local cultural knowledge systems with the one-size-fits-all system of Western knowledge, a process described by Haarman (2007) as modernity's "replacement ideology."

On the one hand, modern science and technology provide us with a host of material benefits, including advanced medical technology, global transportation, e-communication systems and improved agricultural productivity. On the other hand, environmental ethicists (e.g., Skutnabb-Kangas *et al.*, 2003) and scientific and governmental advisory panels, such as the Intergovernmental Panel on Climate Change (2007) and the United Nations Secretary General's High-Level Panel on Global Sustainability (2012) report that this has come at a very high cost. Modernization is strongly associated with increased global warming, air/water/soil pollution, proliferation of weapons of mass destruction, nuclear power crises, global financial crises, cultural, linguistic and biological extinction, and natural resource exhaustion, to name but a few.

Of concern to me is that science and mathematics curricula tend to direct teachers worldwide toward celebrating uncritically the benefits of the socioeconomic imperatives of modernity and away from revealing the deleterious side-effects. Few teachers feel compelled to prepare their students with higher-order abilities for engaging critically and imaginatively in social decision-making about ethical dilemmas facing society's adoption of modern science and technology. Furthermore, there is very little curriculum interest in The West for revealing the multicultural heritage of modern science and mathematics, particularly its non-Western genesis in Arabia, Persia, China and Africa (Lyons, 2009). In Australia, bilingual curriculum programs for rural and remote Aboriginal schools have been all but abandoned, signaling that cultural assimilation into the Western modern worldview has become de rigueur.

We appear to be at a crossroads in the evolution of our planet: either we continue on the tragic path of diminishing our cultural, linguistic and biological diversity and voraciously consuming non-renewable energy resources or we decide to engage deeply and wholeheartedly in sustainable development marked by careful conservation of the Earth's natural and cultural resources and peaceful co-existence. To achieve this goal we need to construct education for sustainability pathways as advocated by, for example, UNESCO's "Decade for Sustainable Development: 2005–2014" (http://www.unesco.org/new/en/education/themes/leading-the-international-agenda/education-for-sustainable-development/) and the Australian Government's national action plan for sustainability (2009).

But educating for sustainability involves much more than teaching children new scientific facts about biodiversity, climate change, cultural diversity, indigenous knowledge and living sustainably. This is a necessary but insufficient condition; the facts need to be processed through higher-order learning such as values clarification, empathic negotiation, critical reflection and mindfulness. Indeed, education *as* sustainability involves holistic teaching that "nurtures the development of the whole person . . . the intellectual, emotional, physical, social, aesthetic, and spiritual" (Miller, 2005, p. 2). A higher level of consciousness honors the whole human being (Palmer and Zajonc, 2010) and seeks synergy between multiple, competing worldviews (Laszlo, 2008).

There is increasing demand for a twenty-first century education *as/for* cultural and environmental sustainability as can be seen in the emergence of interdisciplinary and intercultural studies evidenced by: an integral philosophy of ecology that connects individuals, communities and natural systems in complex networks (Esbjorn-Hargens and Zimmerman, 2009); biocultural diversity conservation which focuses on "the diversity of life in all its manifestations—biological, cultural, and linguistic—which are interrelated (and likely evolved) within a complex socio-ecological adaptive system" (Maffi and Woodley, 2010, p. 5); reconnecting science, reason and spirituality to understand the creative emergence of conscious life (Kauffman, 2008); ethical visions of education to cultivate mind and imagination (Hansen, 2007); integrating physics and biology to understand consciousness (Lanza and Berman, 2009); and educating for social and ecological peace (Wenden, 2004); amongst many others.

Although educating for a higher level of consciousness might seem to be an insurmountable challenge given the historical inertia of formal education systems, there is cause for optimism that it is achievable. In recent decades a paradigm shift has been underway in science and mathematics education, with growing demands for socially responsible curricula and humanistic pedagogies that promote deep meaning-centered learning. Although in its infancy, this paradigm shift is

gaining momentum thanks to emergent theories of mind and society that are giving rise to powerful social epistemologies of teaching and learning. Here I outline
recent trends.

During the 1980s and early 1990s the teaching of science and mathematics
was reconceptualized though the lens of *social constructivism* which emphasizes the
importance of focusing instruction on the learner's cognitive, emotional and social
meaning-making processes (Cobb, 1994; Tobin, 1993). This perspective has contributed to more student-centered classrooms in which teachers engage students
in reflective thinking, experiential learning, collaborative learning, open-ended
inquiry, rich-task activities and problem-posing-and-solving approaches. But a
word of warning! Although social constructivist pedagogies have helped to counter the traditional dominance of behaviorism that governs transmissionist teaching and passive-reception learning roles, it is readily subsumed within standard
curricula that aim to reproduce uncritically and unwittingly the presumed moral
superiority and epistemic certitude of the Western modern worldview, especially
in the instrumental fields of science and mathematics education (Taylor, 2006).

In an endeavor to counter this largely invisible political hegemony, *critical social
theory* was injected into the discourse of curriculum theorists (Grundy, 1987;
Young, 1990). Critical social theory is concerned with creating societies free
from dehumanizing policies and practices that perpetuate social injustice, cultural
exclusion, social inequity, racism, sexism, ageism, scientism and many other forms
of repression. These deeply sedimented ideologies operate invisibly to distort
social norms which serve the (social, economic, political) interests of the powerfully dominant few (e.g., social elites) while marginalizing and disadvantaging the
less powerful and culturally different "other" (e.g., women, ethnic minorities,
children). Critical educators work to emancipate students by engaging them in
classroom dialogue aimed at deconstructing the hegemony of repressive ideologies (after Habermas: see Taylor, 1996; Taylor and Campbell-Williams, 1993). In
science and mathematics education a critical social perspective first became evident in the innovative design of gender-inclusive curricula, and now is giving rise
to the cultural contextualization of curricula by bringing indigenous worldviews
and traditional ecological knowledge systems into the classroom (e.g., Aikenhead
and Michell, 2012). By itself, however, critical social theory does not necessarily
entail deep meaning-centered learning as it can serve to prescribe a counter-
discourse that transmits an alternative (politically correct) ideology to "children
of the revolution."

The beginning of the twenty-first century witnessed a renewed spirit of optimism in the struggle to etch a more secure foothold for meaning-centered learning in the conservative edifice of science and mathematics education. This was
achieved, at least in theory, with the articulation of *critical constructivism* which
combines social constructivist and critical social theories (Kincheloe, 2004;
Taylor, 1998). Thus inspired, the *humanist* teacher aims to create a democratic
classroom ethos of open (empathic and interactive) and critical (reflective and

challenging) discourse that fuels and is fueled by higher-order learning skills such as values clarification and reconceptualization, metacognitive and metaphoric thinking, and imaginative and visionary thinking. Students learn to use a range of genres to give expression to higher-order thinking processes and outcomes, including narrative writing, poetry, plays, stories, drama and role plays, sketches and movie making. Thus, disciplinary knowledge is learned deeply via multiple modes of thinking and representation. And, importantly for science and mathematics education, the epistemic and moral authority (or claims to cultural transcendence) of the Western modern worldview are analyzed (or deconstructed) through critical discourse informed by historical, philosophical and sociocultural perspectives.

A contemporary example of a humanistic pedagogy is a teacher-researcher program of "socially responsible science and mathematics" that is preparing students, as future citizens, to develop a critical consciousness about ethical dilemmas associated with possible misuse of innovations in science and technology. Ethical dilemma teaching focuses on topical issues such as nuclear power generation and the attendant risk of radiation pollution (e.g., Japan's Fukushima accident), and habitat destruction and resultant native species extinction due to land clearance for housing development. Students are taught social skills for engaging in ethical decision-making about the societal uptake of new developments in science and technology (Taylor *et al.*, in press/2013).

In light of these new paradigm developments in school curricula and pedagogies, how can higher education prepare the next generation of teachers with the capacity to inculcate higher-order thinking in their students? This is the challenge for teacher educators wishing to develop in their student-teachers the *eye of wisdom* (Hart, 2009) and the *heart of learning* (Glazer, 1999). As a teacher educator working with professional educators undertaking postgraduate studies, I believe that a key to meeting the pressing need for higher-order professional development is to radically reconceptualize the nature and purpose of postgraduate research.

Transformative Professional Development

An exciting influence on contemporary teacher education that resonates strongly with critical constructivism's humanistic emphasis is transformative learning theory which has its roots in the original work of Jack Mezirow (1991). I have at my feet a pile of books authored/edited by Mezirow and a large number of fellow transformative educators who have continued to expand, enrich and extend his original ideas; as a body of academic work it is clearly burgeoning. Over the past 20 years Mezirow's transformative theory of adult learning has been applied to a range of contexts such as higher education, the workplace and the community (Brookfield, 1995; Cranton, 1994; Mezirow and Taylor, 2009), and recently has been coupled with theories of society, consciousness, spirituality, wisdom, sustainability, globalization, feminism, culture and so on, to generate compelling aesthetic, spiritual and ethical perspectives on the role of education in helping to create a more equitable, peaceful, diverse and sustainable world (Brooks, 2000; Fisher-Yoshida *et al.*, 2009; Gardner and Kelly, 2008). Thus transformative learning theory embraces critical constructivist theory and, a result of its extensive community of scholar-practitioners, a kaleidoscope of applications has been created across the field of education and beyond.

What can we take from this extensive scholarship to shape our university teaching practice, especially in the context of engaging culturally diverse adult learners in postgraduate professional development? The following passage from the introduction to the book, *Expanding the Boundaries of Transformative Learning* (O'Sullivan *et al.*, 2002), is a succinct source of powerful ideas.

> Transformative learning involves experiencing a deep, structural shift in the basic premises of thought, feelings, and actions. It is a shift of consciousness that dramatically and permanently alters our way of being in the world. Such a shift involves our understanding of ourselves and our self-locations, our relationships with other humans and with the natural world; our understanding of relations of power in interlocking structures of class, race, and gender; our body-awareness; our visions of alternative approaches to living; our sense of possibilities for social justice and peace and personal joy.

When I reflect on my own commitment to ensuring that my professional practice contributes to fostering biocultural diversity, then I find myself inspired by the above passage to articulate the following perspective on transformative learning for developing an enhanced mindfulness about ourselves and the world that we are inextricably part of.

1. *Cultural-self knowing*—more fully understanding our worldviews (or ways of knowing, being and valuing), especially values, premises, frames of reference, emotions and ideals residing in our subconscious (and connected to the *collective unconscious*) which underlie our habits of mind, constitute our (cultural/individual) identities, and govern our social inter/actions.
2. *Relational knowing*—understanding and appreciating the value of reconnecting with the natural world and with culturally different others' ways of knowing, valuing and being in the world.
3. *Critical knowing*—understanding how economic and organizational power has historically structured our sociocultural reality (especially class, race, gender and the conventional scientific worldview) and thus governs (controls, restricts, limits, distorts) our identities and our relationships with the natural world and with the culturally different other.
4. *Visionary and ethical knowing*—envisioning (through idealization and imagination and dialogue with the culturally different other) what a better world could/should be.

5. *Enhanced agency*—realizing that it is desirable, feasible and necessary to contribute to making the world a better place and that we have the capacity and commitment to do so.

These are qualities of transformative learning that I endeavor to bring to life in my own university teaching, bringing them to the awareness of my postgraduate students and inviting them to engage in higher-order learning so that they might transform their teaching practices and the lives of their students. I strive to enable them to re-address their standing in the world as professional educators (Palmer, 1993) by focusing their practitioner-research on transformative questions that are both subjective (interior focused) and sociocultural (outward focused); questions such as:

- What are the key social, cultural and political challenges facing my rapidly changing society?
- Whose cultural interests are not being well served by traditional educational policy and practice?
- Who are these students whom I greet every day? What are their worldviews, languages and life-long learning needs?
- Who is the cultural self who teaches? What key life-world experiences and values underpin my own professional practice and aspirations?
- What is my vision of a better world and how can my own professional practice help to realize it?

However, a major obstacle for novice researchers, especially science and mathematics educators, is their restrictive belief about what constitutes legitimate research. Life-long enculturation into *the scientific method* has instilled the conviction that *positivism* is the privileged epistemology of research, not only for the natural sciences but also the social sciences, including educational research (Kincheloe and Tobin, 2009). Positivism is embodied in normative educational research designs that subscribe to the following key epistemological principles.

- The purpose of research is to produce (or verify) objective knowledge about general social laws (i.e., objectivism).
- Legitimate knowledge can be produced only by means of objective, value-neutral inquiry employing quantitative research methods fueled by "scientific reasoning" (propositional, deductive, analytic logic) and governed by quality standards of validity and reliability (i.e., scientism).
- Research is a theory-testing process of manipulating decontextualized variables (i.e., reductionism).
- Bridging the theory-practice gap involves privileging the theoretical voices of expert academic researchers (i.e., elitism).
- Research report writing involves writing scientifically: using third person, past tense, passive voice, free of political polemic and rhetoric; a neutral "reasoned" voice (i.e., "God-speak").

Clearly there is little opportunity in such a deterministic and objectivistic model for the practitioner-researcher to display evidence of his/her transformative professional growth! The primary focus on research outcomes—*knowledge as objective product*—masks the subjective and sociocultural dimensions of an unfolding inquiry. However, my intention is not to deconstruct the positivist research paradigm but to loosen its hegemonic grip on professional educators' worldviews; to open their hearts and minds to alternative epistemologies of inquiry, especially those that promote the emergent process of discovery of "the self who teaches" (Palmer, 1993). Reconstructing my earlier aphorism gives us: *The fish becomes critically aware of the poor quality of water in which it is immersed and is committed to cleaning it up by helping to remove the source of pollution!*

Transformative Research

The field of contemporary qualitative research offers exciting and novel methods for engaging in transformative professional development, especially for practitioner-researchers interested in decolonizing and recontextualizing their society's curricular and pedagogic policies and practices. Here I focus on one such possibility—*arts-based critical auto/ethnography*—which draws on the epistemologies of new research paradigms that have emerged during the past 20 years—*interpretivism, criticalism* and *postmodernism*. This multi-paradigmatic perspective enables practitioner-researchers to combine a variety of innovative research approaches—auto/ethnography, autobiography, narrative inquiry, poetic inquiry, critical action research, self-study, performance ethnography, etc.—to inquire deeply into and radically reconceptualize their own socioculturally situated experiences as consumers (students) and producers (teachers) of education (Denzin, 2003; Ellis, 1997; Green *et al.*, 2006; Pithouse *et al.*, 2009; Prendergast *et al.*, 2009; Roth, 2005). I shall outline briefly each of the research paradigms (for details see Taylor *et al.*, 2012).

At the heart of the *interpretivist research paradigm* is a social constructivist perspective on the researcher's (hermeneutic) endeavor to develop deep, contextual and emergent understanding of the culturally different other by studying how the other's worldview shapes and is shaped by his/her socially situated actions. Ethnographic methods of prolonged immersion, participant observation and informal interviewing are employed. At the same time, the researcher engages in a (phenomenologically) reflexive process of deepening his/her own self-understanding. Autobiographical and narrative methods of writing are employed to explore and record the researcher's own lived experience and emergent self-understanding. Auto/ethnography combines ethnographic and autobiographical perspectives to direct the researcher's heartfelt inquiry into the historical roots of his/her own cultural situatedness and identity.

The *critical research paradigm* arms the auto/ethnographic researcher with conceptual tools for ideology critique, self-decolonization and visionary thinking, as well as with the role of a social activist aspiring to transform his/her sociocultural reality and improve the human condition. An *emancipatory* interest (after Habermas; see Young, 1990) fuels the critical researcher's mission to identify and lay bare the hegemony of powerful systems of social thought and action that have colonized historically his/her society and continue to maintain a powerful presence by virtue of their invisibility (e.g., the traditional Western modern worldview). Adopting a critical reflexive perspective enables the auto/ethnographic researcher to: (i) explore crucial ways in which his/her cultural identity has been molded (or distorted) by formal education systems; (ii) reconceptualize his/her cultural identity, values and aspirations; and (iii) develop a philosophical perspective for transforming the sociocultural structures of his/her future professional practice.

The *postmodern research paradigm* adds both pluralism and playfulness to the auto/ethnographer's work, providing a rich repertoire of modes of inquiry (Barone and Eisner, 2006; Diamond and Mullen, 1999; Galman, 2009; Knowles and Cole, 2008; Richo, 2009). Artful inquiry employs literary genres and logics to evoke in the researcher multiple modes of thinking and feeling and the means to communicate complexity, ambiguity and paradox to the reader in educationally thoughtful ways (Palmer, 1980). Examples include: metaphoric, dialectical and paradoxical thinking, mindfulness and spiritual awareness, poetic and performative writing.

For example, in this chapter my transformative rhetoric includes, in addition to the standard (propositional, deductive, analytic) logic of scientific reasoning, the polemical voice of an advocate of emancipatory education (Lather, 1991) and literary devices such as metaphor (Lakoff and Johnson, 1980) to elicit dialogical thinking (as advocated by Rupert Wegerif in this volume). To the positivist eye, argumentation represented by anything other than scientific reasoning would appear to be transgressive of conventional academic writing standards and thus illegitimate. But the *postmodern turn* in educational research opens the door to the arts, via multivocal and multilingual texts, to help counter this neoconservative challenge (Denzin and Giardina, 2006).

The practice of arts–based critical auto/ethnography involves writing not simply as a process of reporting on a completed inquiry but, importantly, as a process that is constitutive of the act of inquiry: the researcher inquires as s/he writes (Richardson, 2000). The autobiographical aspect fosters excavation of deeply sedimented cultural memories thereby enabling the researcher to identify and examine his/her personal experience of historically established educational policies and practices (Taylor and Settelmaier, 2003; Pereira *et al.*, 2005). Through authoring and reflecting in critical and scholarly ways on their own personal-cultural narratives, researchers can recover and reinvest in their cultural heritage, an important step in the process of personal and professional renewal. To develop one's authority as a producer of cultural knowledge is a step towards decolonizing one's research and professional practice (Mutua and Swadener, 2004).

Arts-based critical auto/ethnographic research has become established as a powerful means for postgraduate educational researchers to engage meaningfully in transformative professional development that embodies higher-order thinking. Drawing on new research paradigms that foreground the researcher's intersubjectivity, and adding sociocultural theories to focus the inquiry, the transformative researcher is provided with powerful developmental tools with which to:

- examine critically his/her culturally situated experiences in life,
- recover and reinvest in the value of his/her cultural heritage, and
- develop a professional philosophy of culturally situated education.

Coda

Doctoral research completed recently by teacher educators working in universities in Mozambique and Nepal serve as exemplars of arts-based critical auto/ethnographic approaches that have yielded philosophies of culturally situated education. Consider these three testimonies.

> When I subsequently returned to Mozambique and to my practice as a science teacher educator at Universite Pedagogica, though conscious that learning never ends, I felt empowered to discuss more deeply with my students issues of science in our cultural context. I have been encouraging them to learn from themselves. To interrogate their own attitudes toward learning and teaching science as well as their colleagues' and teachers' attitudes. To discover hidden subjectivities they have as Africans, especially in the context of the school science classroom.
>
> *(Afonso-Nhalevilo, 2010)*

> My doctoral dissertation addressed the protracted problem of the culturally decontextualised nature of mathematics education which un/wittingly prevents many school students from gaining full access to powerful mathematical ideas. I have developed a mathematics curriculum model to implement creative and innovative pedagogies that help students gain access to much needed mathematical skills and knowledge required for critical and active citizenship.
>
> *(Luitel, 2009b)*

> One of the major outcomes of my doctoral research was an enhanced consciousness of my Mozambican identity. It is something that can be hardly characterized. My identity includes:

> my body and the bodies of others
> my colour and the colour of others
> my language and the language of others
> my country and the country of others
> my relatives and those who I know
> my relatives and those who I don't know
> my soul and the souls of others
> my spirituality and the spiritualities of others
> the others are me and
> I am the others
>
> *(Cupane, 2007)*

These transformative researchers excavated their cultural memories by generating memoirs, poems, stories, performance texts and images. They used these data texts for multiple purposes. First, to interrogate their lived experiences as indigenous people who had during childhood struggled to cross cultural borders into schooling systems governed by the Western worldview of colonial European powers. Second, to reflect critically on their struggles as university teachers to render science and mathematics education culturally meaningful. Third, to explore the hegemony of their deeply sedimented positivist assumptions about what constitutes legitimate research, in the process expanding their epistemologies as they embraced new paradigm research methods. As their research progressed and they developed scholarly sociocultural perspectives, they wrote data-texts to give expression to their developing visions as "culture workers" intent on transforming the professional practices of future generations of teachers and students in their respective countries.

Ongoing scholarly publications by these new generation educational leaders evidence how *research as transformative learning* enabled each of them to develop a vision and commitment to creating culturally situated curricula for empowering African and Asian children to respect, celebrate and grow their cultural capital, and develop identities for belonging to local, regional, national and global communities (Afonso-Nhalevilo, 2010, 2013; Afonso and Taylor, 2009; Luitel, 2009b, in press/2013; Luitel and Taylor, 2006, 2007, 2009, 2010, in press/2013). Time will tell what the long-term impact will be on their professional practice, but there are encouraging signs. In Mozambique, Emilia Afonso-Nhalevilo and Alberto Cupane have introduced an "Innovative Research Methods" course into the master's program of their university, have established a program of research into indigenous knowledge systems (IKS) of Mozambique, and are collaborating with universities in South Africa to conduct culture studies research in science education using new research paradigms. In Nepal, Bal Chandra Luitel has established a program of research specializing in culture studies of mathematics education via new paradigm research approaches; thus far, 20 students have graduated with master's degrees (e.g., Gautum, 2011; Poudel, 2010; Shrestha, 2011). At this stage it would seem that transformative practitioner-research has a firm foothold for fostering meaning-centered learning in Mozambican and Nepali teacher education.

References

Afonso, E. Z. de F. (2002) Rethinking science teacher education in Mozambique: An autoethnographic inquiry. Dissertation for Master of Science Education, Curtin University of Technology, Perth, Australia.

Afonso, E. Z. de F. (2006) Developing a culturally inclusive philosophy of science teacher education in Mozambique. Doctoral thesis, Curtin University of Technology, Perth, Australia.

Afonso-Nhalevilo, E. Z. de F. (2010) *Endless Journey: An Autoethnographic Search for Culturally Inclusive Philosophy of Science Teacher Education in Mozambique.* Saarbrücken, Germany: VDM Verlag.

Afonso-Nhalevilo, E. Z. de F. (2013) "Rethinking the history of inclusion of IKS in school curricula: Endeavoring to legitimate the subject." *International Journal of Science and Mathematics Education.*

Afonso, E., and Taylor, P. C. (2009) "Critical autoethnographic inquiry for culture-sensitive professional development." *Reflective Practice* 10: 273–283.

Aikenhead, G. S., and Michell, H. (2012) *Building Cultures: Indigenous and Scientific Ways of Knowing Nature.* Toronto, ON: Pearson.

Ashcroft, B., Griffiths, G. and Tiffen, H. (2006) *Post-Colonial Studies: The Key Concepts.* New York: Routledge.

Australian Government (2009) Living sustainably: The Australian Government's national action plan for education for sustainability. Commonwealth of Australia, Canberra, ACT.

Barone, T. and Eisner, E. (2006) "Arts-based research." In J. L. Green, G. Camilli and P. B. Elmore (Eds), *Handbook of Complementary Methods in Education Research* (pp. 95–109). Hillsdale, NJ: Lawrence Erlbaum.

Brookfield, S. (1995) *The Critically Reflective Teacher.* San Fransisco, CA: Jossey-Bass.

Brooks, A. K. (2000) "Cultures of transformation." In A. L. Wilson and E. R. Hayes (Eds), *Handbook of Adult and Continuing Education* (pp. 161–170). San Francisco, CA: Jossey-Bass.

Cobb, P. (1994) "Where is the mind? Constructivist and sociocultural perspectives on mathematical development." *Educational Researcher* 23(7): 13–20.

Cranton, P. (1994) *Understanding and Promoting Transformative Learning.* San Francisco, CA: Jossey-Bass.

Cupane, A. (2007) Towards a culture-sensitive pedagogy of physics teacher education in Mozambique. Doctoral thesis, Curtin University of Technology, Perth, Australia.

Denzin, N. K. (2003) *Performance Ethnography: Critical Pedagogy and the Politics of Culture.* Thousand Oaks, CA: Sage.

Denzin, N. K. and Giardina, M. D. (Eds) (2006) *Qualitative Inquiry and the Conservative Challenge.* Walnut Creek, CA: Left Coast Press.

Denzin, N. K. and Lincoln, Y. S. (Eds) (2005) *The Sage Handbook of Qualitative Research* (3rd ed.). Thousand Oaks, CA: Sage.

Desai, G. and Nair, S. (Eds) (2005) *Postcolonialisms: An Anthology of Cultural Theory and Criticism.* New Brunswick, NJ: Rutgers University Press.

Diamond, C. T. P. and Mullen, C. A. (Eds) (1999) *The Postmodern Educator: Arts-Based Inquiries and Teacher Development.* New York: Peter Lang.

Ellis, C. (1997) "Evocative autoethnography: Writing emotionally about our lives." In W. G. Tierney and Y. S. Lincoln (Eds), *Representation and the Text: Re-Framing the Narrative Voice* (pp. 115–139). Albany, NY: State University of New York Press.

Esbjorn-Hargens, S. and Zimmerman, M. E. (2009) *Integral Ecology: Uniting Multiple Perspectives on the Natural World.* Boston, MA: Integral Books.

Fisher-Yoshida, B., Geller, K. D. and Scahpiro, S. A. (Eds) (2009) *Innovations in Transformative Learning: Space, Culture, and the Arts.* New York: Peter Lang.

Galman, S. (2009) "Trading in fables: Literary and artistic methods in self-study research." In C. A. Lassonde, S. Galman and C. Kosnick (Eds), *Self-Study Research Methodologies for Teacher Educators* (pp. 129–149). Rotterdam, The Netherlands: Sense.

Gardner, M. and Kelly, U. (Eds) (2008) *Narrating Transformative Learning in Education.* New York: Palgrave Macmillan.

Gautum, S. (2011) Literacy sucks: Lived experiences of Tharu women. Unpublished dissertation for Master of Philosophy (Education), Kathmandu University, Nepal.

Giroux, G. A. (1993) *Border Crossings: Cultural Workers and the Politics of Education.* New York and London: Routledge, Chapman and Hall.

Glazer, S. (Ed.) (1999) *The Heart of Learning: Spirituality in Education.* New York: Penguin Putnam.

Green, J. L., Camilli, G. and Elmore, P. B. (Eds) (2006) *Handbook of Complementary Methods in Education Research.* Hillsdale, NJ: Lawrence Erlbaum.

Grundy, S. (1987) *Curriculum: Product or Praxis?* London: The Falmer Press.

Haarman, H. (2007) *Foundations of Culture: Knowledge-Construction, Belief Systems and Worldview in Their Dynamic Interplay.* Frankfurt, Germany: Peter Lang.

Hansen, D. T. (2007) (Ed.) *Ethical Visions of Education: Philosophies in Practice.* New York: Teachers College Press.

Hart, T. (2009) *From Information to Transformation: Education for Evolution of Consciousness.* New York: Peter Lang.

Intergovernmental Panel on Climate Change (2007) Climate change 2007: The physical science basis. Downloaded from http://www.ipcc.ch/ on January 2, 2012.

Kauffman, S. A. (2008) *Reinventing the Sacred: A New View of Science, Reason and Religion.* New York: Basic Books.

Kincheloe, J. (2004) *Critical Constructivism.* New York: Peter Lang.

Kincheloe, J. and Tobin, K. (2009) "The much exaggerated death of positivism." *Cultural Studies of Science Education* 4(3): 513–528.

Knowles, J. G. and Cole, A. L. (Eds) (2008) *Handbook of Arts in Qualitative Research.* Thousand Oaks, CA: Sage.

Lakoff, G. and Johnson, M. (1980) *Metaphors We Live By.* Chicago, IL: University of Chicago Press.

Lanza, R. and Berman, B. (2009) *Biocentrism: How Life and Consciousness Are the Keys to Understanding the True Nature of the Universe.* Dallas, TX: Benbella Books.

Laszlo, E. (2008) *Quantum Shift in the Global Brain: How the New Scientific Reality Can Change Us and Our World.* Rochester: Inner Traditions.

Lather, P. (1991) *Getting Smart: Feminist Research and Pedagogy with/in the Postmodern.* New York: Routledge.

Luitel, B. C. (2009a) Culture, worldview and transformative philosophy of mathematics education in Nepal: A cultural-philosophical inquiry. Doctoral thesis, Curtin University, Perth, Australia.

Luitel, B. C. (2009b) *Narrative Explorations of Lived Mathematics Curriculum: An Epic Journey.* Saarbrücken, Germany: VDM Verlag.

Luitel, B. C. (in press/2013) "Mathematics as an im/pure knowledge system: Symbiosis, (w)holism and synergy in mathematics education." *International Journal of Science and Mathematics Education.*

Luitel, B. C. and Taylor, P. C. (2006) "Envisioning transition towards a critical mathematics education: A Nepali educator's autoethnographic perspective." In J. Earnest and D. Treagust (Eds), *Education Reform in Societies in Transition: International Perspectives* (pp. 91–109). Rotterdam, Netherlands: Sense.

Luitel, B. C. and Taylor, P. C. (2007) "The Shanai, the pseudosphere and other imaginings: Envisioning a culturally contextualised mathematics education." *Cultural Studies of Science Education* 2(3): 621–638.

Luitel, B. C. and Taylor, P. C. (2009) "De-frosting and re-frosting the ideology of pure mathematics: An infusion of Eastern-Western perspectives on conceptualising a socially just mathematics education." In P. Ernest, B. Greer and B. Sriraman (Eds), *Critical Issues in Mathematics Education* (pp. 125–152). Charlotte, NC: Information Age Publishing.

Luitel, B. C. and Taylor, P. C. (2010) "'What is ours and what is not ours?' Inclusive imaginings of contextualised mathematics teacher education." In D. J. Tippins, M. P. Mueller, M. van Eijck and J. Adams (Eds), *Cultural Studies and Environmentalism: The Confluence of Eco-Justice, Place Based (Science) Education, and Indigenous Knowledge Systems* (pp. 385–408). Dordrecht, The Netherlands: Springer.

Luitel, B. C. and Taylor, P. C. (in press/2013) "Fractals of 'old' and 'new' logics: A post/modern proposal for transformative mathematics pedagogy." *Philosophy of Mathematics Education Journal.*

Lyons, J. (2009) *The House of Wisdom: How the Arabs Transformed Western Civilization.* New York: Bloomsbury Press.

Maffi, L. and Woodley, E. (2010) *Biocultural Diversity Conservation: A Global Sourcebook.* London, UK: Earthscan.

Mezirow, J. (1991) *Transformative Dimensions of Adult Learning.* San Francisco, CA: Jossey-Bass.

Mezirow, J. and Taylor, E. W. (Eds) (2009) *Transformative Learning in Practice: Insights from Community, Workplace, and Higher Education.* San Francisco, CA: Jossey-Bass.

Miller, J. P. (2005) "Introduction: Holistic learning." In J. P. Miller, S. Karsten, D. Denton, D. Orr and I. C. Kates (Eds), *Holistic Learning and Spirituality in Education* (pp. 1–15). Albany, NY: State University of New York Press.

Mutua, K. and Swadener, B. B. (Eds) (2004) *Decolonizing Research in Cross-Cultural Contexts: Critical Personal Narratives.* Albany, NY: State University of New York Press.

O'Sullivan, E. V., Morrell, A. and O'Connor, M. A. (Eds) (2002) *Expanding the Boundaries of Transformative Learning: Essays on Theory and Praxis.* New York: Palgrave.

Palmer, P. (1980) *The Promise of Paradox: A Celebration of Contradictions in the Christian Life.* San Francisco, CA: Jossey Bass.

Palmer, P. J. (1993) *To Know as We Are Known: Education as a Spiritual Journey.* New York: HarperCollins.

Palmer, P. J. and Zajonc, A. (2010) *The Heart of Higher Education: A Call to Renewal. Transforming the Academy through Collegial Conversations.* San Francisco, CA: Jossey-Bass.

Palmer, P. L. (1998) *The Courage to Teach: Exploring the Inner Landscape of a Teacher's Life.* San Francisco, CA: Jossey-Bass.

Pereira, L., Settelmaier, E. and Taylor, P. (2005) "Fictive imagining and moral purpose: Autobiographical research as/for transformative development." In W.-M. Roth (Ed.), *Auto/biography and Auto/ethnography: Praxis of Research Method* (pp. 49–74). Rotterdam, The Netherlands: Sense.

Pithouse, K., Mitchell, C. and Moletsane, R. (Eds) (2009) *Making Connections: Self-Study and Social Action.* New York: Peter Lang.

Poudel, A. (2010) Exploring mathematics in motherly nature: An autoethnographic inquiry. Unpublished dissertation for Master of Education (Mathematics), Kathmandu University, Nepal.

Prendergast, M., Leggo, C. and Sameshima, P. (Eds) (2009) *Poetic Inquiry: Vibrant Voices in the Social Sciences.* Rotterdam, The Netherlands: Sense.

Richardson, L. (2000) "Writing: A method of inquiry." In N. K. Denzin and Y. S. Lincoln (Eds), *Handbook of Qualitative Research* (2nd ed.) (pp. 923–948). Thousand Oaks, CA: Sage.

Richo, D. (2009) *Being True to Life: Poetic Paths to Personal Growth.* Boston, MA: Shambhala.

Roth, W.-M. (Ed.) (2005) *Auto/biography and Auto/ethnography: Praxis of Research Method.* Rotterdam, The Netherlands: Sense.

Said, E. (1978) *Orientalism.* New York: Random House.

Schech, S. and Haggis, J. (2000) *Culture and Development: A Critical Introduction.* Oxford: Blackwell Publishers.

Semali, L. M. and Kincheloe, J. L. (Eds) (1999) *Indigenous Knowledge: Voices from the Academy.* New York: Falmer Press.

Shrestha, I. M. (2011) My journey of learning and teaching: A trans/formation from culturally decontextualised to contextualised mathematics education. Dissertation for Master of Education (Mathematics), Kathmandu University, Nepal.

Skutnabb-Kangas, T., Maffi, L. and Harmon, D. (2003) *Sharing a World of Difference: The Earth's Linguistic, Cultural and Biological Diversity.* UNESCO-Terralingua-World Wildlife Fund for Nature: http://www.terralingua.org/RecPublications.htm

Taylor, P. C. (1996) "Mythmaking and mythbreaking in the mathematics classroom." *Educational Studies in Mathematics* 31(2): 151–173.

Taylor, P. C. (1998) "Constructivism: Value added." In B. J. Fraser and K. G. Tobin (Eds), *The International Handbook of Science Education* (pp. 1111–1123). Dordrecht, The Netherlands: Kluwer Academic.

Taylor, P. C. (2006) "Towards culturally inclusive science education." *Cultural Studies of Science Education* 1(1): 201–208.

Taylor, P. C. (2008) "Multi-paradigmatic research design spaces for cultural studies researchers embodying postcolonial theorizing." *Cultural Studies of Science Education* 3(4): 881–890.

Taylor, P. C. (in press/2013) "Transformative science teacher education." In R. Gunstone (Ed.), *Encyclopedia of Science Education.* Dordrecht, The Netherlands: Springer.

Taylor, P. C. and Campbell-Williams, M. (1993) "Discourse towards balanced rationality in the high school mathematics classroom: Ideas from Habermas' critical theory." In J. A. Malone and P. C. S. Taylor (Eds), *Constructivist Interpretations of Teaching and Learning Mathematics* (pp. 135–148). Curtin University of Technology, Perth, Australia.

Taylor, P. C. and Settelmaier, E. (2003) "Critical autobiographical research for science educators." *Journal of Science Education Japan* 27(4): 233–244.

Taylor, P. C. and Wallace, J. (Eds) (2007) *Contemporary Qualitative Research: Exemplars for Science and Mathematics Educators*. Dordrecht, The Netherlands: Springer.

Taylor, E., Taylor, P. C. and Chow, M. L. (in press/2013) "Ethical dilemma story pedagogy: Engaging diverse learners in science education for sustainability." In N. Mansour and R. Wegerif (Eds), *Science Education for Diversity: Theory and Practice*. Rotterdam, Netherlands: Sense Publishers.

Taylor, P. C., Taylor, E. and Luitel, B. C. (2012) "Multi-paradigmatic transformative research as/for teacher education: An integral perspective." In B. J. Fraser, K. G. Tobin and C. J. McRobbie (Eds), *Second International Handbook of Science Education* (pp. 373–387). Dordrecht, The Netherlands: Springer.

Tobin, K. (1993) *The Practice of Constructivism in Science and Mathematics Education*. Hillsdale, NJ: Lawrence Erlbaum.

United Nations Secretary-General's High-level Panel on Global Sustainability (2012) *Resilient people, resilient planet: A future worth choosing*. New York: United Nations.

Van Manen, M. (1990) *Researching Lived Experience: Human Science for an Action Sensitive Pedagogy*. London, ON: The State University of New York.

Veerma, G. (2004) "Performing colonial and postcolonial science in India." In K. Mutua and B. B. Swadener (Eds), *Decolonizing Research in Cross-Cultural Contexts: Critical Personal Narratives* (pp. 53–68). Albany, NY: State University of New York Press.

Wenden, A. L. (Ed.) (2004) *Educating for a Culture of Social and Ecological Peace*. Albany, NY: State University of New York Press.

Young, R. (1990) *A Critical Theory of Education: Habermas and Our Children's Future*. New York, NY: Teachers College Press.

13

THE FUTURE OF MEANING-CENTERED EDUCATION

Olga Kovbasyuk and Patrick Blessinger

Introduction

In the introductory chapter of this book, we explained our vision for the book and focused on meaning-centered education (MCE) and meaning-centered learning (MCL) from a macro-analytical and conceptual level in order to give readers a big picture view of the topics. In this chapter, we will focus on MCE-MCL from a micro-analytical and granular level in order to continue constructing the building blocks for MCE-MCL and give readers a more application oriented view of the topic. The specific focus will be on the epistemological underpinnings of MCE-MCL and we will compare them to the objectivist and constructivist paradigms, which are two of the major epistemological paradigms (relative to education and the nature of inquiry) that have evolved since the days of Socrates (rationalist-constructivists) and Aristotle (empiricist-objectivists) (Hyland, 1973; Jonassen, 1991; Vrasidas, 2000). We will then use that framing to discuss the principles of MCL and how those principles can be applied in a practical way.

MCE is an educational philosophy and approach that facilitates the conscious, autonomous integration of new understanding with the learner's prior learning (Ausubel, 1963, 2000). MCE supports the integration of learning across all learning domains (affective, cognitive, socio-cultural) and facilitates the creation of personal meanings about who we are and how we relate to ourselves and the world—the conscious and intentional development of one's life-world. Self-determination and self-regulation are primary indicators of an existential worldview of personality wherein one assumes personal responsibility and endeavors to achieve self-fulfillment (e.g., Leontiev, 2004). The core learning processes supported by MCE are therefore complex, active, constructive, connected, and continuously evolving according to one's life-world context (Shuell, 1990).

Comparison to Other Paradigms

In the last few generations the view of teaching and learning has begun to shift from a passive, unidirectional, unidimensional, authoritarian instructional paradigm to one that is more of an active, multi-directional, multi-dimensional, collaborative learning paradigm (Wulf, 2012). Within the context of this paradigm shift, the following sections discuss two major learning paradigms and how they contrast with each other and with MCE. Along the continuum of each paradigm there are several branches and many nuances but we attempt here to present a very brief overview of each and discuss the points most salient to MCE-MCL.

Objectivist Paradigm

In the objectivist epistemological view of knowledge, knowledge is independent of human subjectivity or human consciousness. Knowledge is external to the mind and created when one learns about or discovers this external, objective reality. Information acquires meaning when this reality (which is the same for everyone) is mapped onto one's mind through interactions with the objective natural world. Thus, under this view, the main goal of instruction is to transfer this pre-existing subject matter knowledge directly to the student in the most efficient and effective way possible (e.g., direct transmission via lecture and textbooks). The focus of learning is on mastery of subject matter content (concepts, principles, theories) as she/he goes through the learning process. The preferred method of instruction is didactical in the sense that the instructor is considered the authoritative expert and the primary source of knowledge for learners (Bednar et al., 1991; Hyland, 1973; Vrasidas, 2000).

In this paradigm, the preferred method of inquiry is the scientific, empirical method which is viewed as the best way to arrive at an accurate and complete understanding of the one "true" objective reality. Examples include listening to lectures, taking notes, reading assigned texts, and taking written tests to demonstrate how much cognitive-based material one has mastered. In this paradigm, learners are viewed mainly as receptacles in the learning process wherein they acquire knowledge by assimilating prior knowledge from subject matter experts (Freire, 1970). The cognitive domain is the primary focus of learning. Ontologically, reality exists independent of the mind, and axiologically, personal values are not important or relevant in meaning making (Bednar et al., 1991; Carson, 2005; Hyland, 1973; Vrasidas, 2000).

Constructivist Paradigm

Constructivism operates along a continuum and has several explicit branches (e.g., personal constructivism, social constructivism). In general, in the constructivist epistemological view of knowledge, knowledge is not created through discovery of an external, objective reality and there is no independently existing knowledge that resides outside the mind, waiting to be discovered. Rather, knowledge is subjective and learning is the process of constructing knowledge by cognitive activity through one's subjective interpretation of personal experiences and interactions with the world. The main goal of instruction is to guide learners to enable them to construct their own knowledge, discover their own truth, and experience their own reality via personal meaning making. The focus of learning is on higher order thinking (e.g., problem solving, evaluating, creating, meta-cognizing) (Krathwohl, 2002), as opposed to lower order thinking (remembering, comprehending, applying). The preferred method of instruction is dialogical and dialectical wherein the instructor is mainly a facilitator and guides the student to create their own knowledge (Bednar *et al.*, 1991; Bredo, 2000; Hyland, 1973; Dewey and Bently, 1949; von Glaserfeld, 1987, 1995; Vygotsky, 1978; Wertsch, 1997; Jonassen, 1991; Vrasidas, 2000).

Within this paradigm, a diversity of learning methods is useful depending on the nature of the problem being investigated. Examples include learning that is active, experiential, inquiry-based, problem-based, project-based, case-based, collaboration-based, and the use of open-ended assessments. Learners are viewed as self-directed and active participants in the learning process. Learners construct their own reality through personal meaning making, reflection, interpretation, and imagination. Learners naturally seek meaning in the learning process and the ultimate responsibility for learning lies with the learner. Thus, the purpose of education is to create the right conditions whereby learners can effectively and creatively synthesize prior and new experiences to construct new knowledge (Elkind, 2005; von Glaserfeld, 1987; Wertsch 1997). The cognitive and socio-cultural domains are the main focus of learning. Ontologically, constructivism sets aside the nature of external reality and its impact on knowledge and learning. Axiologically, personal values are important in meaning making.

Gredler (2009) identified four potential problems with social constructivism: (1) the minimization of direct instruction, (2) difficulty of low-ability students and students of non-dominant cultures to fully participate, (3) the extra burdens placed on instructors to effectively manage this type of classroom environment, and (4) the challenge of minimum guidance instruction to adequately facilitate deep learning. Bandura (2004) noted that although several learning theories exist today for educators, the lack of effective and appropriate implementation models and strategies is still very much needed in order for these learning theories to be fully realizable.

Meaning-Centered Paradigm

In the MCE-MCL epistemological view, knowledge is personified, situated, and attempts to integrate authentic learning elements of both the objectivist and constructivist paradigms (e.g., Cronjé, 2006). Knowledge is created through an awareness of external objective reality but is internally constructed by cognitive, affective, and socio-cultural activities and perceptions. It is through this dynamic interplay of objective and subjective realities that one's life-world evolves (Hannula, 1997). Thus, knowledge is neither exclusively internal to the mind nor exclusively external to the mind. Rather, knowledge is alive, situated, and contextual and exists both subjectively and objectively (Leontiev, 2007). Learning is authorial and entails transformation of the student's authorship in a targeted practice that is recognized and validated by members of a community of practice, in a broader sense. Learning is constantly creative and even transcends pre-existing human culture (Lave, 1991; Lobok, 2001).

With MCE-MCL, the goal of instruction is to co-create, with both instructors and students, an authentic, humane, and holistic learning environment so that individuals can become more self-regulated, self-sustaining, self-determining authors of their own lives. This learning environment is thus individualized and personally meaningful to each unique learner. The focus of learning is on independent, critical thinking, as well as on ethical and psychosocial self-development (e.g., moral and psychological maturing, creation of personal value systems, social and relationship oriented actions). The main method of instruction is dialogical and authorial. The instructor is the author of her/his teaching mode, and collaborator and co-creator of knowledge, so she/he learns alongside the student (Berezina, 2004; Abakumova, 2003; Miyazaki, 2006). Thus, MCE-MCL supports pedagogical pluralism and learning diversity.

With MCE-MCL, there are multiple modes of inquiry and multiple perspectives, depending on the context and depending on the nature of the questions (Dahlberg, 1985; Rogalsky, 2006). The artistic mode (subjective inquiry), the philosophic mode (rational inquiry), and the scientific mode (empirical inquiry) are all acceptable, as long as they are authentic and meaningful to the participants and germane to the context of inquiry. The integration of multiple modes of inquiry, together with interdisciplinary and transdisciplinary learning, can be a useful approach to develop a more holistic and multidimensional understanding of different realities (e.g., scientific truth, moral truth, artistic-poetic truth). Examples include learning that is interdisciplinary and transdisciplinary (e.g., integration of math and art, global learning) as well as the development of new models and theories (e.g., exploration of one's own existential experience, variational learning, probabilistic learning, learning as a dialogue of cultures).

In this paradigm, learners are viewed as the co-owners of the curricula, wherein they help co-define their learning goals and tasks, assess their own successes and failures, and negotiate their own personal meanings within the learning process. With MCE-MCL, the purpose of education is active and creative participation in, and contribution to, the human culture-in-making process. The cognitive, socio-cultural, and affective domains all serve as the main focus of learning in order to form a holistic integration of self with world (i.e., an integrated life-word). Ontologically, reality is within this life-world, and axiologically, personal values, interests, beliefs, aspirations, and other factors define meaning making (Konashkova, 2007; Kebina, 2003).

A solipsistic state of mind that denies objective reality will not lead to a genuine view of reality just as extreme objectivism that denies a world with human values and emotions will not lead to a genuine view of reality. Freire (1970) contends that subjectivity without objectivity is naïve and misinformed and that objectivity without subjectivity leads to a simplistic view of the world without humanity. Freire also contends that such a dichotomy cannot exist in a human world because humans are the consciousness of the world and without that human consciousness, there is no knowing of the world. There is a social reality just as there is a natural reality but those realities can only be understood by way of human consciousness and experience and by the way humans interact with those realities—their life-worlds.

Freire (1970) provides an illustrative example of a student who proclaimed in the middle of a discussion on culture, "Now I see that without man there is no world." The teacher then responded, "Let's say, for the sake of argument, that all men on earth were to die, but that the earth itself remained . . . wouldn't all this be the world?" "Oh no," said the student. "There would be no one to say, 'This is a world'" (p. 69). This illustrates that the physical objects of the world do of course exist without humans but without humans there would be no consciousness to name it and to declare it so. So, what is a world without consciousness? A world without human consciousness is meaningless.

Humans are the consciousness of the world. Without human consciousness, what else or who else is there to make meaning of the world? Humanity, and the language that has evolved out of human evolution, is the voice of the world. Humans cannot exist apart from the world. Hence, this is why the idea of the human–world relationship (i.e., one's life-world) is such an important concept. We are in a continual state of becoming more conscious, and although humans live in a subjective state, it is through a critical analysis of both the subjective and objective realities that we become more aware and more knowledgeable of ourselves, the world, and our existence in the world.

Thus, according to an authorial MCE-MCL approach, learning language for example, involves communicative successes of a student being recognized by the language community rather than the student's acquisitions or discoveries or construction of self-contained, decontextualized vocabulary, grammar, and meta-knowledge about the language (Lobok, 2001). Thus, MCE-MCL is the interplay between diversity and uniqueness—the process of joining individuality with the diversity of human cultures. So, what is needed is both objectivity and subjectivity that is in a constant dialogical relationship just as one needs both theory and praxis in order to critically evaluate and understand the world. And in the dialogical process where one is striving to become a more conscious, self-governing, authentic agent of one's own destiny and transformation, one tries to move towards an authentic, holistic, and humane view of the world achieved through critical dialogue with self and with others.

Meaning-Centered Learning

In short, the MCE epistemology is the philosophical perspective that maintains that human knowledge is created by the continual interplay of cognitive, affective, and socio-cultural factors. MCE is an educational approach that facilitates the conscious, autonomous integration of new understanding with the learner's prior learning (Ausubel, 1963, 2000; Shuell, 1990; Hilgard, 1948). As such, MCE-MCL supports the integration of learning across all learning domains (affective, cognitive, socio-cultural) and facilitates the development of personal meanings about who we are and how we relate to the world and ourselves. Based on the MCE suppositions, and based on the earlier work on MCL by Kovbasyuk (2009, 2010, 2011, 2012), the authors and editors define meaning-centered learning (MCL) as learning that is the self-motivating and self-regulating process of creating personal meaning in one's life-world through reflective, critical, and inquiry-based activities that occur across all learning domains. Thus, according to this proposed meaning-centered learning theory, the learner constructs personal meaning from her/his experiences and their relationship to prior experiences and contexts, taking full responsibility for his/her own learning and self-evolvement as a personality who is capable of authoring one's own life.

Thus, MCL seeks to develop highly mature, integrated, and well-rounded multi-dimensional learners who have the capacity to function in a multiplicity of contexts or situations and as lifelong learners (Fischer, 2000). This includes thinking from different ontological perspectives (what is reality, objectively and subjectively), from different epistemological perspectives (how we know, empirically-sensing and rationally-intuiting), from different logical perspectives (how we reason, "a priori" and "a posteriori"), from different axiological perspectives (how we value, intrinsically and extrinsically), and from different phenomenological perspectives (how we experience reality, individually and relationally). MCL seeks to develop knowledge and learning experiences that traverse across all learning domains and across all disciplinary areas using appropriate modes of inquiry (e.g., scientific, philosophic, artistic) to develop self-regulating personalities who are capable of lifelong sustainable learning. The result is to develop personalities that are knowledgeable, skillful, and capable of making meaningful contributions to their community (citizenship), their profession (leadership), and their fields of study (scholarship).

To that end, ideally MCL seeks to use contextualized and appropriately integrated problem-based and inquiry-based reasoning approaches (e.g., deductive, inductive, reductive, reflective, reframing, analogical) to analyze, synthesize, and evaluate complex phenomena at multiple levels (e.g., individual, group, organizational, national, global) and across multiple learning domains (e.g., affective, cognitive, socio-cultural) in order to equip students with the ability to think and judge critically and creatively, to evaluate common themes/patterns across disciplines, to gain a comprehensive, 360-degree view of an issue/question, to generate new knowledge, and to explain a claim/statement from multiple positions (e.g., apologetic, dialectic, polemic) and from multiple theoretical perspectives (e.g., scientific, philosophic, ethical, psychological, political, sociological, anthropological, historical, humanistic, technological) in order to provide multiple, contextualized answers to complex questions.

MCE-MCL Concepts and Assumptions

MCE, as with any educational philosophy, requires a coherent and well-reasoned set of suppositions (e.g., assumptions, concepts, organizing principles, theories) upon which to base its veracity (Dewey, 1938). We can view MCE through different lenses (e.g., ontological, axiological, epistemological), which allow the theoretical and methodological analyses of three key objects of studies: the human experience and condition in the educational process, humanity and human values in the educational process, and educational culture.

Ontologically, the category of a human being represents the dynamic and ever changing flow of life of humankind. An individual is a part of this flow; she/he is becoming a personality and fulfills her/himself as personality throughout her/his existence. In order to comprehend an evolving personality in the meaning-centered approach, we emphasize that learning is being in culture; it is self-cognition and self-improvement and self-development as the subject of one's own life. The idea of subjectivity as the dominant attribute of a human being lies within the historical movement of the individual "becoming" in order "to be" and engages people as being aware of their incompleteness, thus driving them to improve their life-worlds (Heidegger, 1962; Kierkegaard, 1998; Buber, 1993). This allows us to view the process of strengthening the critical subjectivity of students as a core process in MCE-MCL. Creating authentic conditions for students to live through learning, and make choices with full responsibility for the decisions they make can facilitate the process of students' self-determination to become authors of their own lives.

The ontological dimension of meaning relates to the pedagogy of personality self-development (Kulikova, 2003), which views the process of self-development as internally determined by an individual, to probabilistic education (Lobok, 2001). This is based on the fundamental idea of learning via creative uncertainty (Lobok, 2001), and variational education (Asmolov, 1990) that supports the "variability" of an individual. In *probabilistic education*, the learning space is the space of action "here and now," the space of negotiated agreements and choices which educators and learners make and take full responsibility to act accordingly. *Variational education* provides space for learners to seek new ways out of situations of uncertainty and ways to choose one's own strategies in life. It helps an individual to gain new understanding of self in a constantly changing world. What unites them all is the idea that personal meaning making allows the process and the content of education to be more humane and holistic. The result can hardly be measured in a conventional way—we can only see the result when an individual is exposed to a real life situation and acts effectively with it.

The cultural-anthropological foundations of MCE-MCL lie within its onto-logical aspect, and refer to the deep structures of human subjectivity as an innate attribute. These structures are included in ontogenesis and phylogenies, providing positive and negative states of mind and spirit within the processes of individual development. They help determine the process of personality development and self-development as a way of constructing human lives on the basis of human aspiration for meaning in life and human self-strengthening nature, which we view as a highly spiritual unity. The self-strengthening nature of man is tightly connected with her/his search for personal meaning in life (Frankl, 1998). This search is conditioned by the question "What is a human being?" In our understanding, conscious self-awareness of an individual entails the need to enhance one's life activity via personal meanings, which guide her/him through life. If there are no meaningful life orienta-tions, a person experiences an "existential vacuum," according to Frankl (1998).

The axiological view recognizes the importance of a human being and the humaneness in the human being (Stepashko, 2004) as the conceptual ideas and fundamental values of classic pedagogy. According to classic pedagogy, humans' fundamental values have always been connected with a choice of what kind of life to pursue, and a true choice would always present alternative opportunities. Thus, a person sets goals for her/him by making a choice among all the alternative opportunities in accordance with her/his personal values and motivations.

She/he will try to harmonize personal values and motivations with personal goals in order to minimize possible conflicts among them. The nucleus point of the existential position of a human being is direction and choice. People inten-tionally set goals for themselves and thus make certain choices which direct them towards certain consequences and prevent them from reaching others. Personal values, goals, concerns, and motivations constitute an important source of personal meaning, as human life is constructed around certain things people try to achieve in life. Paul Tillich (1995) wrote "man is utterly concerned about his/her being and meaning" (p. 43). Robert Emmons (2004) concludes that "this very concern of man forms and directs her/his deepest goals and striving" (p. 67). Bakhtin (1990) states that the future is primarily a meaningful category. The future, however, can't be constructed meaningfully by an individual if she/he doesn't comprehend her/his present and past consciously, since both present and past continue to exist and to determine an individual's future to a great extent. Meaning of life includes not only a horizontal line, which connects the past, present, and future of an individual, but a vertical line as well. By a vertical line we mean a human capacity to transcend and to take a position from above her/himself. A "vertical line" determines direction of meaning formation for an individual. In such a way, "if the two lines cross, it becomes possible for man to fulfill the meaning of life" (Trubezkoy, 1999, p. 83).

It therefore becomes evident how crucial it is for an individual to be able to harmonize personal values with personal goals in order to live in accordance with personal meaning of life, which in turn, preconditions human integrity and thus preconditions her/his future life (Emmons *et al.*, 1998; Folkman and Stein, 1997). Pedagogical interpretation of extracted philosophical, psychological, and socio-cultural aspects of the category "value" is concretized via educational processes and content in MCE-MCL, which aims at supporting multiple ways of valuing the "subjectivity" of an individual striving to seek both meaning *in* life and meaning *of* life. The space of MCE-MCL is a space of agency, life activity, responsible choices, and creative solutions. The MCE-MCL content is based on universal human values, cultural values, professional values, and existential values.

MCE-MCL applies to the internal nucleus of an individual, encouraging her/him to seek for personal meanings, but it does not intrude into a person's internal world. According to Berdyaev (1999), human nature is attributed with moral-ity ("man equals to what is moral inside him/her") (p. 35), creativity ("man is a creative creature, born to continue creating the world") (p. 74), and spirituality ("spirit creates man and serves a balanced centre for him/her") (p. 75). These three major human attributes pre-condition the ability of an individual to seek meaning in life. Spirit is the nucleus of a person, which serves to balance her/his life and give it purpose and direction, by making "effort to become," according to Mamardashvili (1996). Human spirit constitutes a vertical line that allows an individual to rise to such existential heights as freedom and responsibility and enables an individual to become an autonomous personality.

The broad MCE philosophical foundations and broad MCL psychological foundations have been defined here on the basis of the authors' suppositions so that the scholar and the practitioner can focus on the more specific concerns of con-textualized applications. As illustrated by the examples and case studies provided by the chapter authors, MCE-MCL can be implemented in a variety of ways. To a large degree, context (e.g., institutional mission and type, organizational and societal culture, type of discipline and course, course learning objectives) and how teacher and learner decide to co-create authentic conditions for mean-ingful teaching and learning will drive how it is implemented. Table 13.1 sum-marizes the key concepts, principles, underlying supporting theories, and learning activities that support MCE-MCL.

TABLE 13.1 Main concepts, principles, theories, and activities that support MCE-MCL

Main Concepts	Main Principles	Main Learning Theories	Main Learning Activities
Contextualism	Pluralism	Active learning	Role play
Situatedness	Diversity	Experiential learning	Field studies
Responsibility	Agency	Inquiry-based learning	Research studies
Reflection	Authenticity	Problem-based learning	Group projects
Relational	Holism	Integrative learning	Writing and speaking
Values	Humaneness	Transformative learning	Community service

MCL Key Principles

Principle 1: Pedagogical Pluralism and Learning Diversity

Contrary to the view that there exists only one stable reality, MCE contends that reality has to be created and recreated, interpreted and reinterpreted. Reality is cognized and experienced via its fractured and heterogeneously existing dimensions, wherein each time we meet a different individual, we meet a different worldview, and thus we deal with a different interpretation of the world. The consequence of such fractured experience is pluralism, since truth is not something that can be monopolized by any one person, group, entity, or view. The continual unfolding of human consciousness through human evolution suggests different realities and perspectives and life that is filled with uncertainty. The source of uncertainty is on one hand, outside an individual, and on the other hand, inside the individual; it is also within the interaction of one's internal and external life-worlds. Experience of differences, which emerges due to the pluralism of perspectives, becomes a defining element in the process of education, which leads us to the principle of pedagogical pluralism and learning diversity.

Pedagogical approaches need not be mutually exclusive. In relation to each other, they may be non-linear and supportive of each other. Hence, they need not be viewed strictly as a continuum or as a hierarchy but rather as overlapping and mutually supportive, emerging from the same pedagogical roots. Depending on the unique context of the learning situation, a variety of approaches could be used at the same time and within the same learning space. One can flow out of and morph into another in the heart, mind, and hands of the MCL teacher. MCL is concerned with drawing learners into a critical dialogue which involves bringing them into a learning space of multiple and different voices using different modes of inquiry and different perspectives. Monologism need not be discarded. It can be contextually applied to teaching and learning, especially in self-reflective practices since self-reflection can be considered as internal dialogue. So, dialogic and monologic often occur at the same time.

Furthermore, dialogues consist not only of small dialogues (e.g., classroom discussions) but they also occur in the larger dialogues that span time and space (e.g., dialogue of cultures (Buber, 1993), ongoing scientific discoveries). As Wegerif (this volume) notes, all these dialogues, whether small or large, whether limited or not limited in the scope of space and time, are all part of the continual dialogue of humanity and the continual evolving personal meaning-making process. This, of course, can only happen when partners in the dialogue are respected as equals and when they are open to each other. This dialogic position of each partner constitutes her/his independence, freedom, and non-completeness. It is dialogic interaction that makes it possible for personality to understand and to be understood adequately. Bakhtin (1999) holds that it is not possible to learn anything about personality as if she/he were an object, but "one can truly learn human life if he/she interacts with partner dialogically, because partners in a dialogue are able to sincerely unfold themselves as subjects" (p. 21). Such attributes of dialogic interaction as freedom and equality between partners provides empathy and deep understanding which, in turn, makes it possible for both partners to be open and sincere with each other. New meanings emerge out of the tensions that exist in this dialogic space through the interaction between different voices. But these meanings are constantly changing as the dialogues are re-interpreted and shared by others. Thus, MCL can be viewed as a teaching and learning process of continual recreation of reality that involves a multiplicity of influences (e.g., affective, behavioral, cognitive, cultural social) all intertwined and playing out at the same time. Effectively managing this process, of course, then becomes an ongoing challenge.

Principle 2: Agency and Authenticity

The meaning of human life is viewed as a generation of self-agency, which is a feature unique to all human life (Humboldt, 1960: cited in Wulf, 2012). Each individual has internal agency within self, but it needs to be intentionally and purposefully activated. This internal capacity of an individual to activate self-agency is the capacity to educate oneself. As Menze *et al.* (1993) hold, "Agency a priori exists in a human being, which means that a human being by nature is an agent of activity and energy, and this is the major feature of her/his substance. This life agency constitutes an individual and drives him/her to educate self" (p. 43).

Thus, educational processes, as Menze *et al.* (1993) note, can be activated due to the human agency directed outside and into the external world. So, internal agency of a human being needs to be self-activated and exposed into the world in order to educate self. Based on this supposition, the principle of agency can be interpreted as merging of the self with the world for self in order to actively and freely interact with the world, in order to develop an authentic life with full self-responsibility for its fulfillment.

Authors of this book resonate with this principle. For example, Tolman (this volume) reminds us that "By viewing the syllabus and related course design as a discussion or ongoing negotiation between an instructor and students, collaboration becomes not just a possibility but a necessary element of education." Hunt (this volume) states that "Separated from the act of meaning, language itself tends to become an empty, pointless exercise." Lee (this volume) states that "The requirements of inquiry-guided learning also satisfy the educational conditions for students' development of self-authorship, that is, the ability to identify a personal sense of meaning and purpose along with the competencies to carry it out."

Humboldt (1960: cited in Wulf, 2012) speaks of authentic education which enables an individual to be in harmony with the world and self. It does not entail that academic components need be universal in various educational programs. In fact, it is natural that academic programs should entail variability within its contextual components, and in order to adequately proceed with this, an individual should be free to choose and define her/his educational process within all the variety and diversity of educational contexts and situations. As Humboldt (1960: cited in, Wulf, 2012, p. 79) notes, "Even a free and independent person would be less engaged in self-education if she/he is exposed to monotonous conditions."

MCL is aimed at supporting the innate capacity of the individual to create an authentic, experiential project of her/his life activity and thus it seeks to provide a variety and diversity of educational situations, which are life situations, where students live and learn to make choices and to take responsibility for these choices. For example, while designing a global learning curriculum between Stanford and Khabarovsk (O'Brien and Kovbasyuk, this volume), students negotiated and developed a number of assignments to work progressively towards developing intercultural competences. They generated a variety of activities such as games and training sessions which were distinctly intercultural in implementation. The curricular emphasis on project-based and problem-based learning and collaborative writing necessitated the development and use of technological tools to meet learning goals. One specific teaching practice that students developed as an integral part of their curriculum was blogging, an activity that involved forming international writing pairs, picking a topic of interest for sharing and reflection, and then collaboratively composing a blog post about that cultural artifact. This blog exchange enabled cross-cultural connections that made possible new understanding of specific knowledge. The participants assessed the results of the survey to realize how helpful it was for them to develop open-mindedness, and both cognitive and affective sensitivity towards others.

Principle 3: Holism and Humaneness

According to Taylor (this volume), global community is at a crossroads in the evolution of our planet: either we continue to diminish our cultural, linguistic, and biological diversity or we decide to engage in sustainable development and sustainable learning marked by careful conservation of the Earth's natural and cultural resources and by peaceful co-existence. In order to achieve this goal we need to construct education for sustainability, which involves raising students' awareness on biodiversity, cultural diversity, indigenous knowledge, and living sustainably. Teaching these and many other issues needs to be processed through higher order learning such as values clarification, empathic negotiation, critical reflection, and mindfulness. Indeed, holistic teaching and learning helps create an educational culture that "nurtures the development of the whole person . . . the intellectual, emotional, physical, social, aesthetic, and spiritual" (Miller, 2005, p. 2). A higher level of consciousness honors the whole human being (Palmer and Zajonc, 2010) and seeks synergy between multiple, competing worldviews.

From an MCL perspective, sustainable learning and learning for environmental sustainability is supported by interdisciplinary and transdisciplinary studies; for example, philosophy of ecology, glocalism as the merging of global and local, new forms of cultural and social complexity (Wulf, 2012), educating for social and ecological peace and ethical visions of education to cultivate the mind and imagination. Diversity and complexity of academic subjects is increasing in a globalized world, and this requires setting new tasks for education: to develop new representations of others, as people with different life perspectives and life-worlds, and to build a constructive dialogue with others to exist and collaborate peacefully. MCL principles are based on learning to learn, learning to act responsibly, learning to live in peace, and learning to live in the diversity of human cultures. MCE-MCL characterizes this emerging educational philosophy and learning theory as holistic, integrative, collaborative, dialogic, contextual, and agency-based.

MCE-MCL Teacher and Learner: Classroom and Curricular Issues and Strategies

Josef Albers notes that "Teaching is first of all not a question of methods or techniques, but of personality, lasting influence is personal radiation" (January 9, 1940; cited in, Reardon and Mollin, 2009, p. 7). This is an apt summary of what MCE-MCL based teaching is about since holistic personality development is one of its chief aims. As such, MCE-MCL provides an evidence-based framework to guide the thinking and designing of teaching–learning in the twenty-first century to support educators and learners.

In order to achieve the aim of holistic personality development, the MCL classroom should be designed to support dialogic, authorial and developmental teaching–learning strategies and behaviors, which embrace the above described principles of MCE-MCL. In the following section we describe how this MCE-MCL paradigm affects multiple levels of teaching and learning: (1) power distance in the classroom is decreased and trust and respect is enhanced, (2) teaching and learning strategies are developed to support active, authorial engagement, and (3) integrated curricula are incorporated in the learning process. In the following sections, examples are provided that model MCL teaching and learning strategies, which lead to the development of the MCL framework and explain a holistic approach to guide the thinking and designing of MCL strategies.

Dialogical Domain

Existential interpretation of a dialogue (Leontiev, 2007) emphasizes that partners in dialogue have to be free and equal to be able to understand each other and to reach empathy, mutual trust, and self-disclosure, which allows each of the participants to unfold him/herself. The quality of subject-to-subject relationships exceeds the utilitarian goal of a dialogue itself. It contributes to humanity, empathy, and trust in the classroom (Campbell, 1967; Combs, 1962; Good and Brophy, 1997). In the MCL classroom, the power distance between educators and learners is critical, and it can be the most difficult change needed for many instructors who need to make the leap from an authoritarian-based view of the classroom to one based on collaborative partnerships (Weimer, 2002). As Tolman (this volume) holds, "Faculty have a list of objections—some legitimate, some problematic—that seem to justify maintaining the educational status quo." A fixed perception of power distance in the classroom would entail inappropriate formality, manipulation, and authoritarianism, and thus would hinder meaning-related interaction. In the MCL classroom, with shared power between learners and educators, each of the participants of the educational process feels confident to explore things, make mistakes and continue trying (Lobok, 2001), thus to develop self. The more that one's self is developed, the more one naturally desires her/his voice to be heard and thus the more that a dialogical learning space is required to facilitate this desire.

The communicative aspect of a dialogue characterizes ways of interaction that help reduce the dissonances between opposite views and this helps to enrich each partner's worldview. We view communicative competence as a crucial attribute for a MCL educator, which, like other professional competences, "does not preclude knowledge or content, but comprises and mobilizes it, infusing it with new life by transferring and applying it to real-world contexts, complex situations, or problem resolution (Cañado, this volume). Communicative competence of an educator consequently involves a shift from knowledge to operative skills, and the ability to admit that another has the right to be different and to hold a different perspective.

Internal reflexivity is also referred to as an internal dialogism of a person (Wegeriff, this volume), thus it is a critical attribute for MCL educators and learners, who can co-design teaching–learning strategies in the classroom. It is the self-understanding and self-accepting personality who is capable of constructing truly dialogic interaction with others (Kulikova, 2003). The MCL educator accepts the diversity of one's own internal world and is capable of developing both "horizontal" dialogue with self (e.g., between emotional and intellectual spheres, between various aspects of self, etc.), and vertical dialogue (e.g., between "stories" of internal world, such as consciousness and unconsciousness). In such a way, the MCL educator conveys his/her integrity and ability to self-develop. Reflective experiences of learners represent their authentic voice, and provide occurrence of new personal meanings, which may facilitate the construction of personality, thus becoming a major driving force in transforming self and the world (Kulikova, 2003). Personal discoveries and inquiry are considered reflective activities, and they add to identity enhancement and self-awareness of learners.

According to Virginia Lee (this volume), "infusing a spirit of inquiry on college and university campuses" would help students "grow into a vital and productive relationship with important and pressing questions of identity and purpose."

Also, establishing linkages between meaning-making in the academic disciplines and in students' own lives early in the undergraduate curriculum would be an excellent strategy to provide authentic conditions for a personality growth.

Lee (this volume) states that some institutions in the USA,

> provide a set of seminars in which students actively explore questions regarding self and identity. At some institutions these seminars comprise the core curriculum, a common set of courses that all students take regardless of academic major. For example, at Dominican University (Chicago, Illinois) the first-year seminar "Dimensions of Self" is the first of four required seminars, one taken each year, in which students explore the search for meaning in ever widening contexts . . . they engage actively with these questions: What is the self? Is the self-made, inherited, given, discovered? What are some of the key influences on a person's physical, emotional, spiritual, and intellectual development? How does the self-interact with community? (Dominican University, n.d.)

Anne Geller confirms that "when students say they find an academic task personal," they may "feel more engaged in the work at hand and with one another" (Geller and Cantelmo, 2011, p. 218).

Authorial Domain

Authorial teaching and learning is the next core domain of MCL. Teachers and students are unique and irreplaceable. No teaching technique will help if teachers are not "authoring their own words, their own actions, their own lives" (Palmer, 1998, p. 33). Authorial teaching comes when we, as educators, reclaim our identity and integrity. "Then teaching can come from the depth of my own truth—and the truth that is within my students has a chance to respond in kind" (ibid., p. 33). As educators, we teach from our own lives, worlds, feelings, ideas, mistakes, values, relationships, and limitations (Maslow, 1973), thus we strive to take full responsibility for what we do and how we learn and judge, what relationships we develop, and what decisions we make. Pedagogical methodology and scientific research can help us learn from each other and from others' experiences but it cannot provide expertise into our own experiences and it, by itself, cannot guarantee good teaching.

The MCL student is viewed as author of her/his own learning and as a critical investigator of the subject, practice, and discourse as opposed to student as a mere receptacle to be filled with existent knowledge. How can the teacher engage the student into such learning to promote active authorial learning while providing freedom for her/him to choose what and how the student wants to learn? We do not think there is an exact prescription to that urgent issue, because educators and learners represent diverse phenomenological experiences. What is important to realize is that MCL educators should not impose or coerce their own views, ideas, and values on students, but they should critically question why students choose something they choose, why they proceed with this or that issue the way they do, why they take or do not take responsibility for their choices. As Vygotsky noticed, understanding of the partner's idea without the awareness of his reasons is incomplete. The MCL teaching strategy comprises risk, which "is essential for learning and development: venturing into unfamiliar territory, confronting and breaking down misconceptions, revealing incompetence, making mistakes, and using developing competencies under increasingly more difficult and complex circumstances" (Lee, this volume).

Developmental Domain

The developmental domain of MCL is an integral one, and it signifies that continual personal self-evolvement and interpersonal interaction and collaboration constitute the core of the learning process. Open type curricula, which are continually re-designed by learners and educators depending on types of activities, modes, and contexts of learning, can represent this MCL domain well.

As Harriet Shenkman explores in her chapter, learning communities "help make what students are learning relevant to their conception of themselves in the world and to their future lives." In the learning communities structure, where students and faculty co-create an engaging learning environment, social integration and collaborative learning strengthen curricular coherence (Tinto, 1997). The social integration and engagement can be achieved in a variety of ways including social events, service learning projects, and residential arrangements. Integration of the curriculum increases effectiveness of teaching and learning (Henson and Eller, 1999) and can be achieved through shared syllabi, joint academic assignments and projects, and common themes across linked courses (Henson, 2001). As a result of such an MCL approach, participation of learners and educators in the variability of the world is increased, the subjectivity of students and faculty is enhanced, and life is cognized through diversity of contexts.

Virginia Lee (this volume) provides another example of an integrated curriculum, which is an essential element to a meaning-centered pedagogical approach. She states that "Integration may include planned integrated syllabi, joint assignments, common readings, joint projects, and themes that are shared during the class and made visible in peer presentations at a culminating event." Another key practice that characterizes MCL curricula is the implementation of integrative assignments which have the intentional aim of cross-disciplinary integration, and thus include integrating knowledge from the different disciplines.

All the MCL domains explain the holistic approach in designing MCL strategies, curricula, and relationships between learners and educators, which makes it more humane while accounting for individual development in personal, social, and cultural spheres. Yet, it remains open for further investigations and explorations to further develop the MCL framework.

The Environment of Meaning-Centered Learning

Learning environments may take many different forms and include various components, depending on the type of education. (Hannafin *et al.*, 1999). A meaning-centered environment is intended to support a more humane, holistic, self-motivating, and self-regulating culture of learning. Authentic contexts are critical to motivate learners and usually take the form of complex, full-scale problems representative of real-world tasks. For example, action-based Model United Nations simulations, Imagine Peace projects, and similar types of learning activities can be used to represent real world problems and thus engage learners in "sense-making" about issues important to society and important to themselves.

Self-efficacy, personal goal setting, self-assessment, and equal valuation among the participants are the key motivational facets of MCL environments. Self-efficacy plays an important role in the motivational aspect of meaningful learning because personal meanings and values are transformed with a person's sense of efficacy for social discourse in a novel social setting (Bandura, 1986). MCL environments are designed therefore to enhance self-efficacy of learners through participation in diverse learning activities and feelings of success.

Human activities, by their nature, are goal directed and purposeful (Locke and Lathman, 1990). People set goals for themselves by making a choice among all the known alternatives. The central points of existential philosophy are free choice and responsibility, which characterize human beings as self-evolving personalities. Thus, in the MCL environment, learning goals are not imposed in an authoritarian manner without regards to the needs of the learners but they emerge as a result of meaningful interactions among the participants.

There are no one-size-fits-all universal assessment standards within MCL environments because developing well-rounded, multi-dimensional learners is more important than one-dimensional formal grading systems that focus only on lower order thinking. Indications of personal learning can be analyzed, according to certain typologies, which are conditioned by general principles of physiological, psychological, and social development. Simple low or high indications cannot completely serve the purpose of selecting the better student from the "underachieving" one. Rather, they provide additional information for exploring relevant and contextualized learning opportunities for learners. Bandura (2001) maintains that the field of psychology is most appropriate and best equipped to understand the integrated and holistic nature of humans, psychosocially and biologically.

For example, the Meaningful Life Orientations (MLO) Model, based on Psychology of Meaning (Leontiev, 2007) can be implemented as a model that examines personal goals and concerns in life, the locus of control over one's own life (self-regulation), and the level of satisfaction with self-fulfillment. The model is a recent adaptation of the "Purpose-in-Life Test" (Crumbaugh and Maholick, 1981), which was designed by scholars on the basis of Frankl's theory of meaning in life. The model can provide unification for people's existential values at the global level, as well as assist in understanding personal values and meanings in life, which can serve as a foundation for developing students' self-concepts and thus, foster their self-evolvement.

Another major attribute of MCL environments is equal valuation between learners and teachers, which means that, ethically, every learner is of equal interest and of equal care to the instructor, and the way to knowing is more important than knowing itself. This last supposition illustrates that the instructor is also always a learner, and her/his main task is to provide the freedom of dialogue, exploration, critical-inquiry, and self-reflection. The efficiency and effectiveness of learning depends on the level of communicative culture and the individual capacity of the learner to gain an insight into the authentic, contextualized problem. Awareness of not knowing is equally valuable as knowing, since it provides a natural opportunity for a learner to move forward in a conscious, intentional way, which is connected with the innate human need to move beyond his/her personal boundaries and expand beyond his/her current capacity (Kolesnikova, 2001).

MCL environments are filled with research, inquiries, collaborative projects, and agency-based learning activities which provide a field of personal meanings, the dynamics and interplay of which illustrate a multiplicity of perspectives and a variational view of the world. Self-efficacy, authentic goal setting, self-assessment, and equal valuation among participants are interconnected and serve to motivate learners instrumentally by providing a chance to make personal choices on an everyday basis, allowing them to consciously and concretely move towards their long-term goals, and this reinforces a sense of self-agency. In each of the cases, the holistic impact on learners' personal growth is reached when internalized values and the level of self-efficacy determine authorship of life.

The main outcome of meaningful education is the learner's "awakened" ability to self-evolve as a mature personality, capable of self-determining the direction and quality and nature of her/his life. This outcome is less assessable in a traditional way as "it is pervasive and it makes a difference in a personality" (Combs, 1999, p. 204). According to Nagata (2006), "It involves experiencing a deep, structural shift in the basic premises of thought, feelings, and actions. It is a shift of consciousness that dramatically and permanently alters our way of being in the world" (p. 16).

Conclusion

In this chapter we focused on MCE-MCL from a micro-analytical level and provided a more application oriented view of the topic. The specific focus was on the epistemological underpinnings of MCE-MCL and comparing MCE with the objectivist and constructivist paradigms as well as on the psychological basis for MCL. The major difference lies in the holistic and humane nature of MCL which supports the integration of learning across all learning domains (affective, cognitive, socio-cultural) and facilitates the development of personal meanings about who we are and how we relate to the world and ourselves. Based on the MCE suppositions, we defined MCL as learning that is a self-motivating and self-regulating process of creating personal meaning in one's life-world through reflective, critical, and inquiry-based activities. Thus, according to MCL, the learner constructs personal meaning from her/his experiences and their relationship to prior experiences and contexts, taking full responsibility for her/his own learning and self-evolvement as a personality capable of authoring one's own life.

The MCL principles of pedagogical pluralism and learning diversity, authenticity and agency, holism and humanness support the MCE strategies via dialogic, authorial, and developmental domains. The MCL environment is designed to provide a humane, holistic, self-motivating, and self-regulating space. Developing a personality is an ongoing journey throughout life. We view MCE-MCL as an opportunity to develop higher awareness about each other and our own educational perspectives, which add resources and opportunities for all of us to contribute to the improvement of the world. It is also an opportunity to increase our consciousness and enlarge our sense of humanity and personal humanness.

References

Abakumova, I. V. (2003) *Teaching and Meaning: Meaning Making in the Learning Process.* Rostov-on-Don: Rostov State University.

Asmolov, A. G. (1990) *Psychology of Personality.* Moscow: Moscow State University.

Ausubel, D. P. (1963) *The Psychology of Meaningful Verbal Learning.* New York: Grune and Stratton.

Ausubel, D. P. (2000) *The Acquisition and Retention of Knowledge: A Cognitive View.* Dordrect; Boston, MA: Kluwer Academic Publishers.

Bakhtin, M. M. (1990) *To the Philosophy of the Action.* Moscow: Nauka.

Bakhtin, M. M. (1999) *Problems of Dostoevsky's Poetics.* Moscow: Nauka.

Bandura, A. (1986) *Social Foundations of Thoughts and Actions: A Social Cognitive Theory.* Englewood Cliffs, NJ: Prentice-Hall.

Bandura, A. (2001) "Social cognitive theory: An agentic perspective." *Annual Review of Psychology* 52: 1–26.

Bandura, A. (2004) "Health promotion by social-cognitive means." *Health Education and Behavior* 31: 143–164.

Bednar, A. K., Cunningham, D., Duffy, T. M. and Perry, J. D. (1991) "Theory into practice: How do we link?" In G. J. Anglin (Ed.), *Instructional Technology: Past, Present and Future.* Englewood, CO: Libraries Unlimited, Inc.

Berdyaev, N. A. (1999) *Man, His Freedom and Spirituality.* Moscow: Flinta.

Berezina E. A. (2004) *Dynamics of Personal Meaning in the Professional Activity of a Teacher.* Kursk: KPU.

Bredo, E. (2000) "Reconsidering social constructivism." In D. C. Phillips (Ed.), *Constructivism in Education. Ninety-Ninth Yearbook of the Society for the Study of Education* (pp. 127–157). New York: Humana Press.

Buber, M. (1993) *I and YOU.* Moscow: Respublika.

Campbell, J. K. (1967) *The Children's Crusader.* Columbia, NY: Teachers College Press.

Carson, J. (2005) "Objectivism and education: A response to David Elkind's The Problem with Constructivism." *The Educational Forum* 69: 232–238.

Combs, A. (1962) *Perceiving, Behaving, Becoming.* Washington, DC: Association for Supervision & Curriculum Development.

Combs, A. (1999) *Being and Becoming: A Field Approach to Psychology.* New York: Springer Publishing Company.

Cronjé, J. (2006) "Paradigms regained: Toward integrating objectivism and constructivism in instructional design and the learning sciences." *Educational Technology Research and Development* 54(4): 387–416.

Crumbaugh, J. S. and Maholik, L. T. (1981) *Manual of Instructions for The Purpose in Life Test.* Munster, IN: Psychometric Affiliates.

Dahlberg, G. (1985) *Context and the Child's Orientation to Meaning: A Study of the Child's Way of Organizing and Surrounding World in Relation to Public Institutional Socialization.* Stockholm: Gleerup.

Dewey, J. (1938) *Experience and Education.* New York: Macmillan.

Dewey, J. and Bentely, A. (1949) *Knowing and the Known.* Boston, MA: Beach Press.

Elkind, D. (2005) "Response to objectivism and education." *The Educational Forum* 69: 328–334.

Emmons, Robert (2004) *Psychology of Ultimate Concerns.* Moscow: Smysl.

Emmons, R. A., Colby, P. M. and Keiser, H. A. (1998) *When Losses Lead to Gains. Personal Goals and the Recovery of Meaning. The Human Quest for Meaning.* Mahwah, NJ: Erlbaum.

Fischer, G. (2000) "Lifelong learning – more than training." *Journal of Interactive Learning Research* 11(3/4): 265–294.

Folkman, S. and Stein, N. L. (1997) *Adaptive Goal Processes in Stressful Events: Memory for Everyday and Emotional Events.* Hillsdale, NJ: Erlbaum

Frankl, V. (1998) *The Unheard Cry for Meaning.* New York: Basic Books.

Freire, P. (1970) *Pedagogy of the Oppressed.* New York: Herder and Herder.

Geller, A. and Cantelmo, F. (2011) "Workshopping to practice scientific terms." In C. Paine, J. Harris and J. Miles (Eds), *Teaching with Student Texts: Essays Toward an Informed Practice* (pp. 210–219). Logan, UT: Utah State University Press.

Good, T. and Brophy, J. (1997) *Looking in Classrooms* (7th ed.). New York: Harper & Row.

Gredler, M. (2009) *Learning and Instruction: Theory into Practice.* Upper Saddle River, NJ: Pearson.

Hannafin, M., Land, S. and Oliver, K. (1999) "Open learning environments: Foundations, methods and models." In C. Relgeluth (Ed.), *Instructional Design Theories and Models* (pp. 115–140). Mahwah, NJ: Lawrence Erlbaum Associates.

Hannula, M. (1997) *Self-Understanding as a Process: Understood through the Concepts Of Self-Understanding as a Narrative Form, the Third Dimension of Power, Coming in Terms with the Past, Conceptual Change and Case Studies of Finnishness.* Turku: Turun Yliopisto.

Heidegger, (1962) *Being and Time.* New York: Harper & Row.

Henson, K. T. (2001) *Curriculum Planning: Integrating, Multiculturalism, Constructivism, and Education Reform* (2nd ed.). New York: McGraw-Hill.

Henson, K. T. and Eller, B. F. (1999) *Educational Psychology for Effective Teaching.* Belmont, CA: Wadsworth.

Hilgard, E. R. (1948) *Theories of Learning.* New York: Appleton-Century-Crofts.

Hyland, D. A. (1973) *The Origins of Philosophy*. New York: Capricorn Books/G.P. Putnam's Sons.

Jonassen, D. H. (1991) "Objectivism versus constructivism: Do we need a new philosophical paradigm?" *Educational Technology Research and Development* 39(3): 5–14.

Kebina, N. A. (2003) *Philosophy of Meaning and Self-Realization of a Personality*. Moscow: Moscow State University.

Kierkegaard, S. (1998) *Delight and Duty*. Rostov-on-Don: Mysl.

Kolesnikova, I. (2001) *Pedagogy Reality: Interparadigm Reflection*. St Petersburg: Detstvo-Press.

Konashkova, A. M. (2007) *Methodological Foundations of Phenomenological Ontology: Architectonics of Meaning*. Ekaterinburg: ESU.

Kovbasyuk, O. (2009) "Theoretical foundations of meaningful approach to raising a personality." *Siberia Pedagogical Journal*. Novosibirsk: NSPU.

Kovbasyuk, O. (2010) "Meaningful education as a resource of global learning." In M. Alagic, G. Rimmington, F. Liu and K. Gibson (Eds), *Locating Intercultures: Educating for Global Collaboration* (pp. 119–140). India: Macmillan.

Kovbasyuk, O. (2011) *Application of Meaning Centered Strategies in Education: Russia and Germany, Comparative Approach. Selected Scholarly Works*. Moscow-Pyatigorsk: PSLU.

Kovbasyuk, O. (2012) "Global learning in the Far East of Russia: Meaning centered strategy." *Journal Regional Problems*. Russia Academy of Science, Birobidjan: RPP.

Krathwohl, D. R. (2002) "A revision of Bloom's Taxonomy: An overview." *Theory into Practice* 41(4): 212–218.

Kulikova, L. N (2003) *Self-Development of a Personality: Psycho-Pedagogical Foundations*. Khabarovsk: KhGPU.

Lave, J. (1991) "Situated learning in communities of practice." In L. Resnick, J. Levine and S. Teasley (Eds), *Perspectives on Socially Shared Cognition* (pp. 63–82). Washington, DC: American Psychological Association.

Leontiev, D. (2004) *Psychology of Meaning*. Moscow: Smysl.

Leontiev, D. (2007) *Psychology of Meaning* (new edition). Moscow: Smysl.

Lobok. A. (2001) *Veroyatnostnyi mir*. Ekaterinburg: Evrika.

Locke, E. A. and Lathman, G. P. (1990) *A Theory of Goal Setting and Task Performance*. Englewood Cliffs, NJ: Prentice-Hall.

Mamardashvili, M. K. (1996) *The Necessity of Oneself*. Moscow: Labirint.

Maslow, A. (1973) "What is a taoistic teacher?" In L. J. Rubin (Ed.), *Facts and Findings in the Classroom*. New York: Walker.

Miller, J. P. (2005) *Holistic Learning and Spirituality in Education: Breaking New Ground*. Albany, NY: State University of New York Press.

Miyazaki, K. (2006) "Another imaginative approach to teaching: A Japanese view." *Academia* 4(5): 22–31.

Menze, C., Bunk, G. P. and Ofenbach, B. (1993) *Menshenbilder*. Frankfurt: Lang.

Nagata, A. L. (2006) "Transformative learning in intercultural education." *Rikkyo Intercultural Communication Review* 4.

Palmer, P. J. (1998) *The Courage to Teach*. San Francisco, CA: Jossey-Bass.

Palmer, P. and Zajonc, A. (2010) *The Heart of Higher Education: A Call to Renewal*. San Francisco, CA: Jossey-Bass.

Reardon, J., and Mollin, D. (2009) *Ch-ch-ch-changer: Artists Talk about Teaching*. London: Ridinghouse.

Rogalsky, E. I. (2006) *Creativity as Meaning of Life*. St Petersburg: St Petersburg State University.

Shuell, T. J. (1990) "Phases of meaningful learning." *Review of Educational Research* 60(4): 531.

Stepashko, L. (2004) *Philosophy of Education.* Khabarovsk: KhGPU.

Tillich, P. (1995) *Selected Works: Theology of Culture.* Moscow: Yurist.

Tinto (1997) "Classrooms as communities: Exploring the educational character of student persistence." *Journal of Higher Education* 68(6): 599–623.

Trubezkoy, E. N. (1999) *Meaning of Life. Meaning of Life. Anthology.* Moscow: Progress Kultura.

Vrasidas, C. (2000) "Constructivism versus objectivism: Implications for interaction, course design, and evaluation in distance education." *International Journal of Educational Telecommunications* 6(4): 339–362.

von Glaserfeld, E. (1987) "Learning as a constructive activity." In C. Janvier (Ed.), *Problems of Representation in the Teaching and Learning of Mathematics.* Hillsdale, NJ: Lawrence Erlbaum.

von Glaserfeld, E. (1995) "A constructivist approach to learning." In L. P. Steffe and J. Gale (Eds), *Constructivism in Education.* Hillsdale, NJ: Erlbaum.

Vygotsky, L. S. (1978) *Mind in Society: The Development of Higher Mental Processes.* Cambridge, MA: Harvard University Press.

Weimer, M. (2002) *Learner-Centered Teaching: Five Key Changes to Practice.* San Francisco, CA: Jossey-Bass.

Wertsch, J. V (1997) *Vygotsky and the Formation of the Mind.* Cambridge, MA: Harvard University Press.

Wulf, C. (2012) *Anthropology of Upbringing.* Moscow: Paxis.

CONCLUSION

Olga Kovbasyuk and Patrick Blessinger

We have been thinking about, reflecting on, and practicing (as educators) the concepts, principles, theories, and activities presented in this book for many years. Along the way we have received many awards for our teaching efforts which have offered us some measure of validation and consolation for our view that meaning-centered education and learning (MCE-MCL) should be at the heart of the teaching–learning process. We have been teaching, learning, researching, presenting, and publishing about education for years and we continue to reflect on the critical issues about how to better educate students. Our desire to concretize what we have been practicing for years was prompted by our collaboration within the International Higher Education Teaching and Learning Association. To that end, we pursued meaningful dialogues about education, comparing the past century of teaching and learning theories and practices with the new century education system.

In the twentieth century, education has been interpreted in a variety of ways: (1) as deviation from a holistic perspective and as an attempt to squeeze new learners into a society which has already failed in various ways (Menegetti, 2007), (2) as a way of introducing young people to the better part of human heritage (Fromm, 2011), and (3) as a process of feeding the soul and heart of a person with the best spiritualizing images (Amonashvili, 2006). All these views as well as other interpretations of education do co-exist in the experience of humankind, as factors of its philosophic and pedagogic culture. Adler (1992, p. 15) noted that "human beings live in the realm of meanings" and thus our focus should be on enhancing and fostering this meaning-making process by making education a personally meaningful experience for each learner.

In the twenty-first century, the industrial age mentality of the past is being changed by the creative type (Kolesnikova, 2011) and thus the aims and functions of education are changing as well. On one hand, education is becoming more pluralistic, organic, non-linear, and non-prescriptive. On the other hand, many learners continue to view education simply as a way to get a diploma in an attempt to get a good job. This dichotomy suggests to us that learning is not altogether personally meaningful to learners and they are not experiencing the full transformative effect of education. Viewing education only in vocational or economic terms does not sufficiently address the whole person or the whole society since education is and ought to be more than just career preparation or job training.

As such, we contend, based on the research presented in this book, that learners should get closer to their own holistic human natures rather than becoming objects at the whims of economic or political forces. It is the meaning-based regulation of human behaviour that is a more authentic measure of humanity (Leontiev, 2005). Meaning-based regulation entails free choice, responsibility, and self-determination, which are vital to the full development of personality and of humanity. Our experience as educators together with our empirical observations have confirmed that when students are engaged in a diverse set of personally meaningful and socially valued activities they are better able to assess what they learned with responsibility to self, to others, and to the local and world communities. This is how the idea to produce a book on MCE-MCL came to life.

In a true dialogue partners equally co-own what they produce when sharing views and meanings. In such a way, we explored the nature and origins of MCE-MCL, explaining the evolution of learning theories and providing a theoretical framing of MCE-MCL, and drawing on, for instance, existential psychology, phenomenology, and other disciplines. We provided an analysis of MCE-MCL in relation to other important educational paradigms, such as objectivism and constructivism, introduced the core concepts and principles of MCE-MCL, and generated our own definition of MCL (see Glossary).

This book is a collaborative effort of international scholars and educators, who joined the project and contributed to the development of an emergent philosophy in education, which aims to create an authentic learning environment that supports a self-regulating and autonomous personality who operates out of her/his own volition and strives to achieve self-fulfilment and self-determination as an indicator of her/his existential worldview (adapted from Leontiev, 2007; Ausubell, 2000; Shuell, 1990).

The chapter authors contributed to theoretical and practical parts of the book, enriching all of us with new ideas and understanding of what MCE-MCL embraces. The MCE-MCL domains explain the holistic approach in designing MCE-MCL learning strategies, curricula, and relationships between learners and educators, which makes it more humane and authentic and accounts for individual development in personal, social, and cultural spheres. Our joint work and research on this book has continued for almost two years, but of course MCE-MCL remains open for further investigations and explorations in the field. We co-created the

Institute for Meaning-Centered Education (http://www.meaningcentered.org) to further develop a research-based understanding of MCE-MCL, its concepts and principles, its meaning-centered learning environment, and its strategies and activities for implementing it in curricula across a range of disciplines.

We are also interested in contributing to the research on the typology of life-worlds, which is relevant to the field of MCE-MCL, since it aims to create supportive conditions for developing the personal life-worlds of learners. The "progressist" life-world (Leontiev, 2004, pp.114–116) aims for the future, as it is characterized by the principle of self-realization, and it therefore represents the idea of harmony between an individual and society and one's personal contribution to the life of the society, which is urgently needed for the evolution of humanity and for sustainable learning and peace on our planet. We invite anyone who shares our vision to contribute to the scholarship and practice of MCE-MCL by collaborating with us in generating new research in this area.

References

Adler, A. (1992) *What Life Could Mean to You* (C. Brett, Trans.). Oxford, UK: Oneworld. (Original work published 1931).

Amonashvili, Sh. (2006) *Truth of School*. Moscow: Izdatelskiy Dom Shalva Amonashvili.

Ausubel, D. P. (2000) *The Acquisition and Retention of Knowledge: A Cognitive View*. Dordrect; Boston, MA: Kluwer Academic Publishers.

Fromm, E. (2011) *The Escape from Freedom*. Moscow: ACT.

Kolesnikova, I. (2011) *Pedagogic Reality: Experience of Interparadigm Reflection*. St Petersburg: Detstvo-Plus.

Leontiev, D. (2004) *To the Typology of Life Worlds*. Conference Proceedings. Moscow: Smysl.

Leontiev, D. (2005) "The phenomenon of meaning: How psychology can make sense of it." *International Journal of Existential Psychology & Psychotherapy* (1)2.

Leontiev, D. (2007) *Psychology of Meaning*. Moscow: Smysl.

Menegetti, A. (2007) *Project Man*. St Petersburg: Ontopsihologiya.

Shuell, T. J. (1990) "Phases of meaningful learning." *Review of Educational Research* 60(4): 531.

GLOSSARY

	Term	Definition	Source(s)
A	Authentic learning	Learning where students are provided with meaningful opportunities to engage in self-directed inquiry, problem solving, critical thinking and reflections in real world and creative contexts.	State University of New York at Oswego School of Education (1998) *Conceptual Framework*. Oswego, NY.
	Authentically meaning-centered language	Language which serves actual social purposes, which acts as utterances (Bakhtin, 1986) or speech acts (Austin, 1962) in real social situations between intending persons.	Bakhtin, M. M. (1986) *Speech Genres and Other Late Essays*. Trans. Vern W. McGee. Ed. Caryl Emerson and Michael Holquist. Austin, TX: University of Texas Press. Austin, J. L. (1962) *How to Do Things with Words: The William James Lectures Delivered at Harvard University in 1955*. Ed. J. O. Urmson. Oxford: Clarendon Press.
	Authorial learning	Learning where the voice of the student plays the major role. Authorial learning is based on the student's unique voice, acceptance of spontaneously emerging teaching–learning situations, and authentic behavior/strategy within such situations. This is possible when the student is an active author of his/her own life world, and culture, and when he/she is an active learner.	

Term	Definition	Source(s)
Authorial teaching	Teaching where the voice of the teacher plays the major role. Authorial teaching is based on the teacher's hope and trust in the student's creativity and authorial learning. Authorial teaching is based on the teacher's recognition of students' unique voices, acceptance of spontaneously emerging teaching–learning situations, and authentic behavior/strategy within such situations. This is possible when the teacher is an active author of his/her own life world, and culture, and when he/she is an active learner.	
Autonomous (self-regulated) learning	An active, constructive process whereby learners set goals for their learning and then attempt to monitor, regulate, and control their cognition, motivation, and behavior, guided and constrained by their goals and the contextual features in the environment.	Wolters, C. A., Pintrich, P. R. and Karabenick, S. A. (2005) "Assessing academic self regulated learning." In K. A. Moore and L. H. Lippman (Eds), *What Do Children Need to Flourish?* (pp. 251–270). New York: Springer.
Autoregulation	The capacity to improve performance based on feedback signals about the discrepancy between the desired and the actual state of affairs.	Leontiev, D. (2007) *Psychology of Meaning.* Moscow: Smysl.
Axiological	Relating to the concept of value (the good of things and how their goodness relates to one another) and to development of personal ethics and aesthetics.	Schroeder, Mark, "Value theory." In E. N. Zalta (Ed.), *The Stanford Encyclopedia of Philosophy* (Summer 2012 Edition). Available online from: http://plato.stanford.edu/archives/sum2012/entries/value-theory/ (accessed December 10, 2012).

C		
Character development	The gradual attainment of a variety of human traits and attitudes that a given culture views as desirable such as self-discipline, tolerance, empathy, curiosity, diligence, fortitude, forgiveness, generosity, gratitude, honesty, humility, purpose, patience, reliability, and thrift.	Lee, V. S. (Ed.) (2012) "Inquiry-guided learning." *New Directions for Teaching and Learning*, 129. San Francisco, CA: Jossey-Bass.
Cognition	The mental ability to think and process and store information and apply knowledge. These processes can be analyzed and understood from different perspectives and within different contexts.	
Cognitive strategy.	An activity that facilitates understanding, such as comparing, describing, and summarizing.	Gredler, M. (2009) *Learning and Instruction: Theory into Practice.* Upper Saddle River, NJ: Pearson.
Competence	The ability to successfully complete the task or meet the requirements of a particular context. Competent performance suggests that one possesses the right combination of knowledge, skills, attitudes, and behaviours to perform competently.	
Connectionism	A synonym for Thorndike's theory of learning. It suggest that connections are made between stimuli and voluntary behaviors. It is also a view of learning that approximates the neural networks in the brain.	Gredler, M. (2009) *Learning and Instruction: Theory into Practice.* Upper Saddle River, NJ: Pearson.
Consciousness	The human state of being aware of one's internal world and one's external world and possessing a sense of self-reflection and a sense of identity in relation to others and the world.	

Term	Definition	Source(s)
Constructivism	An educational view of learning that views knowledge as a human construction and is based on several related perspectives. Radical constructivism, derived from Piaget's perspective of learning, views the learner's knowledge as adaptive. The teacher's role is to challenge the learner's way of thinking. Social constructivist views, in contrast, view knowledge as a social product.	Gredler, M. (2009) *Learning and Instruction: Theory into Practice.* Upper Saddle River, NJ: Pearson.
Contextualism	The totality of the context in which a thought, feeling, or action occurs.	
Critical constructivism	An epistemology that adds a critical social theory perspective to our understanding of how knowledge and the process of coming to know (especially in formal education) is socially constructed and legitimated. It involves critical examination of ways in which truth claims (especially in science and mathematics education) have been structured historically and culturally to serve powerful economic and political interests.	Kincheloe, J. L. (2005) *Critical Constructivism Primer.* New York: Peter Lang.
Criticalism	In the critical research paradigm knowledge production aims first to identify the source of invisible ideologies (or hegemonies) that structure historically inequitable, unfair, unjust social actions and relationships. And second, it aims to emancipate people from their (unwitting) subordination to these normative ideologies by means of active engagement in political-ethical reasoning and openly reflexive communicative relationships.	Young, R. (1990) *A Critical Theory of Education: Habermas and Our Children's Future.* Columbia University: Teachers College Press.

Term	Definition	Reference
Cultural development	In Vygotsky's theory, mastering methods of behavior that are based on signs as a way to accomplish a specific psychological function.	Gredler, M. (2009) *Learning and Instruction: Theory into Practice*. Upper Saddle River, NJ: Pearson.
Cultural meaning (German *Bedeutung*, Russian *Znachenie*)	A fixed semantic unit, generated by a shared cultural context and unambiguously decoded by those who share the cultural code (e.g., language meanings, traffic signs, or church rites).	Leontiev, D. (2007) *Psychology of Meaning*. Moscow: Smysl.
Culture of dignity	A type of culture based on the value of human person, independently of whether something can be gained from that person.	Asmolov, A.G. (1990) *Psychology of Personality*. Moscow: Moscow State University.
Culture of utility	A type of culture striving toward a balance, a self-protection, concerned with survival rather than with living.	Asmolov, A.G. (1990) *Psychology of Personality*. Moscow: Moscow State University.
Curriculum	A planned course of study in a college or university leading to a formal degree.	Lee, V. S. (Ed.) (2012) "Inquiry-guided learning," *New Directions for Teaching and Learning*, 129. San Francisco, CA: Jossey-Bass.
D Dialogic education	Education for dialogue. For education to be dialogic implies that dialogue is not only the means of education, as it often is, but is also an end.	Wegerif, R. (2012) *Dialogic: Education for the Internet Age*. London: Routledge.

Term	Definition	Source(s)
Dialogical learning	The principle of holding different voices or perspectives together in creative tension. Dialogic is a contrasting term to monologic: monologic assumes that there is just one voice, perspective, or truth but for dialogic there is always more than one voice, perspective, or truth.	Wegerif, R. (2012) *Dialogic: Education for the Internet Age*. London: Routledge.
Dialogic space	When two or more voices are held together in the tension of a dialogue this opens up a space of possible responses. In dialogic space children and teachers can co-construct new ideas together or stimulate each other to provoke creative and unexpected responses.	Wegerif, R. (2012) *Dialogic: Education for the Internet Age*. London: Routledge.
Dialogic talk	Engaged, responsive, creative, open-ended shared enquiry. Talk together can be more or less dialogic. The more dialogic it is, the more it is characterized by active listening and the creative emergence of new ideas.	Wegerif, R. (2012) *Dialogic: Education for the Internet Age*. London: Routledge.
Dialogue	This is often used to refer to any conversation but Bakhtin makes a useful distinction between dialogue and conversation, defining dialogue as a shared enquiry in which each answer produces a further question in a chain of questions and answers.	Wegerif, R. (2012) *Dialogic: Education for the Internet Age*. London: Routledge.
Difference	There are two kinds of difference: ordinary difference and constitutive difference. Ordinary difference is the difference between two fixed identities, like the difference between a red cup and a blue cup. Constitutive difference is where the difference between two identities helps to define the identities of the two things from within. So, for example, the difference between	Wegerif, R. (2012) *Dialogic: Education for the Internet Age*. London: Routledge

E

Education — me and you in a dialogue is at least partly constitutive, because I can't have a "me" without a "you" and you also can't have a "you" without a "me" so it is the difference between us that helps to define us.

Leontiev, D. (2007) *Psychology of Meaning.* Moscow: Smysl.

Human cultural institution accounting for individual development in its three intertwined aspects: (1) maturation, (2) socialization, and (3) self-determination.

Empiricism — The gathering of facts through scientific experiments or controlled experience.

Experiential learning — Experiential learning is the process of making meaning from direct, concrete experience. David A. Kolb helped to popularize the idea of experiential learning drawing heavily on the work of John Dewey, Kurt Lewin, and Jean Piaget.

Kolb, D. A. and Fry, R. (1975) "Toward an applied theory of experiential learning." In C. Cooper (Ed.), *Theories of Group Process.* London: John Wiley.

F

Faculty immediacy — Behaviors which increase psychological closeness between communicators (Mehrabian, 1971) and, in an educational context, the verbal and nonverbal behaviors that instructors display in the classroom that influence student perceptions (Baringer and McCroskey, 2000).

Baringer, D. K. and McCroskey, J. C. (2000) "Immediacy in the classroom: Student immediacy." *Communication Education* 49(2): 178.

Mehrabian, A. (1971) *Silent Messages* (1st ed.). Belmont, CA: Wadsworth.

H

Hermeneutics — Greek philosophy. In the course of the Middle Ages and the Renaissance, hermeneutics emerges as a crucial branch of Biblical studies. Later on, it comes to include the study of ancient and classic cultures. With the emergence of German romanticism

Ramberg, B. and Gjesdal, K. (2009) "Hermeneutics." In E. N. Zalta (Ed.), *The Stanford Encyclopedia of Philosophy* (Summer 2009 Edition). Available online from:

Term	Definition	Source(s)
	and idealism the status of hermeneutics changes. Hermeneutics turns philosophical. It is no longer conceived as a methodological or didactic aid for other disciplines, but turns to the conditions of possibility for symbolic communication as such. Now hermeneutics is not only about symbolic communication. Its area is even more fundamental: that of human life and existence as such. It is in this form, as an interrogation into the deepest conditions for symbolic interaction and culture in general, that hermeneutics has provided the critical horizon for many of the most intriguing discussions of contemporary philosophy, both within an Anglo–American context (e.g., Rorty, McDowell, Davidson) and within a more Continental discourse (e.g., Habermas, Apel, Ricoeur, and Derrida).	http://plato.stanford.edu/archives/sum2009/entries/hermeneutics/ (accessed December 11, 2012).
Holism	The idea that the parts of a system cannot be determined or explained solely by the sum of its parts or by simply reducing the system to its component parts. Rather, understanding the whole system helps explain how its parts behave. Holistic thinking attempts to integrate various perspectives of meaning and experience. Holistic education aims to foster the personal development of identity, meaning, and purpose in life.	
Humaneness	Having what are considered the best qualities of human beings: empathy, sympathy, kindness, generosity, mercifulness, ability to love and to sacrifice, to hear and understand, to care and to nurture.	

Term	Definition	Reference
Humanistic pedagogy	Teaching that respects and works with the student's life world, nurturing human development within a democratic, just, meaning-centered and caring classroom ethos.	Plummer, K. (2005) "Critical humanism and queer theory: Living with the tensions." In N. K. Denzin and Y. S. Lincoln (Eds) *The Sage Handbook of Qualitative Research* (3rd ed., pp. 357–373). Thousand Oaks, CA: Sage.
Industrial era—from 1850 to 1950	The period when the industrial/manufacturing sector generated more wealth than the home-based hand-manufacturing sector in some countries.	
Inquiry-guided learning	An array of teaching strategies that promotes the acquisition of new knowledge, abilities, and attitudes through learner's increasingly independent investigation of questions, problems, and issues using the methods and standards of inquiry in the disciplines.	Lee, V. S. (Ed.) (2012) "Inquiry-guided learning." *New Directions for Teaching and Learning*, 129. San Francisco, CA: Jossey-Bass.
Insight	The reorganization of one's perceptual field that results in seeing it in a new way.	Gredler, M. (2009) *Learning and Instruction: Theory into Practice.* Upper Saddle River, NJ: Pearson.
Instruction paradigm	The traditional approach to education characterized by an emphasis on the transmission of content from teacher to student, typically through lecture, as opposed to the authentic production of learning. The instructional paradigm focuses on teaching rather than learning and perceives the means as the end goal.	Barr, R. B. and Tagg, J. (1995) "From teaching to learning—a new paradigm for undergraduate education." (Cover story). *Change* 27(6): 12.
Integrative learning	Integrative learning is an understanding and a disposition that a student builds across the curriculum and co-curriculum, from	Integrative Learning Value Rubric, Association of American Colleges and Universities

I

Term	Definition	Source(s)
	making simple connections among ideas and experiences to synthesizing and transferring learning to new, complex situations within and beyond the campus.	(AAC&U), see http://www.aacu.org/value/rubrics/pdf/integrativelearning.pdf
Intelligence	A person's adaptation to his/her physical and social environment; the developing and changing ways in which a person deals with and adapts to their world.	Gredler, M. (2009) *Learning and Instruction: Theory into Practice.* Upper Saddle River, NJ: Pearson.
Interpretivism	In the interpretive research paradigm intersubjective knowledge is co-constructed by the researcher and co-participants using naturalistic methods drawn from the new ethnography and reflexive narrative inquiry.	Denzin, N. K. and Lincoln, Y. S. (2005) "Introduction: The discipline and practice of qualitative research." In N. Denzin and Y. Lincoln (Eds) *The Sage Handbook of Qualitative Research* (3rd ed., pp. 1–32). Thousand Oaks, CA: Sage.
K Knowledge	In Piagetian theory, the constructive interaction between the subject (person) and the object. It represents the essence of what we know and are aware of.	Gredler, M. (2009) *Learning and Instruction: Theory into Practice.* Upper Saddle River, NJ: Pearson.
L Learner-centered approach	A person learns significantly only those things that are perceived as being involved in the maintenance of or enhancement of the structure of self. Therefore, relevancy to the student is essential for learning. The students' experiences become the core of the course.	Rogers, C. (1951) *Client-Centered Therapy: Its Current Practice, Implications and Theory.* London: Constable.
Learning	The processes by which humans acquire a diversity of knowledge, skills, and attitudes that set them apart from other species.	Gredler, M. (2009) *Learning and Instruction: Theory into Practice.* Upper Saddle River, NJ: Pearson.

	Term	Definition	Reference
	Learning communities	In higher education, curricular learning communities are classes that are linked or clustered during an academic term, often around an interdisciplinary theme, and enroll a common cohort of students. A variety of approaches are used to build these learning communities, with all intended to restructure the students, time, credit, and learning experiences to build community among students, between students and their teachers, and among faculty members and disciplines.	Washington Center at Evergreen State University, see http://www.evergreen.edu/washcenter/lcfaq.htm#21, retrieved July 17, 2012.
	Lifelong learning	Lifelong learning is defined as "all learning activity undertaken throughout life, with the aim of improving knowledge, skills, and competences within a personal, civic, social and/or employment-related perspective."	Mackiewicz, W. (2002). Available at http://www.celelc.org/docs/mackiewicz-valencia_0.pdf
M	Mastery learning	The practice of organizing instructional concepts and skills into units, assessing comprehension and providing feedback, and eventually moving onto more complex concepts and skills over time.	Bloom, B. S., Hastings, J. T. and Madaus, G. F. (1971) *Handbook on Formative and Summative Evaluation of Student Learning*. New York: McGraw-Hill.
	Meaning	All existing definitions of meaning can be grouped into three major areas: meaning as integration of personal and social realities (Phenix, 1964), meaning as interpretation of life (Royce, 1983), and meaning as goal or task in life (Frankl, 1998). The first area is the broadest and includes the second one, which in its turn includes the third one.	Weisskopf-Joelson, E. (1968) "Meaning as an integrating factor." In C. Buhler and F. Massarik (Eds) *The Course of Human Life: A Study of Goals in the Humanistic Perspective*. New York: Springer Publishing Co.
	Meaning as a verb	Grammatically, the word "meaning" is a gerund, a verbal noun ending in -ing that has the function of a substantive and at the	*The Oxford Dictionary of English Grammar.* Sylvia Chalker and Edmund Weiner.

Term	Definition	Source(s)
	same time shows the verbal features of tense, voice, and capacity to take adverbial qualifiers and to govern objects. While *The Oxford Dictionary of English Grammar* says that "if a word [ending in –ing derived from a verb can inflect for plural and lacks verbal force, it is normally considered to be a noun and excluded from the class of gerund," it is treated here, abnormally, to emphasize its character as an action.	Oxford University Press, 1998. Oxford Reference Online. Oxford University Press.
Meaning-centered education	MCE is an educational approach that facilitates the conscious integration of new learning with prior learning across all domains based on personal meanings about oneself in relation to the world. MCE aims to create an authentic learning environment that supports a self-regulating and autonomous personality who operates out of her/his own volition and strives to achieve self-fulfillment and self-determination as an indicator of his/her existential worldview.	Adapted from Leontiev (2007), Ausubel (2000), Shuell (1990). Leontiev, D. (2007) *Psychology of Meaning.* Moscow: Smysl. Ausubel, D. P. (2000) *The Acquisition and Retention of Knowledge: A Cognitive View.* Dordrect; Boston, MA: Kluwer Academic Publishers. Shuell, T. J. (1990) "Phases of meaningful learning," *Review of Educational Research* 60(4): 531.
Meaning-centered learning	A learning theory that holds that human learning is the self-motivating and self-regulating process of creating personal meaning in one's life world through reflective, critical, and inquiry-based activities that occur across all learning domains. Thus, according	Kovbasyuk, O. and Blessinger, P. (Eds) (2013) *Meaning-Centered Education: International Perspectives and Explorations in Higher Education.* New York: Routledge.

		to this meaning-centered learning theory, the learner constructs personal meaning from his/her own experiences and their relationship to prior experiences within multiple life contexts in order to continually self-evolve as a mature personality who is capable of authoring his/her life.	Gredler, M. (2009) *Learning and Instruction: Theory into Practice*. Upper Saddle River, NJ: Pearson.
	Metacognition	Knowledge about and awareness of one's own thinking and learning and the use of strategies to guide and monitor one's thinking and learning.	Lee, V. S. (Ed.) (2012) "Inquiry-guided learning." *New Directions for Teaching and Learning*, 129. San Francisco, CA: Jossey-Bass.
P	Pedagogy	The art and science of teaching, including specific methods of instruction such as lecture, discussion, group work, case study, inquiry-guided learning, or service learning.	Ashcroft, B., Griffiths, G. and Tiffin, H. (2000) *Post-colonial Studies: The Key Concepts*. New York: Routledge.
	Personal agency	The ability of individuals to freely and autonomously initiate action, especially in resisting imperial power.	Leontiev, D. (2007) *Psychology of Meaning*. Moscow: Smysl.
	Personal meaning (German *Sinn*, Russian *Smysl*)	A private and idiosyncratic unit of individual attitude, generated by an individual experience context, not necessarily shared with anyone.	Kovbasyuk O. V. (2009) "The role of meaning in raising personality." *Selected Scholarly Publications on Timely Issues of Communication and Culture*. Moscow—Pyatigorsk: Pyatigorsk State Linguistic University, pp. 254–267.
	Personality	The total representation of one's physical, psychological, and social qualities. The individual capability to fulfill his/her human mission to constantly self-evolve, engaging in search for meaning in life, and construct his/her life world.	

Term	Definition	Source(s)
Personality self-development	A complex combination of all the internal processes of personal growth, such as: self-cognition, self-regulation, self-improving, spiritual self-strengthening, self-determination, and self-actualization. "Spiritual" is a notion of self-regulation; an internal human core of a personality, which allows her/him to act beyond the threshold of social necessity.	Kovbasyuk O. V. (2009) "The role of meaning in raising personality." *Selected Scholarly Publications on Timely Issues of Communication and Culture.* Moscow—Pyatigorsk: Pyatigorsk State Linguistic University, pp. 254–267.
Perspective	A point of view often determined by a particular theoretical, cultural, ethical, or political orientation.	Lee, V. S. (Ed.) (2012) "Inquiry-guided learning," *New Directions for Teaching and Learning,* 129. San Francisco, CA: Jossey-Bass.
Phenomenology	Phenomenology is the study of structures of consciousness as experienced from the first-person point of view. The central structure of an experience is its intentionality, its being directed toward something, as it is an experience of or about some object. An experience is directed toward an object by virtue of its content or meaning (which represents the object) together with appropriate enabling conditions. Phenomenology as a discipline is distinct from but related to other key disciplines in philosophy, such as ontology, epistemology, logic, and ethics. Phenomenology has been practiced in various guises for centuries, but it came into its own in the early twentieth century in the works of Husserl, Heidegger, Sartre,	Smith, D. W. (2011) "Phenomenology." In E. N. Zalta (Ed.), *The Stanford Encyclopedia of Philosophy* (Fall 2011 Edition). Available online from: http://plato.stanford.edu/archives/fall2011/entries/phenomenology/ (accessed December 10, 2012).

Term	Definition	Reference
	Merleau-Ponty, and others. Phenomenological issues of intentionality, consciousness, qualia, and first-person perspective have been prominent in recent philosophy of mind.	
Philosophy	An organized and justified belief system that provides a consistent and unified view of the external world and the inner world of the individual and the relationship between the two worlds. A philosophy is developed by first defining the nature of reality (ontology) and then epistemological questions (what is knowledge) and other questions are answered coherent with that ontological definition.	Gredler, M. (2009) *Learning and Instruction: Theory into Practice.* Upper Saddle River, NJ: Pearson.
Pluralism	Pluralism connotes a diversity of views, actions, or methods. Pluralism can be represented in many forms (e.g., cultural, linguistic, ethnic, ideological, values). Educational pluralism is the view that teaching and learning philosophies, theories, approaches, and methods may have multiple explanations to account for their nature and origin.	
Positivism	Positivism is the traditional paradigm of the natural sciences which holds that objective (or "positive") knowledge of the real world can be obtained from sense-based experiences via experimental methods.	Mautner, T. (Ed.) (1997) *Dictionary of Philosophy.* London: Penguin Books.
Postmodernism	The postmodern research paradigm deconstructs claims to universal truth (or master narratives) by promoting difference and pluralism, and employs constructively artful modes of reason (new logics) and representation (alternative genres) to produce richer understandings of the complexity of the natural and social worlds.	Taylor, P. C., Taylor, E. and Luitel, B. C. (2012) "Multi-paradigmatic transformative research as/for teacher education: An integral perspective." In B. J. Fraser, K. G. Tobin and C. J. McRobbie (Eds), *Second*

Term	Definition	Source(s)
		International Handbook of Science Education (pp. 373–387). Dordrecht, The Netherlands: Springer.
Pre-industrial era—before 1850	An economics concept that describes the period when the agricultural, home-based hand-manufacturing sector generated almost all wealth in some countries.	Bell, D. (1974) *The Coming of Post-Industrial Society*. New York: Harper Colophon Books; http://en.wikipedia.org/wiki/Post-industrial_society
Post-industrial era—after 1950	An economics concept that describes the period when the service sector generated more wealth than the industrial/manufacturing sector in some countries.	Bell, D. (1974) *The Coming of Post-Industrial Society*. New York: Harper Colophon Books; http://en.wikipedia.org/wiki/Post-industrial_society
Power dynamics	Also referred to as "power relations"; the often unconscious assumptions regarding who makes decisions in the classroom, course design, and classroom activities, and that govern the behavior and relationships of both the professor and the students. These assumptions are often grounded in cultural expectations as well as institutional cultural elements such as the instruction paradigm. In discussing feminist pedagogy, bell hooks notes, "we must acknowledge that our role as teacher is a position of power over others. We can use that power in ways that diminish or in ways that enrich . . . One simple way to alter the way one's 'power' as teacher is experienced in the classroom is to elect not to assume the posture of all-knowing professors."	hooks, b. (1989) *Talking Back: Thinking Feminist, Thinking Black*. Boston, MA: South End Press, p. 52.

Power sharing — A departure from the Instructional Paradigm whereby faculty include students in making decisions (based on a variety of contextual circumstances), ranging from course content, calendaring, types of assignment, and aspects of course governance and assessment.

Weimer, M. (2002) *Learner-Centered Teaching*. San Francisco, CA: Jossey-Bass.

Praxis — The practical application and process by which a learning theory or method is implemented or practiced.

S

Self-actualization — The term was introduced by Kurt Goldstein for the motive to realize one's full potential. In his view, it is the primary motive. Carl Rogers also wrote of a person's tendency to actualize his potentialities. Abraham Maslow further explained this idea in his hierarchy of needs theory as the ultimate level of psychological and personal development.

Self-concept — The organized consistent conceptual gestalt composed of perceptions of the characteristics of "I" or "me" and the perceptions of the relationships of the "I" or "me" to others and to various aspects of life, together with the values attached to these perceptions. It is a gestalt which is available to awareness though not necessarily in awareness. It is a fluid and changing gestalt, a process, but at any given moment it is a specific entity.

Rogers, C. (1959) "A theory of therapy, personality and interpersonal relationships as developed in the client-centered framework." In S. Koch (Ed.), *Psychology: A Study of a Science. Vol. 3: Formulations of the Person and the Social Context*. New York: McGraw-Hill.

Self-determination — An area of existential psychology and philosophy, which explores new ways of life, on the basis of human consciousness. Dmitry Leontiev calls self-determination one of the indications of existential worldview for a personality, who takes responsibility for her/his own life and strives for her/his self-fulfillment.

Leontiev, D. (2007) *Psychology of Meaning*. Moscow: Smysl.

Term	Definition	Source(s)
Self-efficacy	The sense that one can successfully execute a behavior that is required to produce an outcome.	Gredler, M. (2009) *Learning and Instruction: Theory into Practice*. Upper Saddle River, NJ: Pearson.
Self-regulated learner	see "Autonomous learning."	
Speech-act theory	The idea that language is not primarily a bundle of facts but a series of intentional acts, first propounded by J. L. Austin (1962), and elaborated by John R. Searle (1969).	Austin, J. L. (1962) *How to Do Things with Words: The William James Lectures Delivered at Harvard University in 1955*. Ed. J. O. Urmson. Oxford: Clarendon Press. Searle, J. R. (1969) *Speech Acts: An Essay in the Philosophy of Language*. Cambridge: Cambridge University Press.
Student-centered instruction	Student-centered instruction is an instructional approach in which students influence the content, activities, materials, and pace of learning. This learning model places the student (learner) in the center of the learning process. The instructor provides students with opportunities to learn independently and from one another and coaches them in the skills they need to do so effectively. The SCI approach includes such techniques as substituting active learning experiences for lectures, assigning open-ended problems and problems requiring critical or creative	Collins, J. W., 3rd, and O'Brien, N. P. (Eds) (2003) *Greenwood Dictionary of Education*. Westport, CT: Greenwood.

thinking that cannot be solved by following text examples, involving students in simulations and role plays, and using self-paced and/or cooperative (team-based) learning.

Sustainability Meeting the needs of the present without compromising the ability of future generations to meet their own needs.

United Nations World Commission on Environment and Development (WCED) (1987) *Our Common Future*. Oxford: Oxford University Press.

Hutchings, P. (1996) *Making Teaching Community Property*. Washington, DC: AAHE.

T

Teaching circles A group of faculty members, often cross-disciplinary or departmental, who collaborate throughout an academic year/semester to address common questions and problems regarding student learning.

Textoids "Synthetic fragments of language which exhibit none of the complex richness of natural language" (Hunt, 1989). Chris Anson (1986) has expanded the idea to suggest that readers and situations may render texts otherwise whole and natural into textoids, devoid of human purpose and "stripped of their human richness and complexity." See also Hunt (1993).

Anson, C. M. (1986) "Reading, writing, and intention." *Reader* 16: 20–35.

Hunt, R. A. (1989) "A horse named Hans, a boy named Shawn: the Herr von Osten Theory of Response to Writing." In C. M. Anson (Ed.), *Writing and Response: Theory, Practice, and Research* (pp. 80–100). Champaign-Urbana: National Council of Teachers of English.

Hunt, R. A. (1993) "Texts, textoids and utterances: Writing and reading for meaning, in and out of classrooms." In S. B. Straw

Term	Definition	Source(s)
		and D. Bogdan (Eds), *Constructive Reading: Teaching Beyond Communication* (pp. 113–129). Portsmouth, NH: Heinemann-Boynton/Cook.
Theory of mind	This concept posits that central to our humanity is our ability to understand the mental states of others around us, to infer their intentions from their actions, and to grasp when they do, and when they don't, share our perceptions of the world.	Premack, D. G. and Woodruff, G. (1978) "Does the chimpanzee have a theory of mind?" *Behavioral and Brain Sciences* 1: 515–526.
Transformative learning	Transformative learning involves experiencing a deep, structural shift in the basic premises of thought, feelings, and actions . . . an expansion of consciousness.	Morrell, A. and O'Connor, M. A. (2002) "Introduction." In E. V. O'Sullivan, A. Morrell and M. A. O'Connor (Eds), *Expanding the Boundaries of Transformative Learning: Essays on Theory and Praxis* (pp. xv–xxx). New York: Palgrave.
Triangulation	The use of multiple methods, data types, and theories in the same research study to arrive at more accurate and complete findings.	
V Values	A personal value is a personal belief about what is good or fair or just that helps to guide one's actions. A cultural value is a belief about what is good or fair or just that is shared by a culture. A value system is a set of coherent values. Values can be based on ethics, ideology, aesthetics.	

Variational education	A type of exploratory education that probes different paths and various situations in culture to provide a person greater possibilities for choosing one's destiny.	Asmolov. A. G. (1990) *Psychology of Personality*. Moscow: Moscow State University.
W Worldview	A component of the individual picture of the world, composed by the constructions of the general regularities effective in the world.	Leontiev, D. (2007) *Psychology of Meaning*. Moscow: Smysl.

INDEX